The tercentenary of Henry Purcell's death falls in 1995, and this volume of specially commissioned essays has been collected to celebrate Purcell's music in this tercentenary year. The essays are representative of the best recent research and explore the following areas: the autograph manuscripts, Purcell's compositional technique, the relationship between Purcell and his teacher John Blow, a reassessment of Purcell's court odes, performance practice and word-setting, and eighteenth-century reception history, particularly regarding *King Arthur*. The volume is richly illustrated with music examples and photographs of important manuscripts. This is also the first collection to analyse Purcell's compositional techniques through detailed study of his manuscripts and the first to report on the discovery of two important autograph manuscripts. The book opens with an assessment of Purcell's elusive personality.

Purcell Studies

Watercolour portrait of Henry Purcell, Royal Academy of Music

Purcell Studies

edited by

CURTIS PRICE

King Edward Professor of Music,
King's College London

CAMBRIDGE
UNIVERSITY PRESS

Published by the Press Syndicate of the University of Cambridge
The Pitt Building, Trumpington Street, Cambridge CB2 1RP
40 West 20th Street, New York, NY 10011–4211, USA
10 Stamford Road, Oakleigh, Melbourne 3166, Australia

First published 1995

Printed in Great Britain at the University Press, Cambridge

A catalogue record for this book is available from the British Library

Library of Congress cataloguing in publication data

Purcell studies / edited by Curtis Price.
    p.   cm.
  Includes bibliographical references and index.
  ISBN 0 521 44174 9 (hardback)
  1. Purcell, Henry, 1659–1695 – Criticism and interpretation
I. Price, Curtis Alexander, 1945– .
ML410.P93P87 1995
780'.921–dc20   94-17174 CIP

ISBN 0 521 44174 9 hardback

Contents

List of Contents

Illustrations

Preface

This collection of essays is published to commemorate the tercentenary of the death of Henry Purcell on 21 November 1695. Rather than being simply an appreciation of his music, which, thankfully, no longer needs apologists, or a survey of his huge output in every genre known to late seventeenth-century England, this book offers instead a selection of the latest scholarly research. It is intended as a sequel and complement to *Henry Purcell (1659–1695): Essays on his Music*, edited by the late Imogen Holst and published thirty-six years ago to mark the tercentenary of the composer's birth. The present volume naturally measures the development of thinking about Purcell since 1959 but is by no means a replacement for the earlier book; several essays in the Holst collection are now rightly regarded as classics.

Nevertheless, the essays assembled here do generally take a different tack and go some way towards filling a perceived gap. Several years ago, I wrote that 'the most urgent *desideratum* for Purcell research is forensic study of the early manuscripts, to answer the kinds of questions tackled by the editors of the *Neue Bach-Ausgabe* in the 1950s and by those presently at work on the *Hallische Händel-Ausgabe*'.[1] I might have mentioned several other areas in which Purcell research seemed at the time to lag behind that into the music of other Baroque composers of similar stature. No one had undertaken a comprehensive study of Purcell's compositional technique as evidenced by corrections in the autographs, working drafts and revisions of his own works – research analogous to Robert Marshall's on Bach, which appeared more than twenty years ago. Musical education and early development – subjects of great import to those working on Monteverdi, Schütz, Bach and Handel – seemed unpromising for Purcell, owing to lack of sources or, rather, to uncertainty over how to interpret the evidence. Purcell's obviously close but

---

1. Review of Franklin B. Zimmerman, *Henry Purcell: A Guide to Research,* in *Early Music* 17 (1989), 577.

still puzzling relationship with his teacher and friend John Blow had not been investigated without prejudice as to the direction in which their influence flowed. No one had seriously challenged Jack Westrup's generally negative assessment of Purcell's early court odes: 'the awkward gait and pompous conventionality' which, he claimed, 'involved the acquisition of a more brilliant manner, for which Purcell's training had not fully prepared him'.[2] And, with one notable exception,[3] there had been no major study of Purcell's music in light of recent developments in reception history. Advocates of historically based performance tended to derive the 'Purcellian style' uncritically from contemporaneous French practice, rather than seek guidance from internal evidence or become aware of earlier English practice and tradition. The essays in this volume help supply these desiderata and, though some are prolegomena to larger studies as yet not fully realized, or are necessarily tentative in their conclusions, each is representative of the several burgeoning areas of Purcell research. Inevitably, there is some overlap between the essays, particularly those on the autograph manuscripts and the court odes, but I have resisted the temptation to remove the common ground, preferring instead to allow the contributors to develop their own arguments fully so that each essay can stand on its own.

When planning this book a few years ago, I could not have hoped that it would include reports on two important new autograph manuscripts (see chaps. 4 and 5). The discovery of these sources would have especially pleased Peter le Huray who, sadly, did not live to finish his contribution to this volume, which is dedicated to his memory.

C.P.

2. *Purcell*, rev. edn by Nigel Fortune (London, 1980), p. 172.
3. Richard Luckett, "'Or rather our Musical Shakspeare": Charles Burney's Purcell', in *Music in Eighteenth-Century England*, ed. Christopher Hogwood and Richard Luckett (Cambridge, 1983), pp. 59–77.

In search of Purcell's character

CURTIS PRICE

Any study of Purcell will always be hampered by lack of information about the man himself. His curriculum vitae – genealogy, court appointments, marriage, dates of major compositions and so forth – is fairly well documented, but little is known about his relationship to his contemporaries, his character or what he thought about the other arts and sciences flourishing simultaneously in post-Restoration England. His biography is as rich in anecdote as it is poor in primary sources but, since the appearance of Westrup's Master Musicians book in 1937, which largely rejected unverifiable tradition, scholars have shied away from making inferences about Purcell's character from the music, or even from considering how his life circumstances may have affected his art. Not unrelated to the void at the centre of Purcell's personality is the apparent gap between the high esteem in which musicologists and performers hold his music and the paucity of works in the standard repertory. Only Dido's Lament, 'Nymphs and shepherds' and the Trumpet Voluntary (actually by Jeremiah Clarke) have entered the canon. Roger Norrington crystallized these related issues in a pair of questions: 'was Purcell a "musician's musician"? is that why he is not very popular today?'[1] One cannot answer the first without attempting to define Purcell's musical personality, and I believe that a more general appreciation of his music will not arrive until that personality is better fixed in the public imagination.

It may be possible, without creating yet another myth, to sketch Purcell's character by re-examining the testimony of actual acquaintances – Thomas Tudway, Henry Playford, Henry Hall, John Dryden, Jacob Talbot and especially Roger North – filling in the details with some of the more plausible anecdotes. It is curious that, from the many lamentations, odes and other tributes which appeared shortly after his death, no clear personality

1 In a talk given at the Purcell Experience, Queen Elizabeth Hall, London, 20 November 1993.

emerges; quite the opposite: only a 'God-like Man' worshipped by the 'learn'd' in the art. Henry Hall was one of the few to offer an earthly comparison ('Our first reforming Music's *Richelieu*'), which time has rendered inapt. The image of a peerless yet characterless genius was projected throughout the eighteenth century by the poems printed at the beginning of the first volume of *Orpheus Britannicus*, one of the most widely distributed of all collections of English music.[2] The only story about Purcell which seems to have lodged in the public consciousness is that concerning the circumstances which supposedly led to his death. The tale has always been prefaced by a disclaimer, as in H. C. Colles's entry in the third edition of *Grove's Dictionary of Music and Musicians* (1927), which is also censored: 'there is no need to attach any importance to the tradition reported by Hawkins, that the composer caught cold from being kept waiting for admittance into his house late at night'. In 1937, Westrup recounted more of the story: 'Purcell was a man of intemperate habits and given to late hours, that his wife, indignant at these excesses, refused to admit him after midnight, and he consequently caught a cold which brought on his death.'[3] Its unjustly criticized first purveyor, Sir John Hawkins, freely admitted that the 'tradition' was inconsistent with firmer evidence of a lingering death, but his purpose for including it in *A General History of the Science and Practice of Music* (1776) was a well-intentioned attempt to move away from the panegyric and give Purcell a human face. Since the original version is often misrepresented, it is worth quoting *in extenso*:

> It is said that [Purcell] used to keep late hours, and that his wife had given orders to his servants not to let him in after midnight: unfortunately he came home heated with wine from the tavern at an hour later than that prescribed him, and through the inclemency of the air contracted a disorder of which he died. If this be true, it reflects but little honour of Madam Purcell . . . and but ill agrees with those expressions of grief for her dear lamented husband, which she makes use of to Lady *Elizabeth* Howard in the dedication of the Orpheus Britannicus.[4]

Here one sees a jovial pub-crawler but also a hen-pecked husband, the 'God-like Man' brought low by a scold and a cold. Hawkins does himself less credit in recording uncritically a second-hand account of Purcell's reaction to the news of Stradella's murder. When informed that 'jealousy was the motive to it', Purcell lamented Stradella's fate and, 'in regard of his great merit as a

---

2 From which the quotations earlier in this paragraph are taken.
3 J. A. Westrup, *Purcell*, rev. edn by Nigel Fortune (London, 1980), p. 40.
4 Sir John Hawkins, *A General History of the Science and Practice of Music*, 1776 (rev. edn London, 1853), vol. II, 748.

musician, said he could have forgiven him any injury in that kind; which, adds the relator [of the story], "those who remember how lovingly Mr. Purcell lived with his wife, or rather what a loving wife she proved to him, may understand without farther explication"'.[5] The sting in the tail – the implication that Purcell was an adulterer and his wife a hypocrite – needs to be considered in light of the 'death by cold' tradition.

As is suggested below, Purcell was hardly a shrinking violet, but neither was he as socially gregarious as Dryden nor as publicly grand as Wren. The likeliest reason the composer did not cut more of a figure round and about London was his sheer prolificacy: on average, he must have produced more than one page of full score every day of his working life, an astounding achievement, considering the generally high quality of his output. If Purcell's labours kept him chained to his desk and prevented much contact with the chroniclers of the age, one can nevertheless reconstruct a distinctive personality from the writings of those few who knew him, as Tudway did, 'perfectly well'. Purcell possessed tremendous self-confidence and was well aware of his talent. He could be somewhat testy and irritable, not only with colleagues and his immediate superiors but even, on one occasion, with Queen Mary herself.[6] He may have had a certain contempt for his public, which is perhaps surprising for a composer who wrote so many popular tunes. He was, as Robert Shay argues below, a musical conservative, very proud of his mastery of the *stile antico*. He was also intensely interested in the latest French and Italian music but never followed fashion for its own sake; rather, he was confident that he could produce better music than anyone, English or foreign.

There is, then, a contradiction at the heart of Purcell's musical personality which may account for his wonderful synthesis of the traditional modal counterpoint in which he was trained and the modern Bolognese tonal style which he tried to emulate. Hence his obeisance to 'the most fam'd Italian masters' in the foreword to the *Sonnata's of III Parts* (1683) and other later acknowledgements of having drawn inspiration from foreign musicians, in contrast to his pride at having mastered double counterpoint, which is hardly a prominent feature of contemporaneous French and Italian music.[7] Further evidence of the ambivalence which characterizes Purcell's musical style is offered by the dedication to the score of the semi-opera *Dioclesian* (1690), an encomium to French and Italian music. Signed by the composer, it was

5 Hawkins, *A General History*, vol. II, 653–4. I am grateful to Peter Holman for pointing out the relevance of the Stradella anecdote in this context.
6 See below, chap. 7, p. 159.
7 See, for instance, the Dance for the Followers of Night in *The Fairy Queen*, which Purcell headed '4 in 2', drawing attention to the fact that it is a double canon.

actually written for him by Dryden.[8] The rough draft included a passage which would have insulted Purcell's forebears and teachers ('leave the hedge notes of our homely Ancestours'). This was cut from the published version, presumably at the composer's insistence, since Dryden was notoriously plain-spoken in his contempt of earlier English music. Leaving aside the conventional politeness which prefaces and dedicatory letters required, what did Purcell really think about foreign music? His fellow Chapel Royal chorister and later the Professor of Music at Cambridge, Thomas Tudway, came close to giving an answer. In his *History of Music* he wondered what Purcell would have made of the introduction of Italian operas on the English stage had he lived to see them: 'He would have been so far from despiseing them, that he woud never have ceas'd, till he had equall'd, if not outdone them.'[9]

To complete this character sketch one must turn to Roger North who, if he knew Purcell little better than did Tudway, is the only writer to hint at a darker, brooding side to the composer. In a discussion, only recently available in print,[10] of the initial reception of the semi-operas, North wrote that these works were not 'sustened by performance', that is, they were badly executed. Implying, in contradiction to almost all other contemporary witnesses, that the semi-operas met with mixed success, he records the composer's own reaction: 'Mr Purcell used to mark what did not take for the best musick, it being his constant observation that what took least, was really best, and his freinds would desire him to touch those passages by that caracter.' (I interpret this to mean that Purcell could tell his best music by the coolest reception, and his friends would ask him to play the passages in question on the harpsichord.) The person North describes had evidently suffered some disappointment; indeed, the younger composer John Eccles may have challenged Purcell's popularity in the theatre for a while in 1694.[11] Yet, more significantly, one sees here a proud man who did not trust his audience to recognize the full sophistication of his music, an audience which instead applauded the easy melodies and catchy dance rhythms while ignoring those passages which had cost him much more labour. What is remarkable about Purcell's development as a composer is that he never compromised his gift for counterpoint, never completely gave in to French 'airyness' or to addictive Italian figuration and sequences.

Of course, we do not really know whether Purcell, when friends gathered round the harpsichord, pointed proudly to the bed-rock of fugue, the rich

---

8 Discussed in detail in Curtis Price, *Henry Purcell and the London Stage* (Cambridge, 1984), pp. 264–5.
9 Christopher Hogwood, 'Thomas Tudway's History of Music', in *Music in Eighteenth-Century England*, ed. Christopher Hogwood and Richard Luckett (Cambridge, 1983), pp. 44–5.
10 *Roger North's Cursory Notes of Musicke (c. 1698 – c. 1703): A Physical, Psychological and Critical Theory*, ed. Mary Chan and Jamie C. Kassler (Kensington, N.S.W., 1986), p. 229.
11 See Price, *Henry Purcell and the London Stage*, pp. 164–8.

dissonance and beautifully detailed inner parts which are so much admired in his music today. But North certainly does imply that the composer felt the need to draw attention to qualities in his music that most listeners could not fully appreciate. Here is a true child of the age of the Royal Society, when the mathematical underpinning, the scientific rationale of art, architecture and literature were meant to be understood by the consumer. Dryden was similarly proud of the web of classical allusion which gave force to his political writing, as was Wren of the classical geometry embodied within St Paul's Cathedral. Purcell was no theorist, but he too relied upon 'classical' Renaissance procedures to give integrity to music which, at its very best, may have met with uncomprehending silence.

1

Purcell's great autographs

ROBERT THOMPSON

Purcell's three great autograph scorebooks – Cambridge, Fitzwilliam Museum Music MS 88, British Library Add. MS 30,930 and British Library, Royal Music MS 20.h.8 – are amongst the most studied of all English musical sources, and it may seem presumptuous to suggest that very much of importance remains to be learned about them.[1] Nevertheless, little if anything has been published on the physical make-up of the volumes and their relationship with other manuscripts, or on Purcell's handwriting in relation to the manuscripts' paper types and structure.[2] The tercentenary of Purcell's death is as good a pretext as any to investigate how these aspects of the manuscripts contribute to our understanding of the nature and purpose of the musical texts they contain.

The basic physical features of the three books are set out in Table 1.1 (p. 21). Like all large English music manuscripts of the period they are made of heavy, high-quality paper from the Angoumois region of south-western France. Mere identification of watermark types reveals nothing that is not already apparent, but two further aspects of their paper and structure are much more interesting.[3] First, the two sources in the British Library belong to a group of contemporaneous manuscripts containing identical paper, most of which show some connection with court musicians (see Table 1.2); secondly, there are significant differences in structure between Add. MS 30,930 and the other two sources.

---

[1] See for example Nigel Fortune and Franklin B. Zimmerman, 'Purcell's Autographs', in *Henry Purcell (1659–1695): Essays on his Music*, ed. Imogen Holst (London, 1959), pp. 106–21.

[2] Discussions of Purcell's hand, valuable even when some of their conclusions are no longer tenable, appear in Fortune and Zimmerman, 'Purcell's Autographs'; Augustus Hughes-Hughes, 'Henry Purcell's Handwriting', *The Musical Times* 37 (1896), 81–3; and G. E. P. Arkwright, 'Purcell's Church Music', *The Musical Antiquary* 3 (1910), 63–72, 234–48.

[3] Virtually all paper used for music in England between 1660 and 1688 came from the Angoumois: see Robert Thompson, 'English Music Manuscripts and the Fine Paper Trade, 1648–1688', Ph.D. thesis, King's College London (1988), pp. 31–60.

The five manuscripts listed in Table 1.2 are all wholly or partly made of paper with a pair of fleur-de-lis watermarks and corresponding countermarks comprising the Jesuit symbol 'IHS' and the initials of the papermaker Etienne Touzeau.[4] The different manuscripts display slight variations in the marks, but there are enough similarities in the precise relationship between the marks and the chain lines on the mould and an unusual alternation of 'fat' and 'thin' forms of the letter 'S' in the countermarks to allow one to determine that all the paper came from the same pair of moulds, showing the inevitable wear and tear to be expected over the seven months or so a mould lasted.[5] Judging from some slight distortion apparent in the watermarks, the paper of Add. MS 30,930 was made later than that of Oxford, Christ Church MS Mus 628, R.M. MS 20.h.8 and John Walter's book, now at Chichester, which is dated 1680.[6] The Blow autograph, Christ Church MS 628,[7] is probably the earliest of the five sources in Table 1.2, but the appearance of the same paper type in Harleian MS 1501, copied by Pietro Reggio in 1681, argues not only against a date much before 1680 for the Blow copy but also against the assumption that this paper type was in some special way linked to the court musical establishment. Of the great Purcell autographs, only Fitzwilliam MS 88, which seems for other reasons to be the earliest of the three volumes, consists of different paper with a 'bend' watermark and the

---

4 Marks of the same general type are illustrated in E. Heawood, *Watermarks, Mainly of the 17th and 18th Centuries* (Hilversum, 1950), nos. 1760, 1784–8, 1795–6. At this time the watermark was normally placed in the centre of the left-hand half of the oblong mould and any countermark in the corresponding position in the right-hand half. Paper makers always used two moulds at each vat, so that two similar but not identical watermark and countermark combinations can be found in even a small quantity of paper produced in the same operation. See Allan Stevenson, 'Watermarks Are Twins', *Studies in Bibliography* 4 (1951–2), 57–92. The Jesuits at Angoulême were said to make 'the finest paper the world had ever seen'; see W. E. J. Berg, *De réfugiés in de Nederlanden na der herroeping van het Edict van Nantes* (Amsterdam, 1845), p. 142, quoting *Hollandse Mercurius* (1672), p. 30. In 1673, Dericq Janssen leased a paper mill called 'l'Abbaye'; see C. M. Briquet, *Les Filigranes*, facsimile edn by Allan Stevenson (Amsterdam, 1968), vol. II, 701. Etienne Touzeau was working for Dericq Janssen at the St Michel mill by 1671: see G. Babinet de Rencogne, *Recueil de documents pour servir à l'histoire de commerce et de l'industrie en Angoumois, Bulletin de la société archéologique et historique de la Charente*, 5ième série, tome ii (Angoulême, 1880), 103–14.
5 There is no direct evidence of the life of a mould in the seventeenth century, but the eighteenth-century English paper maker James Whatman, who would have used the same methods as earlier craftsmen, stated that his moulds had to be replaced after about seven months; see T. Balston, *James Whatman, Father and Son* (London, 1957), pp. 60, 120.
6 Walter's autograph inscription, 'Jo: Walther His Book Anno Domino 1680', is in fact on a cutout pasted into the modern cover, along with another reading 'Io Walter Ano 1630', which certainly came from a different source. Thus, although Walter copied some of the music in the volume, there is no proof that he owned it in 1680. John Walter's significance as a copyist is shown in Bruce Wood, 'A Note on Two Cambridge Manuscripts and their Copyists', *Music & Letters* 56 (1975), 308–12.
7 Discussed in H. Watkins Shaw, 'The Autographs of John Blow (1649–1708)', *Music Review* 25 (1964), 85–95.

countermark of the unidentified Angoumois craftsman 'RC'. R.M. MS 20.h.8 and the Fitzwilliam source are similar, however, in being so regularly constructed that their collation can be treated like that of a printed book whereas Add. MS 30,930 defies bibliographical description, its early history apparently differing so much from that of the other two manuscripts as to suggest that Purcell did not commence the three as parallel volumes devoted to different kinds of music. Instead, each appears to have a distinctive character, perhaps not merely reflecting a conscious division of repertory into different genres but also illustrating either a different stage in Purcell's fast-moving professional career or a particular aspect of his musical life.

One of the Etienne Touzeau books, R.M. MS 20.h.8, provides the best starting point for a survey of the three big autographs because it contains a sequence of welcome songs which can be precisely dated (see Table 1.3): if Purcell entered these works either before the performance or as a record shortly afterwards, then R.M. MS 20.h.8 offers an invaluable guide to the development of his handwriting between 1681 and 1689. Although Purcell had already composed a few anthems with strings and, indeed, a welcome song for September 1680,[8] his commencement of R.M. MS 20.h.8 appears to coincide with the time when he began to be regularly entrusted with the composition of these large-scale works, and the book may have been issued to him so he could make fair copies in full score. Apart from its repertory, there are other indications that R.M. MS 20.h.8 was used by Purcell in the execution of his duties at court and that he may not have regarded it, at least at first, as his personal property: it is the only one of the three great scorebooks not to have his name on the flyleaf in a more or less ostentatious style and in which he quite regularly handed over part of the copying to two or more assistants. Perhaps significantly, his interest in the score, reflected in the diminishing amount of music added to it and his increasing use of some-times unreliable assistant copyists, decreased after he lost the posts of organist and composer in 1685.[9] The status of R.M. MS 20.h.8 as a court music book is confirmed by its close relationship with a significant group of fair-

---

[8] *Welcome, Vicegerent.* Early anthems with strings include *My beloved spake,* found in an early auto-graph copy in British Library Add. MS 30,932 fol. 87 and *Behold now praise the Lord,* Add. 30,932 fol. 121, whose handwriting suggests that it is a little earlier than the first vocal music copied in Add. MS 30,930.

[9] Franklin B. Zimmerman, *Henry Purcell, 1659–1695: His Life and Times,* rev. edn (Philadelphia, 1983), p. 129. The main subsidiary copyist of R.M. MS 20.h.8 was also responsible for a manuscript containing anthems by Purcell, Blow and Gibbons which in 1896 belonged to W. H. Cummings: see Hughes-Hughes, 'Henry Purcell's Handwriting', p. 81. This was probably no. 25 in Cummings's sale catalogue of 1917, which was claimed to be an autograph in spite of being dated 'Saec XVIII': it was sold to Quaritch for £27. See British Library, S.C. Sotheby 1240, p. 3.

copy scores, all in the same principal hand and containing what is undoubtedly a court repertory dating from the mid-1680s: a collection of Purcell anthems with strings in Royal College of Music MS 2011, originally in two volumes,[10] and British Library Add. MS 33,287, also once in two volumes, the first containing songs with instruments by Purcell, Blow and Turner and the second court odes and welcome songs by the same composers with the addition of Humfrey. For many of Purcell's works Add. MS 33,287 is the only source besides R.M. MS 20.h.8, from which they were often clearly copied.

The earliest dated work in R.M. MS 20.h.8 is the welcome song *Swifter Isis, swifter flow*, probably performed on the King's return by river from Windsor in late August 1681. The manuscript is neat and careful: the description 'fair copy' would seem to be fully merited, and the conclusion that this score is a formal record rather than an item of performing material is superficially attractive. But in several ways this conclusion is inadequate. For the last chorus of *Swifter Isis* Purcell provided only an outline score, suitable for rehearsing, directing or playing the harpsichord but hardly what is wanted in a formal record copy, and there are other places where messy or missing passages have not been corrected, as they easily could have been, with paste-overs.[11] The copyist of Add. MS 33,287, who only a few years later was to use the Purcell autograph as his main or only source, could not supply the missing bars. These problems, together with one or two details of instrumentation the later copyist apparently added from memory,[12] should serve as warnings against equating 'autograph' with 'definitive text', if indeed the concept of a definitive text is one that would have been recognized in 1681. At the same time the problems strengthen the autograph's claim to be regarded as a contemporary score serving some immediate practical purpose, rather than a retrospective fair copy, and therefore add to, rather than detract from, its authority. This evidence in turn has a bearing on the history of the other two great autographs.

[10] Hughes-Hughes, 'Henry Purcell's Handwriting', p. 81. Royal College of Music MS 2011 is similar in style and quality to Add. MS 33, 287 and two subsidiary hands are common to both sources. The same principal copyist was responsible for British Library R.M. MS 24.e.5, a score of Purcell's *Raise, raise the voice*: a page of R.M. 24.e.5 is reproduced in *The Works of Henry Purcell*, vol. X, rev. Bruce Wood (London and Sevenoaks, 1990), xv.

[11] What the composer actually wrote in this final chorus is shown clearly in *The Works of Henry Purcell*, vol. XV, ed. R. Vaughan Williams (London, 1905), 47–51. Elsewhere in R.M. MS 20.h.8 an extremely messy erasure on fol. 235v (inverted) makes it impossible to copy four bars of the treble voice part on fol. 235; there are also ugly and inconclusive alterations at the end of the symphony of the incomplete 'We reap all the pleasures', fol. 224 (inverted).

[12] In *Swifter Isis* Add. MS 33,287 specifies flutes as the obbligato instruments for the bass solo 'Land him safely on her shore' and 'Oboe & 3rd treble' for what appears in the autograph simply as a third treble part in the ritornello before 'Welcome, dread Sir, to town'.

Two features of Purcell's text hand change markedly during his composing career. Both Arkwright and Hughes-Hughes noted Purcell's use of a kind of reversed 'e' in what appeared to be early autographs such as Fitzwilliam MS 88 and the version of the funeral sentences in Add. MS 30,931.[13] This type of 'e' is entirely absent from both R.M. MS 20.h.8 and Add. MS 30,930, so we may conclude that by mid-1680 Purcell had abandoned it in favour of a more modern form. Another distinctive feature, a reversed 'r', is much in evidence in both of these manuscripts: a more modern form creeps in alongside the old in *Fly, bold rebellion* of 1683, but only after the 1684 welcome song *From those serene and rapturous joys* does this kind of 'r' become exclusive. Especially when other forms of evidence can be found to support them, these features of handwriting provide a useful insight into the history of Fitzwilliam MS 88 and Add. MS 30,930. (For the early 'e' and 'r', see ill. 2.3, p. 46 below.)

Add MS 30,930 appears to be the most personal of Purcell's early scorebooks, its earlier and principal contents consisting of devotional songs (some in Latin), seven sonatas and the fantazias. In contrast to the restrained and anonymous heading of R.M. MS 20.h.8, the inscription 'The Work's of Hen: Purcell Anno Dom. 1680' takes up nearly half a page; there is no professional reticence here. The manuscript's most striking physical feature is the evident disorder of its folios, with blank ruled leaves interrupting what are in fact complete pieces. The absence of any original pagination or quire numbering must have contributed to this problem, which dates from the nineteenth century: seventeenth- and eighteenth-century copyists appear to have had no difficulties with the now disordered vocal music section.[14] In 1849, Joseph Warren described the entire book in some detail without mentioning any misplaced blank pages.[15]

The British Library has no record of the work carried out when the manuscript was last re-bound in 1895, but a number of features enable one to establish the present collation with reasonable certainty and to make an informed guess as to its earlier arrangement.[16] In many places the stitches are

13 Arkwright, 'Purcell's Church Music', pp. 241–3; Hughes-Hughes, 'Henry Purcell's Handwriting', pp. 82–3.
14 Manuscripts demonstrably copied from Add. MS 30,930 include Oxford, Bodleian Library MS Mus.c.28 (discussed below) and Tenbury MS 1175 (housed at the Bodleian Library), which bears such inscriptions as 'Transcribed from the Original Score 1680 in the handwriting of the Author' (p. 242). Royal College of Music MS 517, in the hand of E. T. Warren Horne, might have been copied from either the autograph or Tenbury 1175, both of which belonged to him.
15 William Boyce, *Cathedral Music*, ed. Joseph Warren (London, 1849), vol. II, 18.
16 I am grateful to Mr Arthur Searle, Curator of Music Manuscripts at the British Library, for providing a great deal of information about the history of the manuscript after it came into the British Museum's possession in 1878. The current foliation apparently dates from September of that year when, according to a note on fol. 72v, there were 'ii + 72 folios', the present number of copied folios.

visible; the two watermark and countermark combinations ought to match and should of course be the same way up in the same sheet of paper: the staves were ruled in two blocks of six and one of four, and folios which are the two halves of the same sheet of paper ought both to have the block of four either at the top or the bottom. At the very least one can see which pairs of folios do not belong together; in a few places the present collation is completely artificial. Table 1.4 sets out the relationship between the music contained in the score and the arrangement of its pages, with suggestions for the original arrangement where the present collation is obviously wrong. Amongst other things, this analysis highlights the amount of space left for five-part fantazias in original gathering M and elsewhere and shows the almost complete state of the two sonata gatherings J and K. The fragmentary folio 37*, which contained the beginning of Sonata IV (Z 805), can be seen to be the end of gathering K, and a folio appears to have gone from the beginning of gathering J, where the rest of Sonata IV may have been.[17]

Many features of Add. MS 30,930 suggest that Purcell kept it for some time as a set of unbound gatherings whose pages could be removed or re-ordered as he found convenient, although the consistency of its paper type equally suggests that he went to some trouble to keep it separate from other working papers. There are too many variations in the apparent size of the original gatherings for the book to have been a bound volume supplied by a stationer; there are marked contrasts between the neatest and untidiest examples of Purcell's copying, which may reflect work done before and after binding.[18] Discoloured pages and highly selective or strangely ordered concordances also suggest that various parts of the collection were from time to time separated and possibly bound into smaller individual books. There is no evidence that the present Add. MS 30,930 was bound as a single volume until the late eighteenth century,[19] but the absence of any contemporary

---

17 The remaining fragment of Sonata IV on fol. 37* may be part of a discarded copy, or it may have belonged to a copy Purcell wished to separate and send elsewhere. The bars lost when he cut round the end of Sonata III could easily have been copied onto a small slip of paper and pasted in place.

18 Judging by the neatness of Purcell's writing, the first vocal works to be copied were nos. 10–13 (works contained in gathering D) followed by nos. 1–4 (contained in gathering A). No. 16, *Hear me, O Lord, the great support*, begins similarly but changes markedly after the first page; all other vocal pieces are, to varying extents, less carefully written than 1–4 and 10–13. Amongst the instrumental works, the G major overture and suite appear to have been added after binding; less predictably, so do the Pavan, Chacony and the third three-part fantazia.

19 The earliest document listing the complete present contents is a list made by E. T. Warren Horne, written on the back of part of a pamphlet entitled *A Short State of the Case respecting the intended Canal from Cromford in the County of Derby to communicate with the River Trent through the Erewash canal*, Add. MS 30,930 fol. 72. The Cromford canal was constructed between 1789 and 1795; the Erewash, which clearly pre-dated the pamphlet, between 1777 and 1779. See J. R. Ward, *The Finance of Canal Building in Eighteenth Century England* (London, 1974), pp. 38, 39.

pagination or binding scheme suggests that, when the whole or part of the manuscript was first bound, most of whatever music had been copied all lay within gatherings, so that a mistake in the collation would not be disastrous.

Indirect confirmation on this account of the history of Add. MS 30,930 comes from the early concordance of the vocal music closest to it in readings, Bodleian MS Mus.c.28. Here the copyist transcribed first all the complete English works which lie entirely within gatherings, nos. 1, 2, 3, 10, 11, 12 and 15. The neat handwriting of the first six of these suggests that they were amongst Purcell's earliest copies in Add. MS 30,930 and were made on flat, unbound sheets. Only then does the Mus.c.28 copyist add works entered in Add. MS 30,930 over two gatherings, nos. 9, 14 and 16. In general, the readings of MS Mus.c.28 are so close to the autograph that is seems likely to be a direct copy made as performing material by a musician belonging to Purcell's immediate circle,[20] and to reflect the order in which Purcell entered the works in his score, first writing inside loose gatherings he had formed from the paper and then adding later works on the unused pages from the end of one gathering to the beginning of the next. There is also evidence that certain parts of the section containing instrumental music were separated at some stage: the three sonatas contained complete in gathering J were copied into Christ Church MS Mus 3 in the mid-1680s by Richard Goodson, who at about the same time copied the fantazia on one note (Z 745) – which Purcell wrote on a single sheet of paper now at the centre of gathering P – into Christ Church MS Mus 620.[21] It is difficult to understand why Goodson should have limited his sonata copies, undoubtedly made directly from the surviving autograph score, to the three sonatas contained completely in gathering J unless he had only that gathering available.

Many of Purcell's headings, including the initial 1680 title-page, probably postdate at least some of the music and indicate the composer's plans for the further development of his collection as well as the manuscript's contents at the time of binding, whether as one volume or more. Even if complete blank gatherings and gatherings containing only what appears to be later music were not supposed to be where they are now, it is remarkable how much space Purcell seems to have been prepared to allocate to fantazias, suggesting

[20] This close relationship is apparent throughout, but especially in *Hear me, O Lord, the great support*, where the Mus.c.28 copyist transcribes only Purcell's neatly copied first page, ending with a triple time signature subsequently erased but still visible in the autograph, and then leaves space for the rest of the work. Though musically accurate, Mus.c.28 makes no attempt at all to match Purcell's careful underlay, which suggests that it was used as an open-score organ part.

[21] Both of these Christ Church manuscripts are composite volumes whose oldest layers are much earlier than their later contents imply.

that he anticipated copying sequences of three- and five-part works to match the four-part series, which itself does not seem to have been finished. All this sits uneasily with the notion of Purcell closing the book, as it were, on the outmoded fantazia form in 1680 and implies, instead, that he intended copying other fantazias into this manuscript. His interest in the fantazia reaches back beyond the four-part consort suites of Locke, which he might reasonably have been expected to take as his models,[22] to the earlier free-standing fantazia and the In Nomine,[23] but also extends forwards, in the fantazia on one note, to develop the possibilities of the genre beyond anything previously achieved. Nor should it be assumed that Purcell's fantazias were silent exercises: at least one of his senior colleagues living in 1680, John Hingston, had himself composed with distinction for the viols and in 1683 Hingston named what he called his 'best chest of viols' amongst the other instruments of which he made specific bequests in his will, those important enough not to be included in the unspecified residue of his goods.[24] Although Purcell's professional colleagues and neighbours could undoubtedly have assembled a consort to play through his fantazias, this music would hardly have advanced his professional career at court or amongst a wider public; its composition seems to reflect his desire to understand in depth not merely the established procedures but the unfulfilled potential of the polyphonic fantazia and to make its complex contrapuntal texture a natural part of his own musical language.[25]

As well as large and ultimately unanswerable questions about Purcell's perception of the polyphonic tradition and his reasons for composing his own

---

[22] British Library Add. MS 31,435, a source of Locke's 'Broken Consort' and of the fantazias only from his 'Consort of Four Parts', is marked in each of the string parts with comments such as 'Mr Locks Fa: Exa: by Mr Purcells Score Book' (fol. 19); it also contains music by Christopher Gibbons and the second of Purcell's three-part fantazias in an early version. The Locke score in question might have belonged to Thomas Purcell but, given Henry's interest in fantazias, it is likely that he studied it even if he was not its owner.

[23] Warwick Edwards, 'In Nomine', *The New Grove*, vol. IX, 230–3 points out similarities between In Nomines by Purcell and Parsons, and his list of In Nomine composers makes it abundantly clear how long the form had been obsolete by Purcell's time.

[24] London, Public Record Office, Prob 11/375 fols. 134–135. Hingston leaves to 'my beloved friend Mr Thomas Blagrave £10 & my best chest of vyolls'; other unspecified viols would have gone to his heir and executor Richard Graham. The relative insignificance of the bequest of £5 to 'my Godson Henry Pursall (son of Elizabeth Pursall)' probably means that by 1683 Purcell was well advanced in his career and needed no material help; Hingston perhaps expected Purcell to inherit his court appointments and thought that was enough.

[25] Michael Tilmouth, 'The Techniques and Forms of Purcell's Sonatas', *Music & Letters* 40 (1959), 109–21, points out the extent to which contrapuntal procedures were absorbed into Purcell's style. It may well be significant that the 'period of almost rash harmonic and textural experiment' identified by Peter Dennison in his sacred music precedes the composition of the fantazias: see *The Works of Henry Purcell*, vol. XIII (rev.) (London and Sevenoaks, 1988), ix.

fantazias, Add. MS 30,930 raises serious questions of detail about the chronology and nature of Purcell's revisions. These questions concern the devotional songs, the majority of which also appear in Christ Church MS 628, and the sonatas later to appear in the 1697 publication, especially the substantially revised sonatas VII and VIII (Z 808 and 809).

Christ Church MS 628, an autograph of John Blow, contains music by himself, Pelham Humfrey and his pupil Purcell (see Table 1.5). Its strange mix of genres implies a private rather than a professional purpose. The manuscript has the appearance of a presentation copy and seems on the basis of paper type to be roughly contemporaneous with Add. MS 30,930; only the fact that Blow includes some anthems of his own believed to have been written by 1677 shifts the balance in favour of Christ Church MS 628 being the earlier of the two manuscripts and the Purcell readings there being earlier than those in the autograph.[26] Most early secondary sources of these songs appear to derive from the Blow copy or from earlier separate autographs related to it, like the copy of *Plung'd in the confines of despair* in Birmingham University, Barber Institute MS 5001, rather than from the Add. MS 30,930 version, a fact that underlines the major autograph's essentially private quality. The alterations made by Purcell in compiling Add. MS 30,930 are relatively minor, some introducing apparently superior readings or interesting variations of detail.[27] Rhythmic simplifications lead one to suspect that Purcell may have notated this private scorebook less exactly than other copies and, therefore, that one might be ill advised to take it as definitive.

The sonatas in Add. MS 30,930 also have significant early concordances. The set of parts of Sonatas I-III (Z 802-4) in Oxford, Bodleian Library MSS Mus. Sch. e.400-403 date from about 1685 but probably contain a version of the music earlier than that in the autograph;[28] the score of Sonatas IX,

---

[26]   A date before 1677 can be assigned to *When the Lord turned again* and *The Lord is my Shepherd* on the basis of their ascription to 'Mr Jo: Blow' in British Library Add. MS 50,860, copied by William Tucker. The similarity of paper between Blow's autograph Christ Church MS 628 and other manuscripts dated 1680 may suggest that these anthems were in fact composed a little later and copied in Add. MS 50,860 nearer Tucker's death in 1679. If so, ascriptions to 'Mr' Blow (as opposed to 'Dr' Blow) cannot necessarily be relied on as evidence of date.

[27]   The Blow autograph is not collated in the Purcell Society edition, but comparison of the variants in Barber Institute MS 5001 will indicate the kind of changes Purcell made. For example, in *Plung'd in the confines of despair* Add. MS 30,930 contains variants in bars 46 and 69 which might be considered genuine improvements: see *The Works of Henry Purcell*, vol. XXX (rev.) (London, 1992), 184, 186, 218. Variants in these bars, like most others in Barber Institute MS 5001, are also present in Christ Church MS 628.

[28]   Bodleian MSS Mus. Sch. e.400–403 appear from their paper type to have been commenced in the early to mid-1680s; the Purcell sonatas are part of an anthology of twelve, by various composers, added after Corelli's Op. 2 of 1685. Sonata I of the 1697 set appears in A minor. See Thompson, 'English Music Manuscripts', pp. 452–60.

VII and VIII (Z 810, 808, 809), in that order, in Christ Church MS 3, however, is a direct copy from Add. MS 30,930, containing, of course, the manuscript versions of sonatas VII and VIII rather than the printed version published in 1697. Correction slips in Add. MS 30,930 altering a unique original reading of Sonata IX have on their reverse fragments of the printed version of Sonata VIII, a fact that led Christopher Hogwood to question the generally accepted view that the printed version was later than the surviving manuscript reading.[29]

Hogwood's suggestion is borne out by variations of handwriting and ink in Add. MS 30,930. In Sonatas I–III (gathering K) the pre-1683 form of reversed 'r' predominates in the tempo directions; in Sonatas VII–IX (gathering J) the later form is found. The two sequences differ significantly in both music hand and ink colour and seem highly unlikely to have been copied at the same time. All secondary sources of Sonatas VII–IX, including the Goodson copy and that in John Walter's book, both of which date from the mid 1680s,[30] transmit Purcell's altered version of Sonata IX, made using correction slips of the same paper type as the rest of the manuscript and copied, on the reverse, with part of the printed version of Sonata VIII written in pale ink similar to that of the earliest and neatest entries in the surviving volume. In contrast, the alteration to Sonata IX appears from its hand and ink colour to have been made almost at once. The present gathering J is intact as far as Sonata VIII is concerned, so the correction slips did not come from a single page torn out of the present manuscript; on the contrary, they seem to have belonged to a complete copy of Sonata VIII, contemporaneous with or possibly earlier than the existing scores of Sonatas I–III, which perhaps came at the end of a gathering that lay between J and K, or one that was never included in the binding. If the printed version of Sonata VIII was indeed meant to be Purcell's final revision, it is hard to see why he cut up a sheet containing it to correct Sonata IX but made no alteration to his manuscript text of Sonatas VII and VIII before he allowed Goodson, then Oxford Professor of Music, to make a copy from his manuscript incorporating alterations to Sonata IX but not to the other two. Any notion that such revisions are definitive ought to be questioned: Joseph Warren made it clear that when he owned the autograph the slips were held in place by pins, not glue, a method quite familiar in seventeenth-century documents and, of course, reversible.

---

[29] Henry Purcell, *Ten Sonatas in Four Parts*, Nos. 1–6, ed. Christopher Hogwood (London, 1978), p. vi.

[30] The copy of Sonata IX in this manuscript is not in Walter's hand but in that of another copyist who also transcribed, amongst other music, Draghi's St Cecilia's Day Ode for 1687 (pp. 24–63), Purcell's music for *Timon of Athens* (pp. 88–104) and his *Hail, bright Cecilia* of 1692 (pp. 106–14; incomplete). So, in spite of being copied at the beginning of the manuscript, the sonata may have been added nearer to 1690 than 1680.

The pinholes are still visible. Purcell's procedures in copying the devotional songs indicate that he was quite willing to alter what was already 'finished' music, and it is possible that the so-called 'correction slips' were deliberately pinned rather than glued to permit alternatives. Other revisions in the sonatas may be seen as offering alternatives either contrapuntally erudite (as in the largo of Sonata VIII) or technically challenging, as in the canzona of Sonata VII, perhaps made especially for Goodson and for the use of the Oxford Music School. In the case of Sonata VII those responsible for the 1697 publication naturally chose the technically simpler version without the octave leaps in the canzona, although such figuration can have caused no problems to capable amateur players, let alone Purcell's professional colleagues.[31]

The earliest of the large Purcell autographs, Fitzwilliam MS 88, contains most of Purcell's surviving copies of music by other composers.[32] An earlier copyist transcribed a number of verse anthems with strings before September 1677, when an index of them was compiled; Purcell appears to have worked on the score after this copyist, because his ascriptions from the outset are to 'Dr' Blow. However, early features in his hand, including not only the reversed 'e' but also an unusual hook-shaped bass clef,[33] suggest that he began not long after 10 December 1677, when Blow received his Lambeth doctorate: the inscription on the opening title page, 'A Table of all the Anthems contain'd in this book Sep: ye 13th Anno Domini 1677' may well record the state of the manuscript when the original copyist finished with it and passed it on to Purcell, who had perhaps carried out much of his own copying by 1680, if the presence of his early reversed 'e' in the text hand is a reliable guide. At least half the music copied in this book by Purcell was entered there well before the date indicated on the reverse flyleaf in the inscription 'God bless Mr Henry Purcell 1682 September ye 10th', although handwriting evidence suggests that additions were still being made to the manuscript at and after

---

31   In *The Works of Henry Purcell*, vol. VII (rev.) (Borough Green, 1981), xi, Michael Tilmouth points out that the original editor of the 1697 set did not make reference to Add. MS 30,930.

32   See Zimmerman, *Henry Purcell*, pp. 47–8.

33   The hook-shaped bass clef appears in the early autographs of the funeral sentences, British Library Add. MS 30,931 fol. 81, *My beloved spake*, Add. MS 30,932 fol. 87, and *Who hath believed our report*, Add. MS 30,932 fol. 94; in Purcell's copy of Humfrey's *By the waters of Babylon*, Add. MS 30,932 fol. 52 and at the beginning of the second work in the reverse section of Fitzwilliam MS 88, Blow's *God is our hope and strength*. Bruce Wood has convincingly suggested that Purcell's first version of the funeral sentences was made for the burial of Christopher Gibbons on 24 October 1676, a date quite consistent with the paper type of the early autograph. Most significantly, the early bass clef occurs in Christ Church MS Mus. 554 fol. 3, a single-sheet organ part of *God is our hope and strength* in Purcell's hand ascribed to 'Mr' John Blow. This part may have been one of Purcell's exemplars in copying the work into Fitzwilliam MS 88, resulting in a temporary reversion to his earlier clef form.

that time.[34] Why then did Purcell, between late 1677 and 1680, laboriously copy into score not only works by his mentors and contemporaries Locke and Blow but earlier music by Tallis, Byrd, Gibbons and Tomkins, much of it transcribed from the Barnard printed partbooks?[35] The explanation generally offered or implied, that Purcell transcribed these works for his own private study, does not seem adequate:[36] the composer who in the late 1670s could produce the verse anthem *My beloved spake* and by 1680 was refining his contrapuntal technique in the fantazias surely had little to learn from such relatively straightforward anthems as Byrd's *Prevent us, O Lord,* which he must already have thoroughly known from singing different parts and playing the organ. Even if he had wanted to study the compositional technique of more complex works like Gibbons's *Hosanna to the Son of David,* he could have done so by making an untexted score.[37] Instead, he produced a carefully edited version of the Barnard pieces in which virtually all the problems of underlay Barnard poses the performer have been solved, though often after more than one attempt and with some difficulty.[38]

The special quality of Purcell's work here is highlighted by comparison with the great Windsor scorebook, Cambridge, Fitzwilliam Museum Music MS 117 (see Table 1.6). Most of the copying in this score was finished by 1683, when fine calligraphic indexes were made for either end of the book;[39] and the paper, much of which bears the mark of the Angoulême factor Abraham Janssen, probably dates from no earlier than 1679.[40] There is no evidence that the copyist William Isaack did anything other than start at either end, with anthems and services, respectively, and keep going: in 1671 he was described as one of the 'most diligent' members of the choir at

---

[34] At the 'anthems with instruments' end Purcell appears to have added Blow's *Cry aloud and spare not* and *Sing unto the Lord O ye saints,* and at the reverse end the first seventeen of thirty-three works, before 1680. Only the final additions at either end appear to have been made after 1683.

[35] See Robert Shay, 'Purcell as Collector of "Ancient" Music: Fitzwilliam MS 88', chap. 2 below. Although we disagree about the date of Purcell's contributions, the present discussion owes much to Dr Shay's work and advice.

[36] For example in Zimmerman, *Henry Purcell,* p. 47; J. A. Westrup, *Purcell,* rev. edn by Nigel Fortune (London, 1980), p. 26.

[37] As he apparently did of Monteverdi's 'Cruda Amarilli', a fragment of which appears in Purcell's hand on the back of a correction slip in the autograph copy of his B♭ Benedicite, Bodleian Library MS Mus.a.1. See Franklin B. Zimmerman, 'Purcell and Monteverdi', *The Musical Times* 99 (1958), 368–9.

[38] See chap. 2 below, for a detailed discussion of Purcell's editing.

[39] See the dates given in the index. On fol. 241, Blow's *Hear my voice O God* is inscribed 'July ye 18th 1683'. This is one of thirty anthems added between fols. 201 and 277 after the compilation of the original index.

[40] An ascription to 'Mr' John Blow in the service music section (fol. 374) may indicate that the copying of this end of the manuscript began rather earlier.

St George's Chapel,[41] an assessment amply borne out by this huge and largely accurate copying project, which could well have taken the whole four years from 1679 to 1683.

Almost all the anthems, whether full, verse or with instruments, found in Fitzwilliam MS 88 are also in Fitzwilliam MS 117, often in closely related readings. If, however, one applies the strictest possible criteria of correspondence in text, underlay, barring and incidental detail, one can see that two distinct and well-separated sections of Fitzwilliam MS 117 are almost certain to have been copied directly from Purcell's autograph, and that two other works common to both sources but not copied from the Purcell have been subsequently corrected from it.[42] At a very late stage, after the indexing and pagination of Fitzwilliam MS 117 was complete, string parts derived from Fitzwilliam MS 88 to four anthems by Humfrey were copied on separate sheets now bound at the beginning of the volume. It seems probable, then, that the scorebook travelled to Windsor on more than one occasion during the time when Isaack was working on his own score: Purcell is known to have spent some time there in 1682 and as the court went to Windsor every summer it is likely that his visits there were fairly regular.[43] The difference in precision between the anthems copied by Isaack from Purcell's autograph and those he either scored himself from parts or copied from other scores is striking and underlines the exceptional care taken by Purcell.

However Purcell's score book reached Windsor, the purpose of its journey was more probably professional than private; it is hardly likely that he took it with him in order to copy music that would have been readily available in London. The score might have been used in the performance of verse anthems with strings; the group of musicians who went in 1682 included string players, and the Purcell score was the source not only of entire verse and full anthems in Fitzwilliam MS 117 but also of string symphonies added to

---

41 Shelagh Bond, *The Chapter Acts of the Dean and Canons of Windsor, 1430, 1523–1672* (Windsor, 1966), p. 295.

42 The six-part version of Byrd's *O Lord make thy servant Charles our King* in Fitzwilliam MS 117 appears at first unrelated to the faulty five-part version scored by Purcell from the Barnard prints. Isaack undoubtedly began with Purcell's copy, however, as he not only faithfully copied Purcell's arrangement of the text (which Barnard modified from the original 'O Lord make thy servant Elizabeth our Queen' without suggesting how the underlay might be adapted) but also copied, in the same ink, Purcell's successful attempt to supply a missing entry, designated by him 'Tenor Cantoris', at 'Give him his heart's desire' (see ill. 2.3, p. 46). No doubt warned by Purcell that there was a part missing, Isaack had allowed a second tenor stave throughout. He then found a copy of the missing tenor part, really the first tenor, with another version of the text, and filled in the rest of this blank stave in a different coloured ink. Finally he altered the text of the second tenor part, Purcell's careful underlay of which he had diligently copied, to correspond with the first tenor he had found elsewhere.

43 Zimmerman, *Henry Purcell,* p. 87.

works previously copied without them. A further clue to the possible purpose of Purcell's copies of earlier music is that three of the first four anthems by Blow copied into the reverse end of Fitzwilliam MS 88 – *God is our hope and strength*, *O God, wherefore art thou absent* and *Save me O God* – appear consecutively near the end of a list of anthems copied for the Chapel Royal between 1670 and 1676, and also in Fitzwilliam MS 117.[44] Purcell's copies have alterations in the layout of these works, for example re-ordering the parts of *God is our hope and strength* so that the generally lower pitched of the two bass parts is on the bottom stave and redistributing entries between the two treble parts in *O God, wherefore are thou absent*, which has the effect of keeping the highest part in the chorus at the top of the score. It is difficult to imagine any reason other than practical for making these changes, and such editorial work may have been amongst the first professional tasks assigned to Purcell between 1677 and 1680.

Each of the three great autographs has a character of its own. Purcell's initial task in Fitzwilliam MS 88 appears to have been primarily editorial, concerned with establishing good performance texts of both earlier and contemporary music in the Chapel Royal and Westminster Abbey repertory; some of this work was passed on to St George's Chapel, Windsor, through the scorebook copied by William Isaack.[45] Only later did Purcell begin to use Fitzwilliam MS 88 for fair copies of his own music.[46] The purpose of British Library R.M. MS 20.h.8, which is largely devoted to Purcell's own music, is less readily apparent: the book seems too unwieldy to have been used in performance, though it could perhaps have been laid flat on top of the harpsichord. Its occasional incompleteness argues against consistent use as either a fair copy from which performing parts were subsequently made or as a reference copy. Where it is incomplete there is generally enough detail for a good musician to have used it to accompany or direct a performance, as in the final chorus of *Swifter Isis, swifter flow* where Purcell carefully provided both a complete harmonic outline and clear directions at points where the music departs from a straightforward homophonic texture. All this suggests that R.M. MS 20.h.8 was not merely a file copy which Purcell did not have time to finish. Another incomplete copy in the score is *Rejoice in the Lord alway*, fols. 37v–39v, which lacks all the inner string and chorus parts

---

44 Andrew Ashbee, *Records of English Court Music*, vol. I: *1660–1685* (Snodland, 1986), 162–4.

45 Peter Holman, 'Bartholomew Isaack and "Mr Isaack" of Eton: a confusing tale of Restoration Musicians', *The Musical Times* 128 (1987), 381–5, suggests that another member of the Isaack family copied New York Public Library MS Drexel 5061, the only extensive secondary source of the Purcell fantazias.

46 The inscription 'God bless Mr Henry Purcell 1682 September ye 10th' on the final flyleaf may possibly record the date when the manuscript ceased to be an official copy and became Purcell's private property.

but has the verses complete apart from the middle voice of the chorus interjections. Although it is not surprising that Purcell should compose by writing down treble and bass parts first, it is not so obvious why he should follow this procedure in making a fair copy unless he wanted to ensure that, whatever happened, the essential features of the music were written down first: in *Rejoice in the Lord alway* the immediate purposes would appear to have included rehearsing the singers in their solo parts and playing the continuo instrument, possibly at rehearsal rather than performance, throughout. In all probability R.M. MS 20.h.8 had a variety of functions in the Whitehall musical establishment: it contains a complete range of vocal music, from anthems and welcome songs with instruments to solo pieces, suitable for most occasions on which singers might be required to perform at court, and could well have been used by Purcell for coaching, rehearsal and accompanying. Whatever else is missing from the larger scale pieces, solo vocal parts are usually present. For most of the contents the score does in fact provide a complete and accurate text, but where Purcell appears to have been overtaken by events, he has generally given priority to providing a performing outline of a whole work or section rather than a complete copy of a part of it.

Fitzwilliam MS 88 and R.M. 20.h.8 are clearly connected with Purcell's professional work as a composer and performer at court. In contrast, Add. MS 30,930 for the most part reflects the more private side of Purcell's musicianship; the exploration of both early and modern forms of instrumental music, and the composition of devotional songs which evidently won the approval of his master John Blow. Whereas the other two volumes were probably kept at Whitehall or, in the case of Fitzwilliam MS 88, possibly at the Abbey, Add. MS 30,930 was perhaps kept at Purcell's home and contains some of the music Purcell might have played or sung with his family or friends. Its unofficial, informal character is reflected in the irregular collation of its eventual binding. The great autographs nevertheless have two overriding characteristics in common: they are not retrospective collections of works in a form the composer thought definitive, and there is no evidence that Purcell himself regarded them in anything other than a practical light, either as performing material or as sources for copying parts for performance. In short, the three manuscripts have more the character of a workshop than a museum and, in spite of their status as autographs, they neither render all secondary sources redundant nor provide a solution to all editorial problems. They offer us something less immediately useful but ultimately more valuable, a privileged insight into Purcell's working life as both performer and composer.

Table 1.1. *Purcell's major autograph scores*

Manuscript/dimensions	Watermark/ countermark	Stave ruling[a]	Probable original collation[b]
Add. MS 30,930 408 × 260 mm	Fleur-de-lis/IHS with ET	16 staves: one block of four, 11 (13.5) 10.5 (13) 13 (13) 11 = 83.5; two blocks of six, 10 (13.5) 11.5 (13.5) 11 (13.5) 11 (13) 12 (13)11 = 132	Irregular: see Table 1.4
R.M. MS 20.h.8 410 × 250 mm	Fleur-de-lis/IHS with ET, as Add. MS 30,930	16 staves: four blocks of four, 12 (13) 11.5 (12.5) 11.5 (13) 11 = 85	46 gatherings mostly of six folios
Fitzwilliam MS 88 436 × 277 mm	Bend on shield/RC	15 staves: three distinct blocks of five, 11 (13.5) 11 (13) 10.5 (14) 11 (14) 10 = 108	25 gatherings all but one of six folios

a Dimensions in millimeters; unbracketed measurements give the width of the staves; bracketed measurements the width of the gaps between them; = shows the overall measurement of the rastrum.
b Collation is not readily apparent in any of these MSS and is deduced from watermark/ countermark and stave ruling matches. A number of folios have been removed from all three manuscripts. The present collation of Add. MS 30,930 is partly artificial; that of Fitzwilliam MS 88 entirely so.

Table 1.2. *Manuscripts consisting of 'identical' paper made by Etienne Touzeau*

Add. MS 30,930	'The Work's of Hen: Purcell Anno Dom. 1680'
R.M. MS 20.h.8	
West Sussex C.R.O. MS Cap. VI/I/I	'Jo: Walther his Book Anno Domino 1680'; ruled identically with R.M. MS 20.h.8
Christ Church MS 628	This paper up to p. 80 only: thereafter fleur-de-lis/IHS with RC. Blow autograph.
British Library MS Harl. 1501	'Scritto a richesta di Monsieur Didie in Londra Anno Domini 1681'. Reggio autograph.

Table 1.3. *Contents of British Library R.M. MS 20.h.8*

Folio		Hand:(P = Purcell: A–C unidentified)
2	Flyleaf inscribed 'A Score Book Containing Severall Anthems wth Symphonies'	P, after 1683
3	Flyleaf: 'The Table' (incomplete)	P, after 1683
4	Heading: 'Anthems'	
	It is a good thing to give thanks	P
7v	O praise God in his holiness	P
13v	Awake, put on thy strength	A (a few bars P)
16v	'Dr Blow': O pray for the peace of Jerusalem	P
17v	In thee O Lord do I put my trust	P
22v	The Lord is my light and my salvation	P
25v	I was glad when they said unto me	P
28v	My heart is fixed O God	P
32v	Praise the Lord O my soul	P
37v	Rejoice in the Lord alway	P
39v	Why do the heathen so furiously rage	P
43	Unto thee will I cry	P
48	I will give thanks unto thee O Lord	P, after 1684
52	They that go down to the sea in ships (incomplete)	P
	I will give thanks unto the Lord	Index only
	O Lord, grant the King a long life	Index only
53v	My heart is inditing	P, 1685
67	O sing unto ye Lord	A
75	Praise ye Lord O Jerusalem	A
81	Praise the Lord, O my soul (incomplete)	A
	Manuscript inverted	
246v	Flyleaf: 'Score Booke'	P
	'Anthems and Welcome Songs and other Songs all by my father'	? Edward Purcell
245v	A welcome Song in ye Year 1681 For ye King: Swifter, Isis	P
238	A Welcome Song for his Royall Highness at his return from Scotland in the yeare 1682: What shal be done in behalf of the man	P
232v	A Welcome Song for his Majesty at his return from New Market October ye 21 1682: The summers absence unconcern'd we beare	P
226	How pleasant is this flow'ry plain	P
224	Wee reap all ye pleasures (incomplete)	P
222v	Heark how ye wild Musitians sing	P
218	Heark Damon heark	P
217	Above ye Tumults of a buisy state	P
216	(The 9th Ode of Horrace imitated) (A dialogue betwixt ye Poet & Lydia): While you for me alone had Charmes	P
215	(A dialogue between Charon & Orpheus) Hast, gentle Charon	P
213v	(ye Epicure) Underneath this Mirtle shade	P
212v	(The Concealment) No: to what purpose should I speak	P
211v	Draw neare you Lovers that complaine	P
211	(Jobs Curse) Let ye Night perish	P

Folio		Hand:(P = Purcell: A-C unidentified)
210	Amidst ye shades	P
209	See where she sits	P
207	A Song yt was perform'd to Prince George upon his marriage with ye Lady Ann: From hardy Climes & dangerous toyles of Warr	P; 28 July 1683
201	(Mr Cowley's complaint) In a deep visions intelectuall scene	P
198v	(Song) out of Mr Herbert: With sick and famish'd Eyes	P
197v	Ye Welcome Song perform'd to his Majesty in ye Year 1683: Fly bold Rebellion	P
190	A Latine Song made upon St Cecilia whoes day is commerated yearly by all Musitians made in ye year 1683; Laudate Cecilliam	P
188	Oh, what a Scene do's entertain my sight	P
186v	Tho' my Mistriss be fair	P
185v	(A Serandeing Song) Soft notes & gently rais'd	P
184	A Seranading Song: Silvia, thou brighter eye of Night	P
183v	Goe tell Aminta gentle Swain	P
182v	The Welcome Song perform'd to his Majesty in ye Year 1684: From those serene & rapturous joyes	P
175	(Song on a Ground) Cease Anxious World your fruitless pain	Mostly P; last line, on 174v, A
174v	The Rich Rivall out of Mr Cowly: They say you're angry	A
174	O solitude my sweetest choice	A to end of 174; then P
173	When Teucer from his Father fled	P
172	(Sighs for our Late Sov'raign King Charles ye 2d): If Pray'rs & Teares	P
170v	(The Thraldome out of Mr Cowley)	P; title only
169v	In some kind dream	P
169	(The 34 chapter of Isaiah paraphras'd by Mr Cowley): Awake and wth attention hear	P
166	Welcome Song 1685 being ye first Song perform'd to King James ye 2d: Why are all ye Muses mute	P to end of 162v; then B
157	Here's to ye Dick	A
155	Welcome Song 1686: Yee tunefull Muses	B
144v	If ever I more riches did desire	P
140	(Anacreon's Defeat): This Poet sings the Trojan Warrs	P
139	Welcome Song 1687; Sound the Trumpet, Beat ye Drum	P
128	The Resurrection: out of Cowley's Pindaricks: Begin ye Song	P; outline of beginning only
127	[Cazzati] Crucior in hac flamma	P
125v	A Song that was perform'd at Mr Maidwells a schoolmaster on ye 5th of August 1689 ye words by one of his scholars: Celestial Music	P to middle of 124, then C
116v	Now does ye Glorious day Appear	A (1689)
105v	Of old when Heroes thought it base: Mr H Pursell 1690	A
90	Arise my muse arise	A (1690)

23

Table 1.4. *British Library Add. MS 30,930: current and possible original collation*

Unwritten folios are not numbered in the manuscript and are here indicated thus: 62/i.
Torn-out pages of which there is any evidence are shown in the same way.

Folios tabulated within square brackets [57/i] are hypothetical; original gatherings that no
longer exist are identified in italics, e.g. *original gathering E1*

------------ = visible stitching

Up = block of four staves at the top of the page
Lo = block of four staves at the bottom of the page

Where the stave ruling is the same throughout a gathering the description is given for the
first folio only.

a = fleur-de-lis watermark a   IHSa = countermark a
b = fleur-de-lis watermark b   IHSb = countermark b

All references to 'top' or 'bottom' or to inverted watermarks (↓) assume that the manuscript
is viewed the right way up for the vocal music and inverted for the instrumental, following
the current British Library foliation from front to back.

	Folio	Watermark	Ruling		
Gathering A					
	3	IHSa	Up	3r–4r:	Plung'd in the confines (1)
	4	a↓		4r–5v:	O all ye people (2)
	5	b			
	6	b↓		6r–7r:	When on my sick bed (3)

	7	IHSb↓		7v–8r:	Gloria Patri (4)
	8	IHSb		8v–11r:	Jehova, quam multi sunt hostes (5)
	9	IHSa↓			
	10	a			
Gathering B					
	11	IHSb	Lo	11r–12v:	Beati omnes (6)
	12	IHSb	Up		
	13	IHSb	Up		Domine, non est exaltatum (incomplete) (7)

	13/i	b	Up		
	13/ii	b	Up		
	[13/iii	b]		Guard stub	
Gathering C					
	[13/iv	IHSb]		Guard stub	
	13/v	IHSb		[All this gathering Lo except for 13/ix and x]	
	13/vi	b↓			
	13/vii	IHSb			
	13/viii	IHSa			
	13/ix	IHSb	Up		

	13/x	b	Up		
	13/xi	a			
	14	b			Lord not to us (8); 14v blank
	15	IHSb↓			15r blank; 15v: Ah! few and full of sorrows (9)
	15/i	b			Blank; clearly misplaced
	16	b			Continuation of 'Ah! few and full'

The evident disarrangement here is best considered after the following gathering.

	Folio	Watermark	Ruling	
Gathering D				
	17	b	Lo	Last part of 'Ah! few and full' (incomplete); 17v blank
	18	b↓		18r–20r: O Lord our Governor (10)
	19	IHSb		
	20	IHSb		20v–21v: O, I'm sick of life (11)

	21	b		
	22	b		22r–23r: Lord, I can suffer (12)
	23	IHSb↓		23v–24r: Hear me, O Lord and that soon (13)
	24	IHSb		24v–25v: Since God so tender a regard (14)

Continuity of the music shows that folios 14–17 were originally consecutive.
Gathering D might thus have been preceded by a six-folio gathering as follows:
Original Gathering C2

	[13/iv]	IHSb↓		
	13/vi	b		
	13/vii	IHSb		
	14	b		Lord not to us (8)
	15	IHSb↓		15v–17r: Ah! few and full (9)
	16	b		

The three blank bifolia may have made up a separate, unused, six-folio gathering:
Original Gathering C1

	13/v	IHSb	Lo
	13/viii	IHSa	Lo
	13/ix	IHSb	Up
	13/x	b	Up
	13/xi	a	Lo
	15/i	b	Lo

Gathering E				
	25	b↓	Up	25v–27v: Guarded. 25v–27v: Early, O Lord (15)
	26	IHSa	Lo	
	26/i	IHSb	Lo	
	26/ii	IHSa	Lo	
	27	IHSa↓	Up	Continuation of 'Early, O Lord'

	27/i	[a]		stub: C17 paper
	28	a↓	Lo	28v–29v: Hear me, O Lord, the great support (16)
	28/i	a	Lo	
	28/ii	b	Lo	Guarded
	28/iii	IHSb	Lo	Guarded

'Early, O Lord' must run consecutively from 26r to 27, and 'Hear me, O Lord' from 28 to
29. These requirements are met by the following hypothetical structure:
Original Gathering E1

	25	b↓	Up	
	26	IHSa	Lo	
	27	IHSa↓	Lo	
	27/i	[a↓]		stub
	28/i	a	Lo	
	28/iii	IHSb	Lo	

28/iii does not match 25, but is guarded and could be pasted in the wrong way up.

	Folio	Watermark	Ruling	
Original Gathering E2				
	26/ii	IHSa	Lo	
	26/i	IHSb	Lo	
	28/ii	b	Lo	
	28	a	Lo	
Gathering F				
	29	IHSa	Lo	29v: Conclusion of 'Hear me O Lord'
	29/i	IHSa		
	------	-----	-----	-----
	29/ii	a		
	29/iii	a		
Gathering G				
	29/iv	b↓	Lo	
	29/v	b		
	------	-----	-----	-----
	29/vi	IHSb		
	30	IHSb↓		End of Sonata X (inverted)
Gathering H				
	30/i		Guard stub	
	30/ii	IHSb	Up	
	30/iii	b	Lo	
	30/iv	IHSb↓	Lo	Misplaced unused gathering
	30/v	b	Up	
	30/vi	IHSa	Up	
Gathering J				
	31	b	Lo	Sonata X
	32	b↓		Sonata IV (fragment; second copy)
	33	b↓		
	34	b↓		Sonata VIII
	------	-----	-----	-----
	35	IHSb↓		35v: Sonata VII
	36	IHSb↓		
	37	IHSb↓		37v: Sonata IX
	[37/i	IHSb]		
Gathering K				
	37*	Part of leaf:		37*v: end of Sonata III; 37*r: part of Sonata IV
	38	IHSb	Up	Continuation of Sonata III
	39	b	Up	Sonata III
	40	IHSa	Up	
	41	a	Up	Sonata II
	41/i			stub: C17 paper
	42	b	Up	
	43	IHSb↓	Up	'Sonnata's': verso discoloured
Gathering L				
	43/i	a↓	Up	
	43/ii	IHSa	Lo	
	44	b↓	Lo	fragments

Folio	Watermark	Ruling	
44/i	IHSb↓	Lo	
44/ii	a	Lo	
45	IHSa↓	Up	End of In Nomine [in 7 parts]

Folio 45 here must originally have come next to 46, as it does now.
Gathering M

46	a	Lo	46r: In Nomine [7 parts]: 46v blank
47	IHSa	Lo	47v: End of In Nomine [6 parts]
47/i	IHSa	Lo	
47/ii	a	Lo	
47/iii	a	Lo	
47/iv	IHSa	Lo	

48 must come inside 47. 48–48/ii have been misplaced, this gathering probably originally being:

Original Gathering M1

46	a	Lo	46r: In Nomine [7 parts]; ends fol. 45
47	IHSa	Lo	
48	b	Lo	48r-47v: In Nomine [6 parts];
			48r: 'Here Begineth ye 6 7 & 8 part
			Fantazia's'
47/i	IHSa	Lo	
47/ii	a	Lo	
48/ii	IHSb	Lo	
47/iii	a	Lo	
47/iv	IHSa	Lo	

The reasons for matching 48 with 48/ii are given after Gathering P below.
Gathering N

47/v	a↓	Up	
47/vi	IHSa	Lo	
47/vii	a↓	Lo	
47/viii	IHSa	Lo	
47/ix	a	Lo	
47/x	IHSa↓	Lo	
47/xi	a	Lo	
47/xii	IHSa↓	Up	

Gathering P

48	b	Lo	In nomine [6 parts]: 'Here Begineth ye 6,
			7 & 8 part Fantazia's'
48/i	b		
48/ii	IHSb		
49	IHSa		
50	a		Fantazias of 5 Parts: [Fantazia on one note]
50/i	a		50/i and iii both guarded
[50/ii]			
50/iii	a		

27

Folio	Watermark	Ruling

Gathering P is artificial. 48 and 48/ii, both guarded, offer the most likely pairing and really belong in the previous written gathering after 47, as shown above. 49 and 50 are another apparent pair, the implications of which are shown below. 48/i has probably lost its partner; 50/i and iii are problematical.

Gathering Q

51	IHSa	Lo	'Here begineth ye 5 part: Fantazies'
[51/i]			
51/ii	IHSb		
51/iii	b↓		51/iii–52 form an artificial bifolium
51/iv	a↓		
52	b		52: dance movements
52/i	IHSa↓		
52/ii	IHSb↓		
53	IHSa		53r: dances; 53v: end of overture
53/i	a		

The bifolium 51–53/i must be misplaced as it interrupts the overture; 52 and 53 need to be continuous for the dances. The original arrangement may have been thus:

Original Gathering P1

48/i	b	Lo	
49	IHSa		49v: End of Fantazia on one note
50	a		50r: Beginning of Fantazia on one note
[50/ii	IHSb]		

Original Gathering Q1

51	IHSa	Lo	'Here begineth ye 5 part: Fantazies'
51/iii	b↓		
51/iv	a↓		
52/i	IHSa↓		
52/ii	IHSb↓		
53/i	a		

Original Gathering Q2

[51/i	a]	Lo	
51/ii	IHSb		
52	b		Dances
53	IHSa		53r: dances; 53v: overture ends

Gathering R

54	IHSb	Lo	54r: Overture
54/i	IHSa		
54/ii	b↓		
54/iii	a↓		
54/iv	IHSa↓		
54/v	IHSb↓		
54/vi	a		
54/vii	b		

Gathering S

55	a↓	Up	Chacony ends
56	b↓	Lo	56r: Chacony begins
56/i	IHSb↓	Lo	
57	IHSa↓	Up	57r: Pavan

28

Gathering T

[57/ib]			
58	b↓	Up	fantazia (incomplete) Feb.ye 24th 1682/3
59	a↓	Up	

60	IHSa↓	Up	
61	IHSb↓	Up	
62	IHSb↓	Lo	62v: end of June 22 fantazia

Gathering V

62/i	b↓	Lo	
62/ii	IHSb	Up	
63	IHSb↓	Lo	63r: June ye 22 1680

64	IHSb	Lo	64r: June ye 19 1680
64/i	b	Up	
64/ii	IHSb↓	Lo	
64/iii	b↓	Lo	
64/iv	b	Lo	

The unused bifolia, 62/i–64/ii and 62/ii–64/i, match and are misplaced; they could have come from anywhere. 63–64 is an artificial bifolium; the two folios match the isolated folios 64/iii and iv. 64 must be continuous with 65. The most satisfactory interpretation of the original structure is the following complete re-ordering into a ten-folio gathering:

Original Gathering TV

64/iv	b	Lo	
64/iii	b↓	Lo	
[57/i	b↓]		
58	b↓	Up	58r: Feb ye 24 1682/3
59	a↓	Up	59r: August ye 31 1680
60	IHSa↓	Up	60r: August ye 19 80
61	IHSb↓	Up	61r: June ye 30 80
62	IHSb↓	Lo	62r: June ye 23 80
63	IHSb↓	Lo	63r: June ye 22 1680
64	IHSb	Lo	64r: June ye 19 1680

Gathering X

64/v	IHSb	Up	
65	IHSb	Lo	65r: June ye 14 1680
66	a↓	Lo	66r: June ye 11 1680
67	IHSa	Lo	67r: June ye 10 1680

68	a	Lo	68r: 'Here begineth ye 4 part fantazies'
68/i	IHSa↓	Lo	
68/ii	b	Lo	
68/iii	b	Up	64/v–68/iii misplaced

Gathering Y

68/iv	b↓	Lo	
69	b↓		69v: [Fantazia 3]
[69/i	a]		
70	IHSa		70v: Fantazia [2]
71	IHSb↓		71r: 'Here begineth ye 3 part fantazia's'
72	IHSb↓		

Table 1.5. *Contents of Christ Church MS Mus 628*

Page		Ascription
1	Gloria Patri	Henry Purcell
3	O all yee people clap your hands	Henry Purcell
8	Goe perjur'd man*a*	Jo: Blow
11	O Praise the Lord*b*	Pellham Humfreys
19	I said in the cutting off of my days*b*	Jo:Blow
26	Thou are my king O God*b*	Pelham Humfrey
32	The Kings of Tharsis*b*	Jo: Blow
39	Plung'd in the confines of despair	Henry Purcell
43	The King shall rejoyce*b*	Pelham Humfrey
52	When the Lord turned again*b*	Jo: Blow
63	Hear my crying O God*b*	Pelham Humfrey
74	The Lord is my sheapherd*b*	Jo: Blow
86	O give thanks unto the Lord*b*	Pelham Humfreys
96	O give thanks unto the Lord*b*	Jo: Blow
111	Since God so tender a regard	Henry Purcell
116	Early O Lord my fainting soul	Henry Purcell
121	O I'm sick of life	Henry Purcell
125	O Lord our governour	Henry Purcell
130	When on my sick bed I languish	Henry Purcell
135	Jehova quam multi sunt hostes	[Henry Purcell]
141	Beati omnes	Henry Purcell

a secular song with two violins
b verse anthem with strings

Table 1.6. *Inventory of Cambridge, Fitzwilliam Museum Music MS 117 (anthem section)*

Relationship with Fitzwilliam MS 88
A = concordance without evident immediate relationship
B = copy corrected from Fitzwilliam MS 88
C = close concordance suggesting an immediate common source
D = direct copy from MS 88 to MS 117

* = derived from Barnard printed partbooks

Numbers indicate sequence in Fitzwilliam MS 88: + in original sequence at the front of the book; otherwise in inverted sequence from the end.

Folio	Page (original)	Title	Ascription	Relationship with Fitzwilliam MS 88
1	—	*Wipe away my sins	Mr Tho: Tallis	
3v	—	*O God whom our offences have displeased	Mr Wm Bird	
5	—	*Blessed be thy name, O God	Mr Tho: Tallis	
9	—	Like as the hart [string parts]	[Pelham Humfrey]	D
10	—	O Praise the Lord [string parts]	[Pelham Humfrey]	D
11	—	O Lord my God [string parts]	[Pelham Humfrey]	D
12	—	Lord teach us to number our days [strings]	[Pelham Humfrey]	D
13	—	How long wilt thou forget me	Dr Gibbons	
14	—	Let thy merciful ears O Lord	[Dr Gibbons]	

[End of additional material bound before the main volume]

Folio	Page (original)	Title	Ascription	Relationship with Fitzwilliam MS 88
15	1	The Lord said unto my lord	Dr Gibbons	
16v	4	Sing unto the Lord	Dr Christopher Gibbons	
19	9	Teach me, O Lord	Dr Christopher Gibbons	
21	13	O Lord, I have loved the habitation	Mr Thomas Tomkins	D (14)
22v	16	Hear my prayer, O God	Mr Adrian Batten	D (16)
24v	20	*Lift up your heads, O ye gates	Mr Orlando Gibbons	D (12)
26v	24	*Prevent us, O Lord	Mr William Bird	D (10)
27v	26	*O Lord make thy servant Charles our king	Mr William Bird	D (11)
29	29	*Hosanna to the son of David	Mr Orlando Gibbons	D (4)
31v	34	*Deliver me from mine enemies	Mr Robert Parsons	
33	37	The king shall rejoice	Dr Wm Childe	
34	39	O lord grant the king a long life	Dr Wm Childe	
36	43	Save me, O God	Dr Wm Childe	
37v	46	I will be glad and rejoice	Dr Wm Childe	
39	49	O Lord God the heathen are come	Dr Wm Childe	
41	53	*O Lord grant the king a long life	Mr Tho. Weelks	
42	55	*O thou God almighty	Mr Edmund Hooper	

Folio	Page (original)	Title	Ascription	Relationship with Fitzwilliam MS 88
43	57	*With all our hearts and mouths	Mr Thomas Tallis	
44	59	*The Lord bless us and keep us	Mr Robert White	
45v	62	Arise O Lord	Mr William Bird	
47	65	*I call and cry	Mr Tallis	A (9)
48	65bis	*O Lord I bow the knees of my heart	Mr Will Mundy	A (13)
49v	68	*Behold it is Christ	Mr Hooper	
50v	70	Bow thine ear, O Lord	Mr Bird	B (8)
52	73	O clap your hands	Dr Wm Childe	
52v	74	Sing we merrily	Dr Wm Child	A (18)
52v	74	*O give thanks	Dr Giles	B (15)
55v	80	Holy, holy, holy	Dr Child	
56v	82	*Sing joyfully	Mr Wm Bird	
58	85	Behold, thou hast made my days	Mr Orlando Gibbons	
59v	88	Holy, holy, holy [8 parts]	Dr Childe	
59v	88	Blessed is he that considereth	Michael Wise	
60v	90	Gloria in Excelsis [in English; 8 parts]	Dr Wm Childe	
62v	94	I will magnify thee	Dr Giles	
65	99	Almighty God which by the leading of a star	Dr Bull	
66v	102	Behold how good and joyful	Dr Childe	
68v	106	Give the king thy judgements	Dr Childe	
70	109	My heart is fixed	Dr Childe	
70v	110	Holy, holy, holy [in e minor]	Dr Child	
71	111	O how amiable	Dr Childe	
72	113	Turn thou us, good Lord	Dr Childe	
73v	116	O praise the Lord	Dr Wm. Child	
74v	118	The earth is the Lord's	Dr Childe	
77v	122	O Lord my God [strings fol. 11]	Mr Pelham Humphryes	A (2+)
80	127	Have mercy upon me O God	Mr Pelham Humphryes	
82v	132	O praise the Lord [strings fol. 10]	Mr Pelham Humphrys	A (1+)
84v	136	Lord teach us to number [strings fol. 12]	Mr Pelham Humphryes	A (6+)
85v	138	God is our hope and strength	Dr John Blow	C (2)
89	145	O God, wherefore art thou absent	Dr Blow	C (3)
90v	148	Save me, O God	Dr John Blow	C (5)
91	149	Haste ye, O God, to deliver me [strings fol. 247v]	Mr Pelham Humphrys	
93	153	O be joyful	Mr Pelham Humphrye	
94v	156	Lord, what is man	Mr William Turner	
96	159	And I heard a great voice [strings fol. 244]	Dr John Blow	
99	165	When Israel came out of Egypt [strings fol. 246]	Dr John Blow	
101v	170	O Lord I have sinned	Dr Blow	A (1)
104	175	O Lord rebuke me not	Dr Childe	

Folio	Page (original)	Title	Ascription	Relationship with Fitzwilliam MS 88
105v	178	Let God arise	Dr Childe	
107v	182	If the Lord himself	Dr Childe	
108v	184	O pray for the peace of Jerusalem	Dr Child	
110v	186	O that the salvation	Dr Child	
111	187	Save me O God for thy name's sake	Mr Henry Purcell	C (17)
113	191	By the waters of Babylon	Mr Pelham Humphrys	
115v	196	Awake up my glory	Mr Michael Wise	
116v	198	Come unto me saith the Lord	B. Isaack	
118v	202	Turn thy face from my sins	Mr Matthew Locke	A (7)
120v	206	O God thou hast cast us out	Mr Purcell	C (27)
122v	210	My God my soul	Dr Blow	
124	213	'Vers of ye litany' (Remember not, O Lord)	Mr Purcell	A (25)
124v	214	I will sing unto the Lord	Mr Hen: Purcell	
125v	216	O Lord God of my salvation	Dr John Blow	C (26)
125v	214	O Lord thou hast searched me out	Dr Blow	
129	223	Like as the hart [strings fol.9]	Mr Humphryes	A (3+)
130v	226	Hear, O heavens	Mr Humphryes	
132	229	Lord thou hast been our refuge	Mr Turner	
134	233	Lord who can tell	Mr Henry Purcell	
135	235	Blessed be the Lord my strength	Mr Hen: Purcell	
137	239	Let God arise	Mr Henry Purcell	
138v	242	O Lord our governor	Mr Hen: Purcell	
141v	248	Lord how are they increased	Dr John Blow	
143v	252	Behold how good and joyful	Dr Blow	
144v	254	Lord let me know mine end	Mr Matthew Locke	A (6)
147v	260	I beheld and lo, a great multitude	Dr Blow	
151	267	Rejoice in the Lord	Mr Humphrys	
152	269	Blessed is the man	Mr Michael Wise	
153	271	How are the mighty fallen	Mr Michael Wise	
154v	274	My soul is weary of my life	Mr Henry Hall	
156v	278	Turn thee unto me O Lord	Dr John Blow	
158	281	O sing unto the Lord a new song	Dr John Blow	D (4+)
162v	288	Sing we merrily	Dr John Blow	D (5+)
164v	294	Lift up your heads	Dr Blow	D (7+)
166	297	Cry aloud and spare not	Dr Blow	D (9+)
170	305	Sing unto the Lord O ye saints	Dr Blow	D (10+)
176	317	When the son of man	Mr Matthew Locke	D (11+)
179	323	Awake, put on thy strength	Mr Michael Wise	
181	327	Blessed is he whose unrighteousness	Mr Henry Purcell	D (20)
185	335	Hear me, O Lord	Mr Hen Purcell	D (22)
187v	340	Bow down thine ear	Mr Purcell	D (23)
190	345	Man that is born of a woman	[Purcell]	D (24)
191v	349	Christ being raised from the dead	Dr Blow	D (28)
192	—	Thou knowest, Lord	Mr Purcell	
195v	355	The Lord is king [symphony added fol. 196; last work in original 1683 index]	Dr John Blow	

Folio	Page (original)	Title	Ascription	Relationship with Fitzwilliam MS 88
201	364	Not unto us	Mr Mathew Locke	
203v	369	I was glad	Mr Hen: Purcell	
206	374	I will magnify thee	Mr Wm Turner	
207	376	The king shall rejoice [symphony fol. 251v]	Mr Humphryes	
208v	379	O give thanks [strings fol. 247v]	Mr Pelham Humphryes	
210	382	When the Lord turned again [strings fol. 248v]	Dr John Blow	
212v	387	The Lord is my shepherd [symphony etc. fol. 249v]	Dr Blow	
214v	391	I said in the cutting off of my days [symphony etc. fol. 250v]	Dr Blow	
216v	395	The kings of Tharsis [symphony fol. 252]	Dr Blow	
219	398	Thou art my king O God	Mr Pelham Humphryes	
220v	401	Hear my crying O God	Mr Pelham Humphryes	
223	406	I will always give thanks	'The Clubb anthem'	
224v	409	My beloved spake	Mr Henry Purcell	
228	416	Arise O Lord	Dr Blow	
231	422	I will hearken	Dr John Blow	
233v	427	Blessed is the man	Dr John Blow	
236v	433	O give thanks 'upon a ground'	Dr John Blow	
241	442	Hear my voice O God ['July ye 18th 1683']	Dr Blow	
245	450	'The symphonyes to some of the foregoing anthems'		
252	465	Out of the deep	Dr Aldrich	
253	466	O give thanks	Mr John Walter	
255v	471	Thy mercy, O Lord, reacheth unto the heavens	Dr John Blow	
258v	477	O give thanks	Dr John Blow	
263v	487	I beheld, and lo in the midst of the throne	Dr John Blow	
266v	493	Hear me O God	Mr John Goldwin	
267v	495	Ponder my words O Lord	Mr John Goldwin	
270	500	God be merciful	Mr Locke	
271v	503	Jesus seeing the multitudes	Dr John Blow	
274	508	I am well pleased	Mr Goldwin	
275	510	O Lord God of hosts	Mr Goldwin	
276v	513	O God thou art my God 'To Mr Purcell's B mi service'	Mr Purcell	A (30)

'Here ends all ye Anthems in this Book'

2

Purcell as collector of 'ancient' music: Fitzwilliam MS 88

ROBERT SHAY

Thomas Tudway reported that 'The Standard of Church Music, begun by Mr Tallis and Mr Bird, &c. was continued for some years after ye Restauration'.[1] Indeed many of the cathedral sources from the 1660s and later show the careful maintenance of a core of older polyphonic anthems, closely related to John Barnard's *First Book of Selected Church Musick*.[2] This makes perfect sense: after the Restoration, the Church of England no doubt found it desirable to connect the unfocused musical scene of the 1660s with earlier times of greatness, venerating Renaissance polyphony – the oldest music widely known and thus deserving esteem. Moreover, the Church had little choice, because no new music was initially available.

Purcell would have certainly encountered many of these older works as he came of age. His relationship with the music of the past, however, extended far beyond casual acquaintance. In the years around 1680 he diligently pursued an interest in old polyphony, copying a number of late sixteenth- and early seventeenth-century anthems and emulating certain aspects of the style of these in his own newly composed works. At the same time he was addressing the viol fantasy, also an antiquated polyphonic genre. The primary testament to this facet of Purcell's development is his collection of anthems in score, Fitzwilliam Museum Music MS 88 (hereinafter referred to as Fitzwilliam MS 88). Purcell's keen interest in older music, as recorded in this much-studied manuscript, is

---

[1] From the preface to vol. II of his six-volume music collection prepared for the Harleian Library in 1715–20, now British Library Harley MS 7338, fol. 2v. For further discussion of Tudway's activities along with excerpts from his prefaces, see Christopher Hogwood, 'Thomas Tudway's History of Music', in *Music in Eighteenth-Century England*, ed. Christopher Hogwood and Richard Luckett (Cambridge, 1983), pp. 19–47.

[2] *The First Book of Selected Church Musick, Consisting of Services and Anthems, such as are now used in the Cathedrall, and Collegiat Churches of this Kingdome*, 10 partbooks (London, 1641; repr. Gregg International, 1972). I have shown the importance of Barnard's *First Book* as a source from which manuscripts were copied during Purcell's lifetime in 'Henry Purcell and "Ancient" Music in Restoration England', Ph.D. thesis, University of North Carolina at Chapel Hill (1991), chap. 2.

remarkable, because few of his contemporaries appear to have been as deeply affected by a sense of historical consciousness and to have responded to this repertory as composers.

THE GENESIS OF FITZWILLIAM MS 88

As one of three large volumes in which Purcell collected his works in fair copy in the early 1680s, Fitzwilliam MS 88 is a source of immense importance.[3] While this manuscript has long been the subject of scholarly inquiry, certain questions have never been satisfactorily answered, especially as regards its date and the possibility that Purcell was not its only compiler. I believe its genesis may be explained more thoroughly than has been done before, shedding light on the importance of the collection as a historical document.

Purcell devoted this large volume to anthems, organizing it into two sections starting from opposite ends: from the front, orchestral anthems; and from the reverse, full anthems together with those verse anthems requiring continuo only.[4] Unlike his other fair-copy collections, Fitzwilliam MS 88 contains a sizable number of works by other composers, both older contemporaries (Blow, Humfrey and Locke) and predecessors (Tallis, Byrd, Orlando Gibbons and others). This dual nature of MS 88, apparently both 'a copyist's anthology and . . . a composer's permanent collection', makes it unique amongst Purcell's autographs.[5] Since much of the original foliation is evident, there is no need to question the manuscript's structural integrity in reconstructing its genesis.[6] The collation is now difficult to determine as a result of rebinding and restoration carried out in 1979, though the original quiring can be deduced from watermark evidence. In short, one may assume that the manuscript remains today in essentially the same structure as when Purcell owned it: a large collection bound as a single volume.

---

[3]   The others are British Library Add. MS 30,930, containing fantazias, sonatas and selected vocal works, and British Library R.M. MS 20.h.8, containing orchestral anthems, welcome songs, odes and other secular music. They are discussed by Robert Thompson and Rebecca Herissone in chaps. 1 and 3 of this book.

[4]   It measures approximately 44 by 28 centimeters and contains 141 folios.

[5]   Eric Van Tassel, 'Fitzwilliam Museum, MS Mu 88: Score in the Hand of Henry Purcell', in *Cambridge Music Manuscripts, 900–1700*, ed. Iain Fenlon (Cambridge, 1982), p. 173. Van Tassel's physical description of Fitzwilliam MS 88 (pp. 170–4) is adequate, although I would note two corrections. (1) The watermarks of the flyleaves, unclear to him, are identifiable, each a fleur-de-lis but with different accompanying initials: on the front flyleaf 'PB' and on the reverse flyleaf as part of an 'IHS' figure 'ET'. (The paper and watermarks are discussed below.) (2) In the main body of the manuscript Purcell sometimes added three additional freehand staves to the fifteen ruled ones, allowing him a maximum of eighteen staves (not seventeen) and thus three systems for a six-part anthem. Van Tassel assumes that the entire manuscript is in Purcell's hand, an idea contested below.

[6]   The original foliation starts from each end of the manuscript. Modern numbering has been added to the reverse end, providing a single running sequence throughout. Since this numbering has been used in previous studies of Fitzwilliam MS 88, I have followed it here.

Flyleaves at each end provide partial lists of contents, as well as dates and other helpful information. At the head of the front flyleaf is the following inscription: 'A Table of all the Anthems contain'd in this book. Sep: ye 13th Anno Domine 167[?].' The last number is, unfortunately, illegible; the date is obviously important, and I will return to it shortly. Following the inscription is the list of the front contents.[7] The titles of the first six works are in the same neat hand as the inscription, while those of six more works were added later in a more casual style that closely resembles established examples of Purcell's handwriting. While the lists on both flyleaves have been categorically stated to be entirely in Purcell's hand, the inscription and first six titles cannot reasonably be identified as such.[8] Indeed, an examination of the handwriting within the body of the manuscript reveals that someone besides Purcell worked on Fitzwilliam MS 88.

A few words on the reverse flyleaf (fol. 143) are also in order.[9] Here are inscriptions clearly in Purcell's hand: 'God bless Mr Henry Purcell 1682' and 'September ye 10th 1682'.[10] Also on fol. 143 is the list of the reverse contents, ending arbitrarily at the bottom of the page. This list is entirely in a hand other than Purcell's and bears no relation to the first hand on the front flyleaf; the writing would appear to be a later, eighteenth-century addition.[11] Purcell was perhaps not so concerned with providing lists of contents, only with finishing the one on the front flyleaf because it had already been started.

In addition to Purcell's inscription and the anonymous list of contents on the reverse flyleaf, several pencil notations on fol. 143 were added well after his time, the last of which is signed and dated 'V. N. 1830'. All these are in the hand of Vincent Novello, collector and publisher of Purcell's sacred music. Novello states here that 'The whole of this very valuable Vol. is in the handwriting of Henry Purcell.' He knew Purcell's manuscripts well and, not

---

[7] A complete inventory of the contents is appended to this essay.

[8] Nigel Fortune and Franklin B. Zimmerman, 'Purcell's Autographs', in *Henry Purcell (1659–1695): Essays on his Music*, ed. Imogen Holst (London, 1959), p. 108.

[9] Fol. 143 is now bound into Fitzwilliam MS 88 reversed and inverted, so the writing appears on what is now the *recto*.

[10] A photograph of part of the reverse flyleaf appears in Franklin B. Zimmerman, *Henry Purcell, 1659–1695: His Life and Times*, rev. edn (Philadelphia, 1983), p. 76.

[11] Besides the obvious difference in style, other evidence strongly suggests that this list is not in Purcell's hand: the indexer uses 'the' exclusively, while Purcell usually abbreviates 'y^e', even for titles at the heads of pieces were there is abundant space, and the ascription 'Mr Munday' (that is, William Mundy) found on fol. 122v, is in the same hand and consistent with the spelling of the list on fol. 143, while Purcell prefers the form 'Mundy' at the end of the anthem on fol. 121. The indexer's hand may also be seen on fol. 9 (system 1, staff 4) filling in a line of text that was omitted by the original copyist. Also previously unnoticed is that the beginning of the list on the reverse flyleaf was written on top of text removed by scraping, perhaps by the later indexer. Vestiges of this layer are visible near the right margin, including what appears to be 'Purcell' among several other words – in his autograph. This may be nothing more than the composer practising his handwriting.

surprisingly, J. A. Fuller Maitland and A. H. Mann endorsed this seemingly authoritative statement in their 1893 catalogue of music at the Fitzwilliam Museum: they described MS 88 as a 'Volume of English Anthems in Henry Purcell's handwriting'.[12] In 1896 Augustus Hughes-Hughes raised the possibility that the first part of the manuscript was in what he described as a later hand, though he avoided declaring that it was not Purcell's.[13] G. E. P. Arkwright attempted to amplify Hughes-Hughes's comments,[14] noting the difference in hands and suggesting that the early portion of the manuscript represented Purcell's formal copying style, probably adopted when he was employed at Westminster Abbey.[15]

In their catalogue of Purcell's autographs, Nigel Fortune and Franklin B. Zimmerman also concluded that Fitzwilliam MS 88 was entirely in Purcell's hand:

> Hughes-Hughes says that the forty-two leaves containing the anthems at the front end of the volume are not in Purcell's hand. We can see why he was led to say this, but would say ourselves that only the first thirty leaves might be called in question and that anyway the assertion requires substantiation. Certainly if these leaves are not in Purcell's hand then many others in the manuscript that are extremely similar to them must also be thrown open to doubt. It is our belief that these leaves (like the rest of the volume) are in Purcell's hand; that they were written in his late 'teens when his handwriting was in a transitional state; and that they are almost certainly his earliest surviving autographs.[16]

This might have been the final word on the subject, but in 1980 Hughes-Hughes's suspicions were substantiated by Katherine T. Rohrer, who noticed two distinct hands within a single anthem:

> A look at fol. 20r, the closing page of Blow's anthem *Sing we merrily*, reveals both hands at work. Apparently the person from whom Purcell inherited the volume left this page incomplete, filling in only the text in the first system

12   *Catalogue of the Music in the Fitzwilliam Museum, Cambridge* (London, 1893), p. 37.
13   'Henry Purcell's Handwriting', *The Musical Times* 37 (1896), 82; Hughes-Hughes does not say whether he means Purcell's or someone else's later hand, though he believes the first forty-two pages are in this hand (and this statement is problematic because neither forty-two nor twenty-one folios mark a line of differentiation).
14   'Purcell's Church Music', *The Musical Antiquary* 1 (1909–10), 243; and *The Works of Henry Purcell*, vol. XIIIA (London, 1921), iii.
15   Purcell replaced Blow as organist at the Abbey in 1679 (Westminster Abbey Muniments [WAM] 33,715, fol. 2). From 1675 to 1678 Purcell was paid for tuning the Abbey organ (WAM 33,709, fol. 5; WAM 33,710, fol. 5; WAM 33,712, fol. 5; WAM 33,713, fol. 5), and in 1676 he was paid 'for pricking out two bookes of organ parts' now lost (WAM 33,710, fol. 5v). J. A. Westrup cautioned against applying the title 'copyist' to Purcell, as earlier biographers had done, since no such position existed at the Abbey; see *Purcell*, rev. edn by Nigel Fortune (London, 1980), p. 25.
16   'Purcell's Autographs', p. 108.

(staves 1, 2, 3 [up through the first three bars], and 4) and the clefs for the first two systems; the rest of the page is in Purcell's hand. The two are so different that it is difficult to believe that the first hand might represent an early version of Purcell's writing.[17]

Except for part of fol. 20, which was finished by Purcell (see ill. 2.1), fols. 1–26 are indeed in another, as yet unidentified hand;[18] so Fortune and Zimmerman's remarks that 'if these leaves are not in Purcell's hand then many others in the manuscript that are extremely similar to them must also be thrown open to doubt' cannot be taken seriously. Purcell's somewhat messy though musically precise writing is immediately recognizable. Nor is Arkwright's view that Purcell had two distinct writing styles tenable, because an examination of fol. 26 (recto and verso, first system) shows this first, formal hand, near the end of its contribution to Fitzwilliam MS 88, becoming more relaxed and hurried, without in the least resembling Purcell's (see ill. 2.2). Furthermore, the earlier hand is that of an expert copyist, not a youthful apprentice,[19] whose spelling is at times more erudite than Purcell's. All of this militates against the possibility that the first hand of MS 88 somehow evolved into Purcell's now well established autograph.

Having indicated that Fitzwilliam MS 88 had at least one previous owner, one must now try to show how and when Purcell acquired the manuscript, a task hindered by the illegible last number of the date on the front flyleaf. Fortune and Zimmerman's reading of this date is generally accepted:

> The date at the head of the front index has for long been a source of dispute: it has been stated, categorically, to be 1673 and 1681 and, tentatively, to be 1687 (a date that cannot be taken seriously). It is a very difficult date to decipher, and it is only after an exhaustive scrutiny that we are for the first time prepared to advance it here as our opinion that the true reading is '1677'. This reading accords, moreover, with the fact that on fols. 9v and

---

17 '"The Energy of English Words": A Linguistic Approach to Henry Purcell's Method of Setting Texts', Ph.D. thesis, Princeton University (1980), p. 112. Rohrer also points to differences in note and clef shapes, spelling and punctuation (pp. 111–13); I would add that the directs of the first hand ascend, while Purcell's descend.

18 Note that this point of division corresponds approximately to the change of hands in the list on the front flyleaf. Curiously, though, the first hand in the table of contents is not the first copyist in the body of the manuscript. A search for another example of this copyist's work has been unsuccessful. His characteristic 'I' and other aspects of the musical hand bear some resemblance to early Blow, as, for example, in Oxford, Christ Church MS Mus. 14; there are, however, many more differences than similarities. A fragment of the 'Club' anthem by Humfrey, Blow and Turner on fol. 26v of Fitzwilliam MS 88 appears to be the work of yet another copyist (shown in ill. 2.2, second system); note and clef shapes resemble neither the first copyist's nor Purcell's.

19 Cf. Van Tassel, 'Fitzwilliam 88', p. 173.

2.1   Fitzwilliam MS 88, fol. 20 (*opposite*)   2.2   Fitzwilliam MS 88, fol. 26v. (*above*)

14v Blow is styled 'Mr' and on fol. 28v 'Dr': Blow received his doctorate on 10 December 1677.[20]

Only the last number is in doubt: a fold in the paper running down the right margin prevented the ink from taking properly. One cannot assume that it was any more legible 100 or 300 years ago. Seven seems the most likely choice, even though the ascending serif does not match that of the two other sevens in the same hand. In any case, the reading of '1677' would only show when the first copyist's contributions were listed and would be of little help in dating Purcell's work.[21] The more important date in assessing his contribution is that on the reverse flyleaf: 1682. Purcell's interest in this manuscript clearly resided not so much in the orchestral anthem section, to which he added five works and completed a sixth, but in that devoted to more traditional anthems, of which he copied thirty-three, probably added closer to 1682 than 1677. Furthermore, I imagine his inscription, 'God bless Mr Henry Purcell', was made either at the beginning or end of the project; since several works are fragments, though plenty of space remained to complete them, the former is more likely. This implies that Purcell's work on the manuscript took place after he inscribed it, that is, in late 1682 and 1683.[22]

Study of the paper of Fitzwilliam MS 88 helps to date the manuscript and suggests possible channels through which Purcell acquired it. The watermarks of the flyleaves[23] date from about 1680.[24] The paper in the main

[20] 'Purcell's Autographs', p. 108; Fuller Maitland and Mann, *Catalogue of the Music in the Fitzwilliam Museum*, p. 37, suggested 1673, while Hughes-Hughes, in 'Handwriting', p. 82, proposed either 1681 or 1687. Arkwright, in 'Purcell's Church Music', p. 242, and *The Works of Henry Purcell*, vol. XIIIA, iii, sided with Hughes-Hughes in suggesting 1681. However, the third number is unequivocally '7'; Hughes-Hughes and Arkwright were pursuing circular logic, contriving a date that was post-1677, because of a mistaken belief that Blow was styled 'Dr' throughout the manuscript. Fortune and Zimmerman's references to Blow include the following errors: the 'Mr. Blow' on fol. 9v is a later pencil notation, perhaps by Novello, and thus not valuable in dating; the next reference to 'Mr' Blow is not on the verso but the recto of fol. 14; and 'Dr. Blow' is not on fol. 28v but on fol. 20 and fol. 31.

[21] In this light the styling of Blow as 'Mr' or 'Dr' is less important in defending a 1677 dating. Since Fitzwilliam MS 88 is the product of two copyists, one can only say that the first worked on the manuscript before 10 December 1677 (when Blow received his doctorate) and that Purcell took over afterwards. He never styles Blow 'Mr' anywhere in Fitzwilliam MS 88.

[22] The probable *terminus ante quem* for Fitzwilliam MS 88 is 1683. By then it was being used as a source by William Isaack, copyist of Fitzwilliam Music MS 117; see Bruce Wood, 'John Blow: Anthems with Orchestra', Ph.D. thesis, Cambridge (1977), vol. V, 410–12; and Peter Holman, 'Bartholomew Isaack and "Mr Isaack" of Eton: A Confusing Tale of Restoration Musicians', *The Musical Times* 128 (1987), 381–5. Wood shows that Isaack copied a cluster of six orchestral anthems directly from Fitzwilliam MS 88. Other correlations may be seen between each of the source's selection of full anthems. For one anthem, Gibbons's *Hosanna to the son of David*, Isaack preserves Purcell's reversal of cantoris and decani parts in Fitzwilliam MS 88 (fols. 136–134v; see also Fitzwilliam MS 117, fols. 29–31v).

[23] See note 5, above.

[24] Edward Heawood, *Watermarks, Mainly of the 17th and 18th Centuries* (Hilversum, 1950), p. 104, plates 240 and 242; for a discussion of the major music paper types of the time and their watermarks, see Robert Thompson, 'English Music Manuscripts and the Fine Paper Trade, 1648–1688', Ph.D. thesis, King's College London (1988). I wish to thank Dr Thompson for generously sharing with me his work on this subject.

body of the manuscript bears the same watermark throughout, a fleur-de-lis and escutcheon (what Heawood calls a 'bend') in combination with the initials 'RC'. While Heawood's exemplar of this paper is a London publication of 1676,[25] it also appears in an inventory of 1674,[26] where it is amongst the most expensive papers listed. The manuscript, originally a large, single unit, could not have been purchased by someone of modest means. Moreover, the pre-ruled five-staff systems are spaced exceedingly generously, three per page, implying that the manuscript was designed for a fair-copy collection in full score. It would not be unreasonable to speculate that the manuscript origi-nated in the Chapel Royal. Started in the mid-1670s, the book could have been given to Purcell about 1682 in exchange for some task rendered for the court, or it could have been handed down to him directly from a colleague.

I would propose the following hypothesis for the genesis of Fitzwilliam MS 88. Sometime in the 1670s, an unidentified copyist started it as a collection of orchestral anthems with five works by Humfrey and two by Blow, the second of which, *Sing we merrily*, was left incomplete (fol. 20). Another copyist added a fragment of *I will always give thanks*, the so-called 'Club' anthem. The first copyist's work ceased sometime before Blow received his doctorate in 1677, and Purcell acquired the manuscript about 1682, perhaps as a hand-me-down from someone in the Chapel Royal. The inscription of the reverse flyleaf was possibly his first marking in the manuscript. He used it mainly as an anthology of works by older composers. Only after copying sixteen pieces into the reverse end did he add one of his own; of those at the reverse end, twelve are full anthems from before the Commonwealth (including three each by Byrd and Gibbons), fourteen are full anthems by Blow, Locke and Purcell himself; and seven are verse anthems of the more traditional type – using continuo only – again representing Blow, Locke and himself. Possibly while adding works by Blow and Locke to the reverse end, Purcell returned to the front to add five orchestral anthems by these two composers, completing another of Blow's that had been left unfinished. Curiously, Purcell did not add any anthems by Humfrey to the collection.[27] His interest in Fitzwilliam MS 88 was mainly as a volume of

---

[25]   Heawood, *Watermarks*, p. 67, plate 23.

[26]   For a transcription, see R. W. Chapman, 'An Inventory of Paper, 1674', *The Library* (series 4) 7 (1927), 402–8.

[27]   In British Library Add. MS 30,932, a guard-book of anthems in miscellaneous hands collected by William Flackton in the eighteenth century, there is a copy of Humfrey's *By the waters of Babylon* in Purcell's hand. The evidence of Fitzwilliam MS 88, however, suggests that Blow and Locke had more direct influence on Purcell than Humfrey, an idea which tends to undermine Peter Dennison's suggestion that Humfrey was central to Purcell's development; see 'Two Studies of Purcell's Sacred Music: (a) The Stylistic Origins of the Early Church Music', in *Essays on Opera and English Music in Honour of Sir Jack Westrup*, ed. F. W. Sternfeld et al. (Oxford, 1975), pp. 44–61.

traditional polyphonic music. It does not include any of his orchestral anthems, which he apparently considered more appropriate for his fair-copy book that included welcome songs, odes and secular music.

SOURCES AND METHODS OF COPYING

Close inspection of Purcell's copying in Fitzwilliam MS 88 reveals that he was working from partbooks rather than from full score. In some cases his sources may be identified. Corrections show that he went over his sources to eliminate mistakes, to adjust problems in underlay and to equalize inconsistent accidentals. Besides giving insight into how he worked, these emendations also suggest why Purcell undertook this project: his concern for preserving a careful record of his own compositions of the early 1680s seems to have extended to those works of others that were evidently a meaningful part of his musical heritage.

Purcell's scoring of a fragment of Orlando Gibbons's *Almighty and everlasting God* (fol. 112) provides the best indication that he was working from partbooks. He finished only one complete system but sketched out the text of the soprano part over one additional system, plus a few words of the bass. He left off quite close to the end of the first point of imitation.[28] This suggests that Purcell was copying one part at a time, completing a point of imitation in one voice, filling in the other parts in appropriate order, and perhaps intending to follow this pattern through successive points. Problems that would not occur in working from a full score, particularly difficulty in avoiding crowding in aligning notes and text, are seen several times in Fitzwilliam MS 88. In William Mundy's *O Lord I bow the knees of my heart*, Purcell was forced to scrape away his initial text layout in order to provide a more accurate underlay (fol. 122v, system 2, staff 3). And, at one place in Byrd's *Prevent us O Lord*, he was unable to provide a complete combination of notes and text, even after corrections (fol. 125v, system 1, staff 2). Purcell appears however to be striving for as accurate an edition as possible, examining his scores for even minor mistakes, such as in Gibbons's *Lift up your heads* (fol. 124v, system 2, staff 4), where he corrects a single note that was a third too high, significantly in a different colour ink from the original, suggesting a subsequent change.

Purcell's corrections to text underlay help lead one to the source from which he copied. The likely candidate is John Barnard's *First Book of Selected*

---

[28] Purcell includes the first six words of the second point of imitation in the soprano part and in the bass omits the last three syllables of 'infirmities', the final word of the first point, just before the cadence of this section.

Church Musick.[29] It appeared inopportunely on the eve of the Civil War in 1641 and thus exerted little influence until the 1660s: copies had apparently been carefully stowed away, because several musical establishments recorded their procurement in the early years of the Restoration.[30] Given the renewed importance of Barnard's *First Book*, Purcell's use of it is not surprising. One of the more interesting corrections in Fitzwilliam MS 88 confirms that Purcell was working from Barnard. Byrd's *O Lord make thy servant* circulated widely in the seventeenth century in both five- and six-part versions. The full SAATTB scoring begins with two tenors in unison; a copyist might easily miss the part that subsequently separates off. While versions including only tenor I were deemed acceptable, Barnard alone provides a scoring with only tenor II, resulting in what Craig Monson has called 'disastrous effect' with 'numerous bare and ungrammatical moments'.[31] Purcell chose this singular version for his copy of *O Lord make thy servant* but, not surprisingly, partially corrected it. On fol. 125, system 2, he added the tenor I part below the system in a different colour ink, clearly showing it to be an emendation (see ill. 2.3).

Problems with underlay, such as those cited above, also stem from difficulties in Barnard's print. A passage of *Prevent us O Lord* is nearly impossible to sort out in Barnard's edition.[32] At the text 'we may glorify thy holy name', the Contratenor Cantoris I and Contratenor Decani II contain significantly more textual activity than any of the other parts, and the singers or scorer are required to intuit melismas to produce a satisfactory reading, even though the print initially suggests a syllabic setting. Purcell worked out most of the problems in Fitzwilliam MS 88 but only after a couple of tries. Out of space, he was finally forced to omit the last two words of this section.

The First Book of Selected Church Musick provided Purcell ready access to the musical past: nine of the twelve pre-Commonwealth works he copied are in Barnard's collection.[33] Having established this as the main source of

---

[29] Barnard has often been suggested as the source for Purcell's copying, but to my knowledge this has not previously been proven; see, for example, Percy Lovell, '"Ancient" Music in Eighteenth-Century England', *Music & Letters* 60 (1979), 403–5.

[30] For example, WAM 33,695, fol. 5, records that Westminster Abbey acquired the Barnard partbooks from John Playford in 1661. John Morehen notes the purchase of the *First Book* at several cathedrals and provides much other information about this source; see 'The Sources of English Cathedral Music, c.1617–c.1644', Ph.D. thesis, Cambridge (1969), esp. pp. 287–8, 297–9, 490–1; see also the preface to his reprint of the *First Book*, pp. iii–ix.

[31] *The Byrd Edition*, vol. XI, *The English Anthems* (London, 1983), 210.

[32] *First Book*, Primus Contratenor Cantoris, fol. 110; and Secundus Contratenor Decani, fol. 107.

[33] The three that are not are Adrian Batten's *Hear my prayer O God*, William Child's *Sing we merrily* and Thomas Tomkins's *O Lord I have loved*. These circulated widely in post-1660 manuscript copies, for example, York Minster MSS M1S (1–8), St Paul's Cathedral, London, 'A2' partbooks, and Durham Cathedral MS Mus. C15. Tomkins's anthem would also have been available in his collected works, *Musica Deo Sacra & Ecclesiae Anglicanae: or, Musick Dedicated to the Honor and Service of God,*

2.3 Fitzwilliam MS 88, fol. 125

these older works, is it possible to account for any changes Purcell made in the copying process? There are no wholesale revisions. Purcell is not concerned with updating the musical language but rather with providing accurate representations of the anthems. His corrections of Barnard rarely diverge from the musical text but make it cleaner and more nearly complete. For instance, Purcell often equalizes accidentals in all parts where Barnard provided them in only one. At the second point of imitation in Tallis's *I call and cry*, he preserves a semitone in all parts by adding necessary accidentals (fol. 127v, system 3), where Barnard provided an accidental only in the tenor.[34]

More important are those rare places where Purcell manipulates an accidental to effect a substantial change. His copy of Nathaniel Giles's *O give thanks* includes an accidental not found in Barnard, creating a bit of chromaticism (fol. 118v, system 3, staff 1). Through this change, an otherwise unassuming passage based on a static E major triad becomes grittier, as the soprano descends through G♯ to G♮. An incongruous detail with no apparent basis in the text or musical rhetoric, it is nevertheless indicative of erudite tinkering. A more easily explained change may be seen at the final cadence of Mundy's *O Lord I bow the knees of my heart* (fol. 118, system 3, staff 3), where in the alto II Purcell altered Barnard's flat to a sharp (that is, a natural) creating an augmented octave cross-relation.[35] Many English pieces from Mundy's day to the mid seventeenth century employ this dissonance at cadences, but this passage shows Purcell's special interest in this anachronism. It may be no coincidence that one of the few passages in his own works in Fitzwilliam MS 88 that Purcell corrected involves this particular cadence: in *O Lord God of hosts*, he changes the soprano line to form a cross-relation (fol. 91v, system 1, staff 1).

Purcell's scoring from individual parts, careful corrections and infrequent though fascinating departures from the apparent source all suggest an auto-didactic course in old polyphony. Like many other composers, he apparently believed the best way to learn how a piece worked was to put it together for

---

and to the Use of Cathedral and other Churches of England, Especially of the Chappel-Royal of King Charles the First (London, 1668).

[34] The idea that Purcell was a careful editor, concerned that his own books and those of the establishments he served preserved accurate musical texts, is further underscored by the recent discovery of an autograph fragment in Westminster Abbey MSS Triforium Music Set I (in the book marked 'Tenor Cantoris 4'), identified by Robert Thompson and myself. On fol. 55 Purcell's hand can be seen editing his anthem *Let God arise*, which had been copied into the Westminster books by William Tucker. Even though this bit of Purcell's handwriting amounts to only minor changes, there is a suggestion here that Purcell was rather diligent in overseeing the production of performing materials at the Abbey, if he did not have a direct role in copying them.

[35] The flat is marked not just in the signature but with a cautionary accidental; *First Book*, Primus Contratenor Decani, fol. 111v, and Secundus Contratenor Cantoris, fol. 105v.

himself anew. Why he chose these particular twelve examples of old polyphony from the much larger body of such works available to him (if only through Barnard) is unknown, but they were amongst the most widely circulated anthems.[36] They provide a compendium of contrapuntal music, ranging from the mid sixteenth century to the years just before the Civil War. The pieces by Tallis and Byrd are examples of classic, late-Renaissance modal polyphony. Those by Gibbons show a new emphasis on vertical orientation. And those by Batten and Tomkins clearly introduce *seconda prattica* elements, with frequent melodic leaps and unprepared dissonance. It was only a short step to Purcell's own polyphonic pieces in Fitzwilliam MS 88. While they certainly show more recent influence, tangibly of Locke and Blow, and at times also from modern continental composers, the ancient roots are clear. In creating such works Purcell positioned himself within a vast and apparently still vital tradition.

ADDENDUM

Some recent manuscript study has shed light on the identity of the first scribe in Fitzwilliam MS 88. Another sample of the fine and distinctive calligraphy of this copyist has finally been located at the head of an established Blow autograph, British Library Add. MS 31,458, providing the title at the extreme top of fol. 1 to Blow's *O sing unto the Lord . . . for he hath done*, slightly obscured by wear and restoration. Especially striking are the matches between the letters 'g' and 'y' with their unusual centred descenders. This is in fact a piece also found in Fitzwilliam MS 88 (fol. 9v), and a comparison of the two versions shows that the musical hands are extremely close in many respects: note size and shape, clefs, time signatures, directs, and the placement of fermatas partially over the ending flourishes. This evidence has led to a rethinking of the possibility of Blow's involvement in Fitzwilliam MS 88 alluded to above (see note 18). I now believe that fols. 1–26 represent a calligraphic variant of the hand of John Blow.

This hypothesis has prompted a fresh and thoroughgoing comparison of the Fitzwilliam MS 88 scribe and Blow. This seemed especially appropriate

[36] Purcell's copying of older music extended beyond Fitzwilliam MS 88. Bodleian Library MS Mus.a.1, a holograph of the Benedicite to his B♭ major Service, includes on the reverse of a cut-and-paste fragment the opening of Monteverdi's 'Cruda Amarilli' in Purcell's handwriting (the first seven and a half bars of the upper four voices are visible); see Franklin B. Zimmerman, 'Purcell and Monteverdi', *The Musical Times* 99 (1958), 368–9. A manuscript once owned by Thurston Dart includes Purcell's copy of John Bull's ten-part canon on the plainsong *Miserere mei Domine*; see Thurston Dart, 'Purcell and Bull', *The Musical Times* 104 (1963), 30–1. See also the account of Purcell's copy of Orlando Gibbons's Prelude in G in chap. 4, below.

since no other sample of this scribe's work has come forth, in itself surprising given the expertise of the copying and the importance the volume must have had at its inception (note especially the quality of the paper and the rare, generous spacing of the staves). In extending the study of Blow autographs to include early ones like Christ Church MSS Mus 14 and 628, parallels may be found for some of the more peculiar aspects of the Fitzwilliam MS 88 hand, such as the beamed dotted-quaver/semiquaver figure with a double flag on the second note. (Compare for example, Fitzwilliam MS 88, fol. 7; Christ Church MS Mus 14, fol. 109r; and Christ Church MS Mus 628, p. 14.) A comparison of the text hands reveals that most of the letters of the Fitzwilliam MS 88 scribe are related in their general shape and curvature to established examples of Blow's hand, taking into account that the writing in Fitzwilliam 88 is a calligraphic style with frequent stops of the pen. In this context the rightward-bulging 'l' proves especially persuasive: it is an extremely rare letter form amongst late seventeenth-century music copyists.

If in fact the first copyist in Fitzwilliam MS 88 is John Blow, then the story of this important source is even more fascinating than previously thought. Robert Thompson and I are currently working on a comprehensive study of Purcell sources, and we hope to have more to report on this in the near future. One other bit of evidence for this idea comes from the reverse flyleaf of Fitzwilliam MS 88: we note the markings above Purcell's famous inscription are not merely pen flourishes but in fact the initials 'JB'.

APPENDIX: INVENTORY OF FITZWILLIAM MS 88

Columns from left to right are (1) item number, (2) folio on which anthem begins, (3) genre (o = orchestral anthem, f = full anthem, v = verse anthem), (4) title or incipit, (5) composer as ascribed by Purcell or other copyist (later, pencil ascriptions are not accounted for), and (6) location of ascription.

front end

1	1r	o	O praise the Lord	Pellham Humfreys	3v
2	4r	o	O Lord my god	Pellham Humfreys	7r
3	7r	o	Like as yᵉ hart	Mr Pelham Humfryes	9v
4	9v	o	O sing onto yᵉ Lord	Mr Jo: Blow	14r
5	14r	o	Sing we merrily	Dr Blow	20r
6	21r	o	Lord teach us to number our dayes	Mr Humfryes	23v
7	23v	o	Lift up your heads	Mr Pelham Humphey^a	26v
8	26v	o	[I will always give thanks]^b	[Humfrey, Blow, and Turner]	–
9	28v	o	Cry aloud and spare not	Dr Blow	31r
10	31r	o	Sing unto yᵉ lord O yee saints of his	Mr Matthew Lock^c	36r
11	36v	o	When yᵉ son of man	Mr Matthew Lock	38v

12	38v	o	The Lᵈ heare thee	Mr Lock	40v
13	40v	o	I will heare what yᵉ Lᵈ	MLock	42r

reverse end

1	142v	v	O Iᵈ I've sinn'd	[John Blow]	–
2	141r	f	God is our hope and strength	Dr Blow	138v
3	138r	f	O God wherfore art thou absent	Dr Blow	136v
4	136r	f	Hosanna to yᵉ son of David	Orlando Gibbon's	134v
5	134v	f	Save me O god	Dr Blow	133v
6	133v	v	Lord let me know my end	Mr Mathew Lock	131r
7	131r	f	Turn thy face from my sins	Mr Matthew Lock	129v
8	129r	f	Bow thine eare O Iᵈ	Mr Will: Bird	127v
9	127v	f	I call and Cry	Tho: Tallis	126v
10	126r	f	Prevent us O lord	William Byrd	125v
11	125r	f	O Lord make thy servant Charles	Mr Will: Bird	124v
12	124r	f	Lift up you heads	Orlando Gibbons	123r
13	122v	f	O Lord I Bow the knees of my heart	Mr Will: Mundy	121r
14	120v	f	O Lord I have lov'd	Mr Tho: Tomkins	119v
15	119v	f	O Give thanks	Dr Giles	118r
16	118r	f	Heare My Prayer O god	Mr Adrian Batten	116v
17	116r	f	Save me O god	HP	115r
18	114r	f	Sing wee Merrily	Dr Child	112r
19	112r	f	Almighty and everlasting god ᵇ	[Orlando Gibbons]	–
20	111r	v	Blessed is he whose unrightousness is forgiv'n	HP	108v
21	108r	f	My God my soul is vexed	Dr Blow	107r
22	106v	v	Heare me O lᵈ and that soon	HP	104v
23	104r	v	Bow down thine eare O lᵈ & heare me	[Henry Purcell]	–
24	102r	f	Man that is born of a Womanᵇ	[Henry Purcell]	–
25	99r	f	Remember not Lord our offences	[Henry Purcell]	–
26	98r	f	O Lord God of my salvation	Dr Blow	96v
27	96r	f	O God thou hast cast us out and scatter'd us abroad	HP	94r
28	93v	v	Christ being raised from yᵉ Dead	Dr Blow	92r
29	92r	f	O Lᵈ God of Hosts	HP	89r
30	89r	f	O God thou art my Godᵇ	[Henry Purcell]	–
31	87v	f	Lord how Long wilt thou be angry	[Henry Purcell]	–
32	86r	v	O Lord thou art my God	[Henry Purcell]	–
33	83v	f	Hear my prayer O Lordᵇ	[Henry Purcell]	–

a Later pen ascription
b Incomplete
c Later pen ascription; recte John Blow

3

Purcell's revisions of his own works

REBECCA HERISSONE

Purcell's extensive output is preserved in a far from satisfactory state. Autograph and holograph manuscripts survive for only a tiny proportion of his oeuvre; for the rest one has to rely on frequently inaccurate contemporaneous and eighteenth-century copies or printed sources. The relative paucity of reliable sources inevitably means that some works are incomplete while others have been lost altogether.

The largest collections of pieces in autograph consist of fair copies[1] and performing scores transcribed into music books, some of which were pre-bound; the sheer volume of music they contain, together with the protection of the binding, almost certainly prevented them from being damaged or lost. Yet many pieces are preserved as unbound rough drafts; the music, frequently in poor condition, is sometimes duplicated in fair copies. While working drafts have survived haphazardly, they are extremely valuable for their corrections, second thoughts and alterations which differ significantly from extant neat copies. The autograph manuscripts provide insight into Purcell's compositional technique and the improvements he attempted to make to his musical language at specific points of his career. Although many of the contemporary non-autograph manuscripts are unreliable, some contain music that is so radically different from autograph copies of the same pieces or from other non-autograph sources that one can only assume they represent a different stage of composition; these manuscripts may also yield important information about the revisions Purcell made to his own works.

There is no definitive list of manuscripts in Purcell's hand. In order to be confident in making assertions about Purcell's compositional technique, one must therefore restrict oneself to analysis of manuscripts whose authorship is not in doubt. This group comprises the following:

---

[1] The term 'fair copy' is not intended to imply a manuscript in which great care was taken over the presentation and appearance, simply to refer to one clearly copied after the main compositional process had been completed.

manuscript	contents	purpose
Cambridge, Fitzwilliam MS 88	full/verse anthems	fair copies
British Library Add. MS 30,930	domestic sacred music, fantazias and sonatas	fair copies and some rough drafts
British Library R.M. MS 20.h.8	full/verse anthems, odes/secular songs	fair copies
London, Gresham College song-book (London, Guildhall Library, Safe 3)	songs from operas and theatre music	?performing score
Oxford, Bodleian Library MS Mus.c.26	*Hail, bright Cecilia* and two anthems	performing score; rough drafts
Birmingham, Barber Institute Library MS 5001	four anthems	rough drafts
British Library Add. MS 30,931	four anthems	rough drafts
British Library Add. MS 30,932	two anthems, instrumental work	rough drafts
British Library Add. MS 30,934	*Who can from joy refrain?*	performing score
British Library Egerton MS 2956	*Of old when heroes*	fair copy
Oxford, Bodleian Library MS Mus.a.1	Benedicite from Service in B♭	rough draft
Cambridge, Fitzwilliam MS 152	one anthem	organ score
Yale University Library Osborn MS 515	*The Stairre Case Overture* and other instrumental pieces	bass viol part-book
London, Royal Academy of Music MS 3	*The Fairy Queen* (partial autograph)	?library score
Oxford, Christ Church MSS 1188–9	one anthem (partial autograph)	part books
Lisa Cox MS, authenticated in November 1993	keyboard works	fair copies and rough drafts

Establishing processes of revision in Purcell's autographs is only possible if one can ascertain which version of any particular piece came first. This is far from easy, since Purcell dated only two of the major manuscripts (the instrumental works in British Library Add. MS 30,930 and Fitzwilliam MS 88),[2] and there is no direct evidence to distinguish between inscriptions referring to the date of composition and those which merely give the date of copying. The music in some of the autographs can be associated with specific performances or other events which suggest at least an approximate date of copying. A record in the accounts of Westminster Abbey for Michaelmas 1681, for instance, mentions a payment of 30 shillings for the copying of 'Mr Purcell's service and anthem', which Franklin Zimmerman has identified as the B♭ service and the anthem *O God thou art my God*.[3] The working copy of the Benedicite in Bodleian MS Mus.a.1 must therefore date from slightly before this time; the song arrangements in the Gresham College manuscript are taken from a mainly theatrical repertory that dates from 1690 to 1695; the Royal Academy of Music partial autograph of *The Fairy Queen* can be dated to 1692 or 1693, when the opera is known to have been performed; and the *Song for the Duke of Gloucester's Birthday*, in British Library Add. MS 30,934, was written for the celebrations of 1695.

Most of the other manuscripts, however, are much more difficult to date. In his 1896 study of Purcell's handwriting, Hughes-Hughes identified a number of autograph manuscripts in which Purcell used letter forms and notational features not found in other autograph manuscripts.[4] In a few manuscripts Purcell used an unusual hook-shaped form of the bass clef; the backwards 'e' is also found in some pieces but not others. These characteristics gradually disappear during the copying of the reverse contents of Fitzwilliam MS 88, and Hughes-Hughes therefore concluded that they were early features of Purcell's writing style that ceased to be used after about 1682. The presence of these symbols in Add. MSS 30,931 and 30,932 led him to classify these manuscripts as the earliest surviving autographs, written at about the same time as the first anthems copied into the reverse end of Fitzwilliam MS 88 (none of which are Purcell's own compositions).

To determine precisely how early these rough drafts were made is difficult, since we do not know when Purcell began to compose. The earliest account of his activities as a composer is in a letter to the singer John Gostling from

---

[2] The organ score in Fitzwilliam MS 152 is also dated by Purcell: 1693.

[3] See Franklin B. Zimmerman, 'Purcell's "Service Anthem", *O God thou art my God* and the B-flat major Service', *The Musical Quarterly* 50 (1964), 207–14; and Zimmerman, *Henry Purcell, 1659–1695: His Life and Times*, rev. edn (Philadelphia, 1983), pp. 84–5.

[4] Augustus Hughes-Hughes, 'Henry Purcell's Handwriting', *The Musical Times* 37 (1896), 81–3.

Thomas Purcell, now generally thought to be Purcell's uncle;[5] it is dated 8 February 1679:

> Sir,
>
> I have re^{cd} y^r fauor of yours of ye 4th wth ye Incloseds for my sonne Henry: I am sorry wee are Like to be wthout you soe Long as yours mentions: but tis very Likely you may have a summons to appeare among us sooner than you Imagin: for my sonne is composing: wherin you will be cheifly consern'd . . .

The letter implies that the anthem Purcell was writing had a virtuoso bass part intended to show off Gostling's talents. Of the early anthems, *Blessed are they that fear the Lord* in British Library Add. MS 30,931 seems best to fit this description, though one cannot be certain.

Where both a rough draft and a neat copy of an anthem survive, the draft is earlier, as one would expect. British Library R.M. MS 20.h.8 and Add. MS 30,930 almost certainly post-date copies of the same music found in Barber MS 5001 and Bodleian MS Mus.c.26. The strongest evidence for this concerns the copies of *Plung'd in the confines of despair*: Purcell deleted the entry of the bass on beat two of bar 69 in the working draft (Barber MS 5001), moving it to the third beat in order to give independent movement; in British Library Add. MS 30,930 he began to write the original bass entry on beat two, then deleted it and continued with the revised version. This suggests strongly that he was either copying from the Barber manuscript itself or from a very close exemplar.[6] Three of the four pieces in the Barber manuscript and *In thee O Lord* from Bodleian MS Mus.c.26 were copied in neat form adjacent to one another in R.M. MS 20.h.8, which suggests they were preserved as a group.

Fitzwilliam MS 88 has long been considered the earliest of the large volumes of fair copies, but this dating was based on the incorrect presumption that all the music in the manuscript is in Purcell's hand. I am strongly inclined to follow Hughes-Hughes in believing that only the music at the reverse end was copied by Purcell,[7] whether or not Purcell's youthful hand was in a 'transitional' state at the time.[8] Scholars have proposed various

---

5 See Zimmerman, *Henry Purcell*, p. 337; but also J. A. Westrup, *Purcell*, rev. edn by Nigel Fortune (London, 1980), pp. 306–8.

6 *The Works of Henry Purcell*, vol. XXX, ed. Anthony Lewis and Nigel Fortune (London, 1965), 218.

7 Hughes-Hughes, 'Henry Purcell's Handwriting', pp. 81–2; see also chaps. 1 and 2, above.

8 See Nigel Fortune and Franklin B. Zimmerman, 'Purcell's Autographs', in *Henry Purcell (1659–1695): Essays on his Music*, ed. Imogen Holst (London, 1959), p. 108; Peter Dennison, 'The Stylistic Origins of the Early Church Music', in *Essays on Opera and English Music in Honour of Jack Westrup*, ed. F. W. Sternfeld et al. (Oxford, 1975), pp. 44–5; and Eric Van Tassel, 'Fitzwilliam Museum, MS Mu 88: Score in the Hand of Henry Purcell', in *Cambridge Music Manuscripts, 900–1700*, ed. Iain Fenlon (Cambridge, 1982), pp. 172–3.

dates for the copying, ranging from 1673 to 1677, 1683 and even 1687, based on their decipherings of the date written on the front contents page.[9] The third figure seems perfectly clear to me: it is a 7. The final figure, which is partially obscured by a paper repair, is almost certainly not a 7, because the shape of the upper half of the figure is entirely different from that of the 7 immediately preceding it and of that included in the list of contents written in the same hand below. I believe the date to be 1672. It is easy to see why scholars should have been uneasy about such an early date: Purcell would have been only thirteen or fourteen when he began to copy the manuscript. The problem is easily eradicated if the twelve pieces first copied into Fitzwilliam MS 88 are attributed to a different scribe.[10]

Purcell may have begun to transcribe works into the reverse end of the book when working as a Chapel Royal copyist, picking up from where the previous scribe had left off. On the reverse flyleaf, Purcell writes 'God bless Mr Henry Purcell 1682 September ye 10th', which is generally taken as the *terminus ante quem* for all the compositions in Fitzwilliam MS 88. But it would be unsafe to date Purcell's music in the reverse contents to this year or earlier: below the date and his signature, someone else has written a partial contents list. It seems extremely unlikely that anyone should have begun to write on the lower part of the page unless something prevented him from writing on the top part of the page. The incomplete contents list given by this scribe stops at Child's *Sing we merrily*, and thus includes only one piece by Purcell. I would suggest that the rest of the manuscript was copied by Purcell shortly after 10 September 1682, since most of the works – with the notable exception of four near the end – appear in other manuscripts known to have been completed by the end of 1683.[11]

If Purcell copied Fitzwilliam MS 88 between 1682 and 1683, then British Library Add. MS 30,930 must be the earliest surviving book of fair copies, since all but one of the fantazias is dated 1680; other parts of the manuscript were added later. He may well have begun the manuscript with the intention of creating a whole volume of instrumental music – certainly the gaps suggest that considerably more music was to be copied – and the incomplete

[9]   See G. E. P. Arkwright, 'Purcell's Church Music', *The Musical Antiquary* 1 (1909–10), 241 and 243; Fortune and Zimmerman, 'Purcell's Autographs', p. 108; J. A. Fuller Maitland and A. H. Mann, *Catalogue of the Music in the Fitzwilliam Museum, Cambridge* (London, 1893), p. 37; Hughes-Hughes, 'Henry Purcell's Handwriting', p. 82; and Van Tassel, 'Fitzwilliam 88', p. 171.

[10] Robert Thompson argues against a date before c. 1675 because the title-page, on which the date appears, has a fleur-de-lis watermark with factor's initials 'HC'; according to his research, factor's marks only begin to appear in the mid 1670s (private correspondence, 14 December 1993).

[11] In particular, the scribe Bartholomew Isaack copied most of the works in Fitzwilliam MS 117. See Van Tassel, 'Fitzwilliam 88', p. 171; and Bruce Wood, 'A Note on Two Cambridge Manuscripts and Their Copyists', *Music & Letters* 56 (1975), 308–12.

Fantazia XIII (Z 774), dated 'Feb ye 24th 168⅔', shows that he continued to add to the book for at least three years.

British Library R.M. MS 20.h.8 was probably begun in 1682, the year that Purcell took up adult employment at the Chapel Royal. He may have needed to make an anthology of his anthems at that time, either for his own record or for performance. The last piece that he entered into the part of the manuscript devoted to sacred music was *My heart is inditing*, composed for the coronation of James II in 1685. The odes and welcome songs at the other end of the manuscript were written for occasions between 1685 and 1687, probably after he had completed the anthems.

COPYING TECHNIQUES AND METHODS OF REVISION

For the most part Purcell was a careful copyist. In neat copies he obviously planned ahead: for instance, where the number of staves is reduced for a verse or solo section, he normally allows for the re-entry of the full chorus or orchestra by leaving empty staves in the last system of the solo section. Yet it is not entirely true to say that 'errors indicating lapses of concentration and miscalculations of available space are quite rare':[12] there is a surprisingly large number of mistakes apparently caused when he misread or lost his place in an exemplar.[13] He also occasionally has to scratch out the beginning of a system because he has not allowed for the greater number of parts which enter at the end, or because he has skipped a line and begun to write one part on a stave that should belong to another.[14]

Purcell appears to have both composed and copied according to the principles he advocated in the twelfth edition of Playford's *Introduction to the Skill of Music* (1694): 'Formerly they used to Compose from the *Bass*, but Modern Authors Compose to the *Treble* when they make *Counterpoint* or *Basses* to Tunes or Songs.'[15] His normal habit was to begin with the top part, add the bass and then fill in the middle parts.[16] This pattern is clearest where

---

12 Zimmerman, 'Purcell's Handwriting', in *Henry Purcell*, p. 104.

13 For instance, in the copy of *Why are all the muses mute* in British Library R.M. MS 20.h.8, fol. 160v, he alters the basso continuo in bars 340–1 having, quite inexplicably, written the music for that part from six bars earlier.

14 See especially the *Sonatas of Four Parts* (Add. MS 30,930), with four staves per system throughout, but where Purcell copies in the basso continuo part (on the fourth system) only sporadically and therefore tends to begin each system in the first violin one stave too high.

15 Henry Purcell, 'An Introduction to the Art of Descant: Or, Composing Music in Parts', in *An Introduction to the Skill of Musick: In Three Books* (London, 12th edn, 1694), p. 129.

16 Robert Ford claims that 'Purcell tended to copy first the top part and then the lower ones, seemingly in their descending order'. Where a piece is complete and has no changes of ink, one cannot be certain

he leaves a piece unfinished: in the *Suite in G* (Z 770), for instance, the first movement is complete, but in the last three movements Purcell writes only the first violin and continuo lines;[17] in *Rejoice in the Lord alway* the verses are complete with inner parts, while the chorus and four-part ritornello have outer parts only.[18] Other pieces were copied in two stages, the inner parts in different ink than the outer. In the *Chacony*, copied just before the *Suite in G* in Add. MS 30,930, the inner parts are written in the same ink as the outer only where the ground shifts from the basso continuo into either the viola or the second violin, and thus where the bottom of the texture is not provided by the continuo. Elsewhere, the inner parts are written in darker ink, and must have been filled in by Purcell after he had finished copying the outer parts.[19] The middle parts of all the ritornellos and the final chorus of *It is a good thing to give thanks* are also in a later ink.[20] Similar patterns are seen in *Bow down thine ear, Blessed is he whose unrighteousness is forgiven,*[21] *I was glad* and *My heart is fixed*.[22]

Changes of ink colour can provide valuable evidence of the precise sequence of revision. The pieces which have been copied with only their outer parts are, without exception, unaltered, even where it is clear that Purcell was composing directly into the manuscript. In this respect he was 'a composer who was able to write down his musical ideas clearly and spontaneously'.[23] But where the inner parts have been added later – sometimes even in neat copies – he frequently alters the top and bottom parts (mainly in order to accommodate the melodies in the middle textures), or goes back to previously copied sections to amend particular passages (see ill. 3.1). The second section of *Bow down thine ear*, 'Amongst the gods there is none like unto thee', at the top of fol. 103v of Fitzwilliam MS 88, was copied after the first part of the anthem in a darker ink. Before beginning to copy this solo verse, Purcell seems to have checked over the earlier material he had copied

---

but, as the following evidence shows, Purcell apparently copied parts in this manner only rarely. See Ford, 'Purcell as His Own Editor: The Funeral Sentences', *The Journal of Musicological Research* 7 (1986), 43.

[17] British Library Add. MS 30,930, fols. 53–54. Tilmouth labels these movements 'Borry', 'Minuet' and 'Jigg'. See *The Works of Henry Purcell*, vol. XXXI, rev. M. Tilmouth (London, 1990), 121–2.

[18] British Library R.M. MS 20.h.8, fols. 37v–38.

[19] British Library Add. MS 30,930, fols. 56–55. See also Thurston Dart, 'Purcell's Chamber Music', *Proceedings of the Royal Musical Association* 85 (1959), 89–90.

[20] British Library R.M. MS 20.h.8, fols. 4–7.

[21] Fitzwilliam MS 88, fols. 104–102, and 111–107.

[22] Barber Institute MS 5001, pp. 292–302 and 308–16. The only exceptions to this pattern are in Sonata VII of the *Sonatas of Four Parts* (Add. MS 30,930, fol. 34v) and *In a deep vision's intellectual scene* (R.M. MS 20.h.8, fol. 201), where changes of ink show on both occasions that Purcell was copying from the top downwards.

[23] Robert Manning, 'Revisions and Reworkings in Purcell's Anthems', *Soundings* 9 (1982), 29.

and made several alterations to the music and text on fol. 102. In *I was glad*,[24] the inner parts of the symphonies are written in the same dark ink that is used to alter the outer parts; Purcell was clearly composing the second violin and viola parts directly into the manuscript, since most of the alterations correct grammatical errors or improve chord spacing within these parts. The same compositional process is evident in *My heart is fixed*.[25]

The techniques of revision so far described all relate to alterations made during copying or at most slightly afterwards. But there are more substantial changes that indicate a systematic process of revision. In five of the surviving autograph manuscripts Purcell attaches paper over the original ruled staves in order to insert new material. Sometimes the reason for covering staves is not connected to the composition itself. In British Library R.M. MS 20.h.8, for instance, paper is placed over the penultimate system of the cantata *In a deep vision's intellectual scene* (fol. 199) not to alter the music at the end of the piece, but to compensate for the fact that Purcell had not allowed himself sufficient room to finish the music before he began the next piece. The slip of paper attached to the top of the first page of *Behold now praise the Lord* in Add. MS 30,932 probably allowed Purcell to use the whole folio, which was blank with the exception of three staves filled by an unknown scribe at the top of the recto.

Several slips of paper are found on pages of the autograph copy of the *Sonatas of Four Parts* in Add. MS 30,930. The last four bars of Sonata III are written on a small piece of paper, continuing from the end of fol. 38. Just beneath the three staves of musical writing on this slip are the opening three bars of the first violin part of Sonata IV, and on its reverse the three-part score of the end of the Adagio and beginning of the Canzona from that sonata (bars 29–33). It is clear that this slip was originally the top part of a complete folio that was bound into the original. Purcell began to copy Sonata IV on the second system of this page but, as he often did in Add. MS 30,930, forgot that the fourth stave of the page had to be left blank for the addition of the continuo part from the end of Sonata III, and so began copying the first violin part of the opening of Sonata IV on that stave. Realizing his mistake after three bars, he smudged out this line before the ink was dry. Several leaves were removed from the manuscript at some point, replaced by blank leaves which have since been misbound so that they interrupt pages copied by Purcell. On fol. 37v, Joseph Warren, a later owner of the manuscript, wrote '10 leaves have been abstracted here, including the whole of the 4th. 5th. 6th. 7th. 8th. Sonatas. The above is the 9th.' (he later

24   Barber Institute MS 5001, p. 292.   25   Barber Institute MS 5001, p. 300.

3.1 Fitzwilliam MS 88, fol. 102. Dark-ink corrections to *Bow down thine ear*

deleted '7th' and '8th'). Warren must at least have been correct about the removal of the fourth sonata, for the material on the back of this slip is obviously the part of the sonata that was originally copied at the end of the first system on the other side of the page.[26]

On fol. 36v Purcell added two more slips of paper to alter the end of the third movement of Sonata IX (bars 106–8). On the reverse of these slips are copies of bars 93–4 and 95–8 of the lower two parts in the Adagio of Sonata VIII.[27] This sonata appears to have undergone considerable revision, and the material on the slip of paper is from the version of the sonata as printed in 1697, not that found in the neat copy in Add. MS 30,930. Tilmouth, in the revised Purcell Society edition of the sonatas, presumes that the printed copy preserves the second setting of both this Largo, and the two movements of Sonata VII in which significant alterations were made,[28] but there are strong stylistic reasons for placing the autograph copy of the sonatas *after* the copy from which the 1697 edition was printed. As Tilmouth points out, one of the main features of the autograph version of the Sonata VII Canzona is a series of octave leaps in the violins. It is difficult to understand why Purcell, who had in the 1683 *Sonnata's* declared a wish to emulate the Italians, should have suppressed such Italianate figuration in this set. Annotations in several manuscripts suggest that he was proud of his abilities as a contrapuntist,[29] so it seems unlikely that he would have edited out a perfectly successful series of inversions on the main theme of the Largo from Sonata VIII. In the 1697 version of the Largo in Sonata VII, Purcell became carried away with the suspension-based sequences set up in bar 7, with the result that the only new thematic feature in the movement (in bars 27–9) sounds out of place (see Ex. 3.1a); in the autograph of this movement, the introduction of new material in bar 22 is much more convincing (see Ex. 3.1b). In the Canzona the passage in bars 31–2 of the printed edition sounds weak and uninspired (see Ex. 3.2a);

---

[26] The dimensions of the manuscript seem to support this hypothesis: the surviving bars of the opening of Sonata IV measure approximately 30 mm each; the writing block of 230 mm allows about eight bars per system, meaning that 24 bars could have been copied on the recto of the missing folio. If another four bars were copied on the first part of the verso, bar 29 of the sonata would be placed at exactly the point at which it occurs on the fragment. See also chap.1, above.

[27] The fragments were identified by Christopher Hogwood. See his comments tipped in at the beginning of the reverse contents of Add. MS 30,930 and also *Henry Purcell: Ten Sonatas in Four Parts*, 2 vols., ed. Christopher Hogwood (London, 1978), vol. I, vi and xvii–xviii, and *The Works of Henry Purcell*, vol. VII, rev. M. Tilmouth (London, 1981), xii and xv. H. Watkins Shaw criticized Hogwood for printing the material under the slip of paper saying that 'the value of such an investigation lies in the knowledge it gives us of a composer's thought and method, but . . . it does not issue as one of the final results of an edition'. See his review, 'Purcell Trio Sonatas', in *The Musical Times* 120 (1979), 496.

[28] *The Works of Henry Purcell*, vol. VII, rev. edn, xv.

[29] See introduction, p. 3 above.

in bars 26–8 of the autograph version, effectively the same music in the violins is made considerably stronger and more vital because of the new bass line (see Ex. 3.2b). It is difficult to believe that Purcell would have deleted this version in favour of the sequence in the 1697 printed parts. This reinforces Hogwood's theory that the version of the sonatas in Add. MS 30,930 is in fact Purcell's revision[30] and also helps to explain the fragments of Sonata VIII. Purcell must have had another copy which he used when writing Add. MS 30,930; having already reworked Sonata VIII, he no longer needed the first copy and could thus use it as scrap paper.[31]

Ex. 3.1   Largo from Sonata VII
              (a) version in printed parts

---

[30]   See *Ten Sonatas in Four Parts*, ed. C. Hogwood (1978), vol. I, vi.
[31]   As Thompson points out, the extra slips of paper were attached by pins, not glue, when Joseph Warren owned Add. MS 30,930, meaning that any of the revisions would have been reversible, and might therefore have been considered as alternative rather than definitive reworkings. See chap. 1, above.

(b)   version in Add. MS 30,930

The two other manuscripts containing slips of paper are less problematic. The unbound copy of the Benedicite from the Service in B♭ is a working draft, with many alterations and corrections. For the most extensive of these, Purcell attached another slip of paper at the end of the recto, covering an earlier version of bars 141–8. The music underneath this slip also shows several alterations, which suggests two stages of revision. The final version of the passage differs significantly from the first, but at the top of the verso the corrections suddenly cease, and the music no longer coincides with the

Ex. 3.2   Canzona from Sonata VII
        (a)   version in printed parts

(b)   version in Add. MS 30,930

version of the service in Fitzwilliam MS 117; evidently another slip of paper was originally attached to this part of the page (until the point where the two versions merge at bar 158) but was subsequently lost.

A final example of methodical revision is found in the Bodleian MS Mus.c.26 copy of *Let mine eyes run down with tears*. Another working draft, this copy reveals that Purcell substantially revised bars 66–83 of the anthem. Of the five slips of paper added, two cover half a page, and one of these (fol. 7a) contains a partial watermark which reveals the paper to be of the same type as the main body of the anthem. The revisions were probably carried out only shortly after the original version was copied, when Purcell was still in possession of the same paper. Previously unidentified fragments of bars 13–16 and the revised version of bars 72–4 of the same piece are found on the reverse sides of fols. 7a and 8b (see Ex. 3.3a). There is no text underlay, but the quaver stems are ungrouped, suggesting that Purcell was copying vocal music. The fragment on fol. 8bv appears to be from a working draft of the second version of the altered verse, which differs only slightly from the form of the verse copied on the sections of paper stuck into the manuscript. But on fol. 7av there are two important differences from the main

Ex.3.3   Sketch fragment from *Let mine eyes run down with tears*
     (a)   transcription of sketch fragment on fol. 7av (shown on p. 64)

version of the text (see Ex. 3.3b). Several notes in the alto line do not correspond with those in the version copied in the main body of the manuscript. And in the fragment the first treble part is copied immediately above the alto, leaving no space for the second treble. The bar lines (written as was Purcell's habit through each line separately, but overlapping so as to join each line together) extend down below the alto part but not above the first treble. This indicates that the music was in score form but that there was no space for the second treble. The immediate conclusion one would draw is that this is a 'sketch' for the anthem – presumably written at the stage before the working copy – and that Purcell decided to add another part to the texture, as well as to make some improvements to the part writing. If this is the case, the 'sketch' must have come from a very early stage of composition, because in the final version the second treble is integral to the texture and gives no impression of having been a later addition. This fragment is an extremely important clue to Purcell's methods of composition, since no other sketch material has yet been discovered.

ANALYSIS OF THE REVISIONS

The majority of the manuscripts which contain significant revisions date from the late 1670s and early 1680s. Purcell's musical language was changing rapidly during this first period of his career, and analysis of the alterations he made to his music can provide a useful insight into the early development of his style. It is not always easy to find logical reasons for the alterations in the

Ex.3.3   Sketch fragment from *Let mine eyes run down with tears*
          (b) final version of sketched passage

manuscripts but, taken as a group, the revised pieces seem to demonstrate so many similar alterations that it is likely the changes were made with a common purpose.

By far the greatest proportion of major revisions to the early works involve the alteration of the harmonic language. Although inevitably an over-simplification, the statement that Purcell's harmonic language underwent 'a gradual progress from the daring harmony, contrapuntally derived dissonance, and frequent modality of the earlier works towards a more tonally directed harmony and a simplified harmonic texture in the later works'[32] is borne out by most of the large-scale revisions he made to his early music. Many passages were restructured to create a better sense of tonal direction, often ironing out sections of extreme chromatic writing and dissonance.

In the midst of life, from the Funeral Sentences, exists in two versions, of which that in British Library Add. MS 30,931 appears to be the earliest (see Ex. 3.4a and b). The second, a neat copy in Fitzwilliam MS 88, is not substantially altered, most of the changes involving details of melody and part writing, but Purcell nevertheless clarifies the harmonic content. The imitative chromatic figure at 'bitter pains of eternal death' remains, but Purcell alters the tenor line in bars 25–8 to simplify the chromaticism (also resulting in

Ex. 3.4   *In the midst of life*
(a) first version

---

32   Kenneth R. Long, *The Music of the English Church* (London, Sydney and Auckland, 1972), p. 272. For similar statements, see Westrup, *Purcell*, p. 245; and Dennis Arundell, *Henry Purcell* (London, 1927), pp. 33–7.

fewer notes, so that the word repetition is less frenzied) and to remove pungent harmonies, such as the false relation with the treble part in bar 27.

The neat copy of the Funeral Sentences in Fitzwilliam MS 88 does not include the last anthem, *Thou knowest Lord*,[33] but comparison of the autograph

33   Ford presumes that Purcell did not make a neat copy of *Thou knowest Lord* because he already had one, but the composer in fact leaves a gap of two sides before beginning the next anthem, *Remember not, Lord, our offences*, which suggests that he did intend to finish copying the sentences into the manuscript. See Ford, 'Purcell as His Own Editor', pp. 53–4.

version in British Library Add. MS 30,931 with non-autograph sources reveals that Purcell revised this anthem to a much greater extent than *In the midst of life*: the first fourteen bars are almost completely rewritten. The original version, although starting in C minor, modulates quickly to the relative major. The tonal path seems uncertain, modulations to C minor and G minor apparently function only to pass to and from E♭ and A♭ major, and the level

Ex. 3.4   *In the midst of life*
         (b) second version

of tension remains low throughout. The second version involves a complete reorganization of the tonal plan, placing much greater emphasis on minor keys, thus aiding a more expressive and emotive setting of the text. In contrast to the predominant E♭ of the original setting, this version, shorter by two bars, revolves around C minor and F minor, moving to A♭ and E♭ only at the end in preparation for 'But spare us': this carefully planned tonal journey leads into the next section of the anthem smoothly and purposefully.

Two autograph versions of the anthem *Hear me, O Lord* are extant. The shorter version in British Library Add. MS 30,930 is almost certainly earlier than the neat copy in Fitzwilliam MS 88.[34] The two settings are essentially identical until bar 11, where they diverge significantly (see Ex. 3.5a and b). Apart from changing the point of imitation in bars 11 and 12, Purcell seems principally to have reworked the harmonic scheme and part writing of 'lest I be like unto them that go down into the pit' in bars 12 to 17. In the first version, he attempted to incorporate word painting on 'go down' with a descending scalic figure. The result is some extraordinarily low pitches (the alto reaches e♭[35] and the tenor B♭), large sections of part crossing and an unstructured harmonic path in which each attempt to resolve onto C minor is put off by the insertion of A♭s. In the revised version, the sequence of keys is considerably simplified,

34 Manning suggests that the differences between the two versions result not from a decision to 'improve' the original but because Purcell rewrote the anthem for private (domestic) use. The musical evidence cited below does not support this idea. See Manning, 'Revisions and Reworkings', pp. 34–5.
35 Pitches are identified with the modified version of Helmholtz adopted for *The New Grove* (middle C = c').

modulating through the circle of fifths. The more direct tonal path means that there are no problems of resolution, less extreme chromaticism and, because of the altered point of imitation, no problems of part writing or range.

The major alteration in *Let mine eyes run down with tears*, where Purcell stuck paper over the original score (bars 66–83), concerns both texture and

Ex. 3.5   *Hear me, O Lord*
    (a)   first version

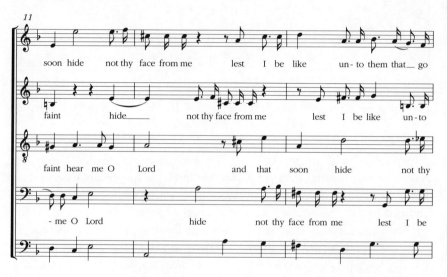

harmonic language. Again there is a lack of harmonic direction in the first version (see Ex. 3.6a): the irregular and unresolved dissonances between the bass and upper parts at bars 71–4 prevent the chromatic scales from forming an audible sequence. Passages such as the repetition of f♯ in the bass against G in the basso continuo (bars 66–7), the anticipation by three parts of the chord at the beginning of bar 71 (which weakens the resolution of the bass), and the stubborn refusal of the basso continuo to move away from A in bars 74–5, also contribute to a weakening of the harmonic path. The revised version of bars 66–83 is considerably more assured in its control of dissonance and resolution, and once again the sequence of keys is simpler and clearer (see Ex. 3.6b). The music remains close to G minor and C minor, with brief

Ex. 3.5   *Hear me, O Lord*
        (b) second version

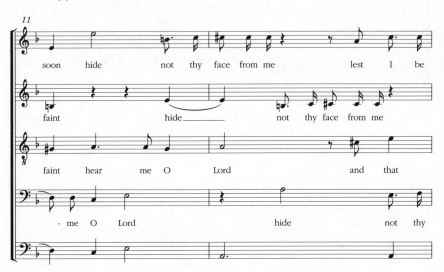

inflexions of F and B♭ major, and dissonance is mostly restricted to suspensions at cadences.

Purcell also frequently altered the imitative texture of works which he revised. As Westrup writes, the 'principle of independent movement colours a good deal of Purcell's part-writing for voices and instruments, particularly in his early work. Sometimes in his youthful anthems it produced mere

Ex. 3.6   Verse section of *Let mine eyes run down with tears*
      (a) first version

(b) second version

clumsiness'.[36] Purcell seems to have been aware that he did not always maintain points of imitation consistently, and both large- and small-scale alterations are made in order to tighten contrapuntal textures or to increase the number and length of imitative entries. One of the simplest examples of this can be seen in bar 29 of *In the midst of life*, where Purcell shifts the treble entry from the third to the fourth beat of the bar, thereby removing the only entry of the principal imitation point that did not begin on a weak beat.

In reworking *Let mine eyes run down with tears*, Purcell simplified the harmonic scheme and distributed the contrapuntal entries more evenly in the verse. In the original version of 'Do not abhor us', the first three voice entries do not overlap but are followed in bar 70 by two further entries at only a quaver's distance, moving to a four-part texture in the next bar. The number of parts then drops again at bar 72, resulting in a lack of textural regulation, so that in some bars the texture is thick, but in others – often in places where the harmony is ambiguous – it is extremely thin. In the second version, Purcell succeeds in controlling both vertical and horizontal components. Each of the voices enters separately with the point on 'do not', and the texture is broken by and interspersed with the original figure on 'remember', now distributed evenly. The parts enter gradually from bar 75, building to the climactic full cadence at 'glory' in bar 79. Then in bars 81–2 each voice enters in turn at a distance of one beat with 'do not break thy cov'nant'.

Purcell changes the point of imitation at 'O let the earth bless the Lord' in the Benedicite of the Service in B♭ by replacing the original broken arpeggio with a scale figure. This facilitated a much more flexible treatment, because the new point works easily against itself in inversion. He draws attention to the new invertible counterpoint by separating out the entries on 'O let the Earth' and 'yea let it praise Him', thereby emphasizing the canon between the bass and tenor in bars 141–2, which is followed in bars 145–6 by one on the inverted point led by the tenor (Ex. 3.7). In the original setting, Purcell made very little of the point on 'O let the Earth', but the newly flexible melody is open to a wide variety of treatments, and he therefore integrated it fully into the melody on 'yea let it praise Him' and the smooth, contrapuntal texture.

Many of Purcell's early works lack the structural coherence that he later developed. The revisions in the early autographs show that he worked hard to improve formal design with effective climaxes in the first years of his career. In Sonata IX (Z 810), for instance, Purcell removes the Adagio at the end of the Canzona and replaces it with three further bars of fast writing, by

---

[36] Westrup, *Purcell*, p. 247.

Ex.3.7 Benedicite from Service in B♭
(a) subject of original version

(b) countersubject of original version

(c) opening section of final version

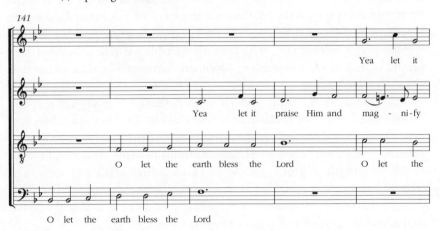

attaching paper over the original score (see Ex. 3.8). As Hogwood suggests, Purcell probably wanted 'to avoid killing the effect of the Grave that followed', as well as to bring the Canzona to a satisfactory conclusion.[37] The original Adagio was quite unprepared, being in a completely different style from the fast imitative writing. The result of this abrupt change, together with the minor-mode inflexions, was to weaken the end of the Canzona. The second ending is stylistically consonant with the rest of the Canzona, yet brings a gradual slowing of pace and thus a decisive end to the movement.

In Fantazia II, Purcell also apparently made an alteration to the last section of the piece. The *Slow* passage from bar 53 is absent from the partbooks in British Library Add. MS 31,435, and there are other small differences which suggest that this is an earlier version of the piece.[38] In the autograph in Add. MS 30,930, bars 53–65 and half of bar 66 are new, but Purcell never completed the final cadence (see Ex. 3.9). His musical judgement is perhaps in question here, since the slow passage, beginning with a chord of E major after a cadence in F, produces a considerable jolt and, as in the original version of Sonata IX, the winding chromatic harmonies confuse rather than affirm the tonal centre.

The autograph anthems also show that Purcell was concerned with balance and formal organization in his early works. In those that underwent major revision – *Thou knowest Lord, Hear me O Lord* and *Let mine eyes run down with tears* – the reworked sections build towards stronger climaxes, mostly as a result of greatly improved part-writing. Smaller revisions also seem to have the same purpose in two verses of *My beloved spake* ('For lo the winter is past' and 'My beloved is mine'), *In thee, O Lord,* and at the climax to the opening alto solo of *Who can from joy refrain.*

In most of the works surviving in rough draft, Purcell seems to have composed directly into the manuscript. Not surprisingly, many of the minor alterations in these manuscripts concern the correction of grammatical errors in the process of composing the inner parts or in checking after copying was complete. Purcell frequently rewrites a few notes to remove parallel fifths or octaves. Examples include *My heart is inditing,* bar 214, where the second treble is altered to remove consecutive fifths with the bass, and bar 360, where one note of the second alto part is changed to prevent parallel octaves with the first treble. At the end of Fantazia VII Purcell alters the third part at

---

[37] Christopher Hogwood, *The Trio Sonata,* BBC Music Guides (London, 1979), p. 91.
[38] Tilmouth thinks that it went through three stages of composition, the second marked by another source (Add. MS 33,236) which has other minor changes. See *The Works of Henry Purcell,* vol. XXXI, rev. Tilmouth, 117.

Ex. 3.8   End of Canzona from Sonata IX

a) first version

b) second version

Ex. 3.9   End of Fantazia II

bar 49, because the original melody, still legible underneath, gave parallel fifths with the second part. Many similar examples are to be found in other autographs, both neat and working copies. Almost always the grammatical error occurs between an inner and an outer part, suggesting that Purcell made mistakes when adding inner parts to pre-existing outer ones.[39]

Some of the minor differences between autograph versions of Purcell's works do not seem to have resulted from a conscious desire to alter or improve a piece. *I was glad* and *Plung'd in the confines of despair* (working drafts in Barber Institute MS 5001 and neat copies in British Library R.M. MS 20.h.8 and Add. MS 30,930, respectively) have a considerable number of minor differences in the continuo lines, mostly changes of octave and addition or removal of dotted rhythms. Purcell did not greatly discriminate between these sorts of details. Occasionally, however, he does appear to alter the continuo or another line deliberately to give more impetus to the music. Such apparently logical alterations are extremely common in both rough drafts and fair copies, and it seems that Purcell consciously checked his works to ensure that momentum was maintained throughout a piece.

Purcell also tried occasionally to separate the continuo from the bass line. The two parts are usually identical in both instrumental and choral music: in the autograph sonatas, for instance, though Purcell left a spare stave for the continuo, showing that he intended to copy it in fully, he generally wrote the part out separately only when it differs markedly from the string bass line. The continuo part therefore 'simplifies the rhythmic and melodic configuration of the bass viol part'.[40] In several other pieces, Purcell altered the continuo in order to clarify the harmony. The *Song for the Duke of Gloucester's Birthday* ends with a lengthy movement on a ground bass. At various places Purcell altered the ostinato, usually to facilitate movement away from the tonic, as in bars 139–50, where a sequence through the circle of fifths is introduced. Originally, he doubled the lowest part of each group of voices in the continuo, resulting in a wide-ranging line moving in continuous crotchets. He then revised the section by placing only harmonic notes in the continuo.

Among the large body of other minor alterations in the autographs are reworkings of melodic details, particularly on the approach to cadences, and

[39] Ford suggests that Purcell 'edited away such technical imperfections as parallel fifths and the like' because 'by the time the composer had reached the ripe old age of twenty one he was already regretting the overindulgence and compositional waywardness of his youth'. There is no evidence of different inks and so on to suggest that Purcell ever returned to a composition to remove consecutives; from my study of the ink, all the alterations appear to have been made at the time of main copying, with the exception of those resulting from the major recomposition of a passage. See Ford, 'Purcell as His Own Editor', p. 54.

[40] As Dart noted in 'Purcell's Chamber Music', p. 83.

those which seem to clarify or enrich the texture. Even where change seems to have resulted in significant improvement, one can only speculate about Purcell's intentions as a reviser of his own music. The autograph manuscripts nevertheless remain invaluable documents through which one may gain a clearer understanding of how he approached the process of composition.

4

New light on Purcell's keyboard music

CURTIS PRICE

The recent discovery by the antiquarian book dealer Lisa Cox of an autograph manuscript of Purcell's keyboard music,[1] which came too late to form the basis of a detailed essay in this book, will probably cause a reassessment of this part of the composer's output and may also shed new light on the last years of his life. As I write (March 1994), the manuscript is embargoed pending sale, but its present owner has kindly allowed me to examine it and to offer the following preliminary report.[2]

Purcell's keyboard music has generally been regarded as the least significant of his entire output, a Cinderella repertory hardly worthy of the organist of Westminster Abbey and the Chapel Royal. Though he did of course play the harpsichord and spinet, there are no accounts of Purcell's virtuosity at the keyboard. Westrup thought the dance movements 'slight and sometimes inconclusive, as though he had become uncertain of his direction; but the best of them are worthy predecessors of Bach's French and English suites'. Among the arrangements of theatre pieces, Westrup found nothing 'of any great significance, though a handful of these gay and dainty movements will pleasantly while away an odd half-hour or so'.[3] It is hard to quarrel with this luke-warm assessment, especially because Purcell himself seemed to take little interest in his keyboard music: during his lifetime relatively few pieces were published, principally the sixteen in Playford's *The Second Part of Musick's Hand-maid* (1689), a volume which Purcell helped revise and correct. The balance of the suite movements was issued by his widow in *A Choice Collection of Lessons for the Harpsichord or Spinnet* (1696). A much larger repertory of transcriptions and arrangements is preserved in manuscripts and published tutors, but many of these works have been judged unauthentic or

---

[1] See Richard Morrison, 'Purcell's Notebook Revealed', *The Times* (17 November 1993), p. 35.
[2] For generous help and advice, I am grateful to Robert Spencer and Simon Maguire.
[3] J. A. Westrup, *Purcell*, rev. edn by Nigel Fortune (London, 1980), pp. 237–8.

spurious.[4] Purcell certainly gave harpsichord lessons, notably to the young Katherine Howard between 27 July 1693 and 16 April 1695, as records of Ashtead Manor show.[5] And the discovery in the mid-1970s of a copy of Walsh and Hare's *The Harpsicord Master* (1697) confirms that he prepared music and written instructions for these lessons: 'plain & easy Instructions for Learners on ye Spinnet or Harpsicord, written by ye late famous Mr H Purcell at the request of a perticuler friend, & taken from his owne Manuscript.'[6] Perhaps his few published keyboard pieces form the tip of the iceberg of a repertory assembled for teaching purposes.

The Lisa Cox manuscript, which reveals a little more of this submerged repertory, is an oblong quarto of some eighty-five pages, with six-line pre-ruled paper in original calf covers. It is in two parts: twenty-one pieces in what is almost certainly Purcell's hand and, reversing and inverting the volume, seventeen keyboard pieces by Giovanni Battista Draghi, also probably autograph. The Purcell section is unsigned and includes few titles or rubrics, but the writing is entirely consistent with holographs from the period 1691–5. The only known example of harpsichord music in his own hand, the manuscript includes five previously unknown pieces,[7] four new keyboard arrangements of known theatre pieces, and Orlando Gibbons's Prelude in G from *Parthenia* (1613). The Gibbons prelude was one of the most widely circulated pieces of seventeenth-century keyboard music; its inclusion in the newly discovered manuscript nevertheless underscores Purcell's keen interest in much earlier music. The contents are listed below, according to the present foliation which begins at the 'Draghi end':

INVENTORY OF THE LISA COX MANUSCRIPT

Draghi end

folio	piece	earliest concordance
1–1v	child-like attempts at composing	
2	blank	
2v–3	Prelude in g	Six Select Sutes (c. 1707) (Kl. 13)[8]

---

4 See Henry Purcell, *Miscellaneous Keyboard Pieces*, rev. edn by Howard Ferguson (London, 1968), pp. 35–6.

5 See Franklin B. Zimmerman, *Henry Purcell, 1659–1695: His Life and Times*, rev. edn (Philadelphia, 1983), pp. 228–9.

6 *The Harpsichord Master (1697)*, ed. Robert Petre (Wellington and London, 1980). See also R. Petre, 'A New Piece by Henry Purcell', *Early Music* 6 (1979), 374–9.

7 Two C major preludes, two C major minuets and a jig in A minor (see inventory, pp. 88–9). The treble part of the A major air (probably a hornpipe) on fol. 38v later appeared in an edition of *Apollo's Banquet* without title-page in the Royal College of Music Library, dating from 1701. The piece is there attributed to 'Eccles' – almost certainly John Eccles.

8 'Kl.' refers to the numbers assigned to Draghi's works in *Harpsichord Music*, ed. Robert Klakowich, in *Recent Researches in the Music of the Baroque Era*, vol. LXI (Madison, 1986).

folio	*piece*	*earliest concordance*
3v–5	Allmand in g	*Six Select Sutes* (Kl. 14)
[leaf removed between 4 and 5]		
5v–6v	Corrant in g	*Six Select Sutes* (Kl. 15)
7–8v	Air in g	hitherto unrecorded
9–10	Jigg in g	*Six Select Sutes* (Kl. 18)
10v–11	Air in A	hitherto unrecorded
11v–13	Allmand in A	*Six Select Sutes* (Kl. 20)
13v–14v	Corrant in A	*Six Select Sutes* (Kl. 21)
14v–15v	Sarraband in A	*Six Select Sutes* (Kl. 22)
15v–16v	Prelude in A	hitherto unrecorded
16v–18v	Jigg in A	*Six Select Sutes* (Kl. 23)
18v–19	Prelude in c	US-Wc M21 M185, p. 82 (c.1705) (Kl. 45)
19v–20v	'ye double'	GB-Ob, Mus. Sch. MS E.397 (Kl. 45)
20v–22v	Alemande in c	GB-Ob, Mus. Sch. MS E.397 (Kl. 46)
23–24	Aire in c	GB-Ob, Mus. Sch. MS E.397 (Kl. 49)
24v–27v	Toccata(?) in G	hitherto unrecorded
28–30	Allmand in G	*Six Select Sutes* (Kl. 8)
30v–32	Hunting Tune in G	*Six Select Sutes* (Kl. 12)

Purcell end [reversing and inverting the book]

43v	Draghi's 'address' and 3 lines of poetry	
43	Prelude in C	hitherto unrecorded
42v	Minuet in C	hitherto unrecorded
42v	Air in C	hitherto unrecorded
42	Minuet in d	*The Double Dealer* (1693) (Z 592/7)
42	arr. of 'Thus happy and free'	*The Fairy Queen* (1692) (Z 629/44)
41v	Hornpipe in e	*The Old Bachelor* (1693) (Z 607/4)
41	Air in C	*The Double Dealer* (1693), transp. arr. from B♭
40v–39v	Prelude by Orlando Gibbons	*Parthenia* (1613), no. 21
39	Hornpipe in g	*The Fairy Queen* (Z 629/1)
38v	Hornpipe in A	*Apollo's Banquet* (1701), attr. to Eccles
38	Minuet in D	*The Virtuous Wife* (c. 1694) (Z 611/8)
37v	'La Furstenburg' in g	*The Virtuous Wife* (Z 611/9)
37	Minuet in d	*The Virtuous Wife* (Z 611/7)
[leaf removed here]		
36v	Prelude in a	*A Choice Collection* (1696) (Z 663/1)
36–35v	Almand in a	*A Choice Collection* (Z 663/2)
35	Corant in a	*A Choice Collection* (Z 663/3)
34v	Jig in a	hitherto unrecorded
34	Prelude in C with fingerings	hitherto unrecorded
34–33v	Almand in C	*A Choice Collection* (Z 666/2)
33	Corant in C	*Musick's Hand-maid* (1689) (Z 665/3)
32v	Sarraband in C	*Musick's Hand-maid* (Z 665/4)

The first part of the Purcell end of the manuscript (fols. 43–37) appears to have been compiled as a beginner's teaching manual, similar to that published in *The Harpsicord Master* (1697). Both open with a simple C major prelude followed mainly by arrangements of theatre pieces. The previously unrecorded minuet in C major on fol. 42v is almost crude: the parallel octaves in bars 2–3 are uncharacteristic of Purcell and perhaps indicate a wish not to trouble some young student with the basics of part-writing. The first piece in *The Harpsicord Master* is a C major prelude 'for ye fingering', whereas in the Lisa Cox manuscript the one prelude with Purcell's own fingering comes later in the second part amongst more difficult music (fol. 34). Also puzzling is the inclusion of the rather demanding Gibbons prelude in the 'simple' section of the manuscript. The second part of the Purcell end (separated from the first by the stub of a missing leaf) includes the more challenging suite movements, most of which were later published in *A Choice Collection* (1696). They are, however, sufficiently different from the printed versions to show that the manuscript was not the direct source of the posthumous publication. The C major Almand on fols. 33v–34 (Z 666/2) looks like a composition draft: the point of imitation in bars 1 and 2 was an afterthought and there are many corrections and cancellations. The C major Corant and Sarraband on fols. 32v–33 (Z 665/3 and 4) were first published in 1689 in *The Second Part of Musick's Hand-maid*. This *terminus a quo*, plus the arrangements of pieces from theatre works with known premières (*The Fairy Queen*, *The Double Dealer* and so forth), suggests that this section of the manuscript was copied between 1692 and 1694, that is almost precisely the period when Purcell was instructing Katherine Howard.

Even without the benefit of a more thorough inspection, one can draw three basic conclusions from the Lisa Cox manuscript. (1) At the height of his fame, Purcell was teaching beginners and keyboard players of intermediate, perhaps even advanced ability. The manuscript thus has a companion in the Gresham College song-book (London, Guildhall Library MS Safe 3), a similarly didactic collection of vocal music written about the same time and comprising, in the main, reworkings of songs composed a few years earlier and then, towards the end, new compositions. (2) Purcell made keyboard arrangements of his own orchestral pieces besides those in *The Second Part of Musick's Hand-maid*. This fact may weaken the opinion that 'some of those [arrangements] that have survived in early MSS are so incompetently made that it is impossible to believe the composer could have had any hand in them'[9] and possibly vindicates Robert Klakowich's praise of the anonymous

[9] Ferguson, *Miscellaneous Keyboard Pieces*, p. 37.

arranger of the pieces in the Clark Library manuscripts as 'a transcriber of musicality and expertise'.[10] For example, the Minuet in D minor from *The Virtuous Wife* (Z 611/7) on fol. 37 of the Cox manuscript is very similar to the Clark Library version, in which Klakowich notes 'the masterly way in which the descending harmonic sequence . . . is punctuated by the introduction of left-hand octaves followed by rests'. Armed with such criteria drawn from what are now known to be Purcell's own arrangements, one can begin looking through the vast anonymous repertory in search of other genuine works. (3) Purcell appears to have had little concept of the keyboard suite on the continental pattern of a fixed sequence of dance-related movements. There is some grouping of pieces by key, but the otherwise haphazard way in which he copied (or indeed composed) pieces into the manuscript suggests that movements were interchangeable and that even the performance of a sequence of numbers may have been alien to the English keyboard tradition. Everything about the Lisa Cox manuscript points to a didactic purpose.

Of the seventeen pieces at the other end of the manuscript, four are unique, while most of the others are found in G. B. Draghi's *Six Select Sutes of leszons for the harpsicord in six severall keys*, published a year or so before his death in 1708. Many of the concordant pieces differ significantly from the printed versions and from other manuscript sources.[11] The letter 'B' is incorporated into the terminal flourishes of most of the pieces in this part of the manuscript; since Draghi was known in England as 'Baptist', this could be his own monogram, a suggestion strengthened by a musical setting in the same hand of an address on the first page at the other end of the volume: 'In Bedford street ouer against ye Cross Keys Tavern at ye signe of ye Catt – Baptist'.[12] Given the high quality of Draghi's keyboard music, the markedly different readings and their evident authority, this part of the manuscript becomes in its own right one of the most important sources of keyboard music composed in England during the period.

Who had the manuscript first? Purcell or Draghi? The two composers were undoubtedly acquainted, being fellow employees of the royal household, contributors to St Cecilia's Day celebrations and competing organists. The physical characteristics of the manuscript give little clue to chronology. The gilt edge of the covers is worn more or less equally at 'top' and 'bottom', the rubbing perhaps slightly more in the Draghi direction, but this proves

---

[10] Robert Klakowich, 'Harpsichord Music by Purcell and Clarke in Los Angeles', *The Journal of Musicology* 4 (1985–6), 189–90.

[11] See Draghi, *Harpsichord Music*, ed. R. Klakowich.

[12] The hand in the Lisa Cox manuscript which I assume to be Draghi's is not the same as that which Klakowich proffers as autograph in his edition.

nothing about the early history of the manuscript. Internal evidence is also inconclusive. The two hands come together on opposite sides of fol. 32, with no indication that either felt a need to save space on previous pages as he approached the barrier of previously copied music: both Purcell and Draghi were extremely wasteful of blank staves. Even without the benefit of a thorough examination, the following hypothesis would nevertheless account for the peculiar layout of the manuscript. After Purcell's death the half-used book passed to Draghi. At that time, the first page (that is, fol. 43v) was blank and someone had made some shaky attempts at copying music on the last two pages (fol. 1–1v). Draghi set his address to music on the blank first page, flipped the book over, then started writing out pieces at the other end, skipping the first two spoiled pages and leaving a third blank. A major weakness of this hypothesis is that the paper bears a watermark which suggests 1680–2 as the date of manufacture.[13] That Purcell (or any hard-pressed composer) would have purchased this elegant little pre-ruled book in the early 1680s and then left it unused for some ten years is highly unlikely, considering the value of fine music paper and the rate at which it was normally consumed. Nor does the hypothesis adequately account for the miscellaneous nature of the Purcell end: the mixture of fair copies, arrangements and composition drafts; the appearance of the simple fingered prelude in the company of much more technically difficult music; no discernible chronological order to the pieces with datable concordances.

Though it might sound preposterous, I would propose that Purcell never actually owned the manuscript nor need it ever have been in his library. An aristocrat (perhaps a member of the Howard family) or wealthy City merchant is far likelier to have bought an expensive blank book designed specifically for keyboard music and let it gather dust for some ten years. Let us suppose that the book was taken down from the shelf about 1693 and used by one of Purcell's pupils, probably the owner's child who had already spoiled the first two pages with some attempts at writing music. At each lesson (almost certainly at the home of the child, if an aristocrat) Purcell would write out a piece or two, compiling over time a mixture of arrangements, copies of previously composed music (including the Gibbons prelude and the two suite movements from *The Second Part of Musick's Hand-maid*), and some new music composed on the spot. Because he did not own the manuscript, Purcell could afford to be uncharacteristically profligate with paper. The pupil was not an absolute beginner, because even the first prelude in the

---

[13] According to Robert Thompson, who has recently examined the watermarks. See also his 'English Music Manuscripts and the Fine Paper Trade, 1648–1688', Ph.D. thesis, King's College London (1988).

book requires fluency in playing scales. The location of the somewhat easier C major prelude with Purcell's fingering in amongst much more difficult music is an anomaly which could be explained if two members of the family, one more advanced than the other, were using the same book for their lessons with Purcell.[14] Here also is a plausible explanation of how the manuscript passed from Purcell to Draghi, a scenario that does not have Mrs Purcell in her hour of need parting with a valuable commodity to a rival composer. Instead, when Purcell died in November 1695 (or even before), his young pupil, now an advanced player, transferred to a new harpsichord master, Draghi, who continued to teach in the same manner – copying out a miscellany of pieces to be learnt seriatim. Draghi's musical address on the first page of the Purcell end could therefore be interpreted not as a mark of possession but as perhaps whimsical directions to his lodgings. This hypothesis would seem far more plausible than imagining that Draghi had the book first, wrote his address at one end, allowed some child to make musical doodles at the other, then copied in a large collection of his keyboard music before turning the volume over to Purcell about 1693.

However this puzzle is finally solved, the Lisa Cox manuscript may tell us a great deal more about Purcell the teacher than about his relationship with one of his most important contemporaries. The discovery of a Purcell autograph has proved as rare during the last two centuries as the appearance of Halley's Comet. Let us hope the new manuscript will not disappear into the void before it can be properly photographed and studied.

---

[14] For this and other insights into the nature of the manuscript, I am indebted to members of my third-year music history seminar at King's College London, during Lent Term 1994. For a more detailed account of this manuscript, which has recently been acquired by the British Library, see my article 'Newly Discovered Autograph Keyboard Music of Purcell and Draghi', *Journal of the Royal Musical Association* (forthcoming).

5

Purcell and Roseingrave: a new autograph

PETER HOLMAN

Preparatory work for a new catalogue of music manuscripts at Christ Church, Oxford has revealed the identity of most of the more prolific copyists who contributed to this important collection during the Restoration period: Edward Lowe, Henry Aldrich, Richard Goodson senior and junior, Henry Bowman, William Husbands and Edward Hull. A number of manuscripts by copyists from outside the Oxford musical scene have also been identified, though in most cases it is not known how or why they found their way to Christ Church.[1] The most timely and welcome discovery in the latter category is a score of Daniel Roseingrave's anthem *Lord, thou art become gracious*, written by Henry Purcell on a single sheet of paper in MS Mus 1215 (see ills. 5.1 and 5.2).[2]

MS Mus. 1215 is a collection of apparently unrelated manuscripts brought together in a modern binding. Purcell's copy of *Lord, thou art become gracious* is the first item; among the others are five anthems by John Ward, copied by a mid seventeenth-century hand; a comic song, 'Hi jinks brisco', in mongrel Italian and English, copied and possibly composed by Richard Goodson the elder; and a dialogue between Love and Despair, 'In spite of despair', by Daniel Purcell. The last was copied by a scribe who seems to have worked for the Drury Lane theatre in the 1690s. His work can be found in British Library Add. MS 31,449, R.M. 24.e.13 (fols. 62ff) and Add. MS 15,318, primary sources of Purcell's music for *The Indian Queen*, the masque from *Timon of Athens* and the music by Daniel Purcell, Jeremiah Clarke and others for *The Island Princess* (1699). He also copied Royal

---

[1] John Milsom and I made a survey of the Christ Church manuscripts in winter 1993–4. In compiling an index of consort manuscripts for the Viola da Gamba Society, Robert Thompson, Jonathan Wainwright and Andrew Ashbee have also studied the various copyists of the collection.

[2] I am grateful to Dr Milsom for allowing me access to the manuscript and to the Governing Body of Christ Church for permission to reproduce it here. I am also grateful to Margaret Laurie, Curtis Price, Robert Thompson and Bruce Wood for helping me to assess it.

College of Music MS 1172, a collection of overtures, act tunes and dances mostly drawn from incidental music written for plays produced at Drury Lane in the 1690s.[3] A second manuscript at Christ Church can also be added to the list of his work: a set of parts in MS Mus 1141A, fols. 30–43 of an anonymous sonata in C major for trumpet, two oboes and four-part strings.

Purcell copied *Lord, thou art become gracious* onto a single bifolio of foolscap paper, roughly 412 mm by 324 mm; a portion of the bottom of the sheet is missing, so the vertical dimension of that section now varies between about 289 mm and 302 mm. He used paper already ruled in the conventional upright folio format with two columns of twelve five-line staves but clumsily converted it to serve as an oblong score by connecting up the columns of staves freehand and extended the staves at the right-hand side of the recto to fit in extra music. Perhaps he was initially worried that he would not be able to fit the anthem on a single sheet of paper; his hand becomes more expansive on the verso. As one might expect, the sheet has been folded vertically between the columns of staves, but it also has been folded horizontally, making it small enough to fit into a pocket or for sending by post – a point to which I shall return.

The sheet is typical of 'Dutch' paper made in the Angoumois region of France in the 1670s; it has a small arms of Amsterdam watermark with a countermark in the form of a monogram showing the letters D and V. A similar combination of watermark and countermark appears in the autograph scores of John Blow's *Great Sir, the joy of all our hearts* and *Arise, great monarch*, respectively the New Year odes for 1681 and 1682, in the library of the Barber Institute, MS 5001, pp. 71 and 53.[4] It is impossible to know how much bearing this has on the date of the Christ Church sheet, but in general there is little evidence that English stationers kept large stocks of the high-quality paper suitable for music over a long period, so it is likely that Purcell copied the Christ Church manuscript at much the same time.

There is no doubt that all the music notation on the sheet is in Purcell's hand, with the exception of the note shapes in the bottom right-hand corner of the recto, and the fragments written upside down in the corresponding position of the verso. A number of the features – the bold 'H-shape' treble

---

3 There is a facsimile of Add. MS 15,318 in *The Island Princess*, ed. C. A. Price and R. D. Hume, Music for London Entertainment 1660–1800, series C, vol. II (Tunbridge Wells, 1985), and of MS 1172 in *Instrumental Music for London Theatres, 1690–1699*, ed. C. Price, Music for London Entertainment 1660–1800, series A, vol. III (Withyham, 1987).

4 I am grateful to Robert Thompson for this information; see H. Watkins Shaw, 'A Collection of Musical Manuscripts in the Autograph of Henry Purcell and Other English Composers, *c*.1665–85', *The Library* 14 (1959), 126–31.

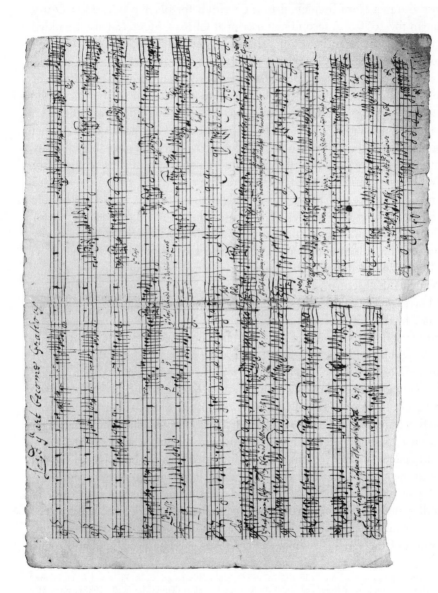

5.1 Christ Church MS 1215, recto of bifolio

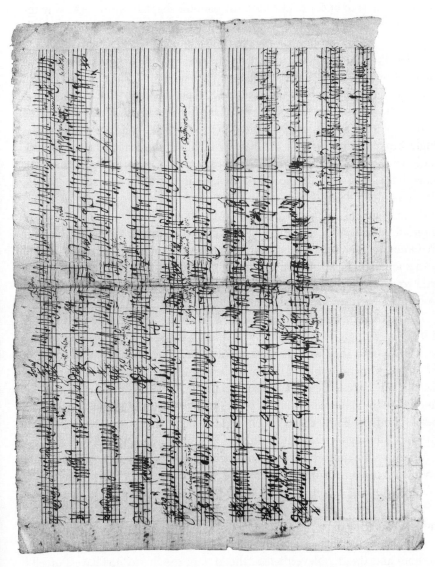

5.2   Christ Church MS 1215, verso of bifolio.

clefs, the idiosyncratic '3' time signatures, the shape of the quavers, with a mixture of curved and straight tails, the balloon-shaped minims, the way the stems of the crotchets and quavers are usually attached firmly to the middle of the note – are common to a range of his autographs. The Christ Church sheet has Purcell's mature form of bass clef, so it was clearly copied later than the early scores of anthems and sacred part-songs in British Library Add. MSS 30,391–2, which have his 'reversed S' type; this early type is only found once in the reversed section of Fitzwilliam MS 88, started no earlier than the autumn of 1677.[5] Similarly, the cross-pieces of the C clefs are made with a single stroke of the pen in a 'Z' shape; a form reminiscent of an arrowhead, made with several strokes, is more common in the early autographs. In general, the music hand is closest to the later items in the reversed section of Fitzwilliam MS 88, probably copied in 1680 or even later, and to the scores of the anthems *Out of the deep* in Add. MS 30,391, fol. 67, and *Behold now, praise the Lord* in Add. MS 30,392, fol. 121, which probably date from about the same time. Purcell's music hand changed little once it reached its mature form about 1680, so it becomes more difficult to date precisely, but there is little reason to doubt the evidence of the paper: the Christ Church sheet probably dates from the early 1680s.

The text hand is more of a problem. The text appears mostly in the form of incipits, though in some places the words have been underlaid, and there one can see that they were added later. The scribe was often forced to write very small, sometimes fitting in words above the line; even so, in a number of places it was impossible to align text and music. It was normal practice at the time (as today) to avoid problems of this sort by inserting the text before the music. Thus it seems that Purcell copied the anthem as a textless piece, without planning to insert the words.

Was Purcell responsible for any of the text? It is difficult to be sure of one's ground when comparing such cramped and crabbed handwriting with the bold and flowing examples in his fair-copy scores. Furthermore, there is no discernible difference in the shade of the ink used for the music and the text, and some of the letter forms are clearly similar to those found in his autographs, particularly the 'a', the 'f', the 's' (which often hangs down below the line) and the 'L'. Nevertheless, the 'd' and the 'h' do not have Purcell's characteristic large loop, the 'p' tends to open at the top rather than at the bottom, the 'R' and 'T' have a more old-fashioned and complex shape than Purcell's and the ampersand is mostly much closer to the modern shape.

[5] At the beginning of Blow's *God is our hope and strength*, fol. 141 (rev); reproduced in *Henry Purcell 1659–1695: Essays on his Music*, ed. Imogen Holst (London, 1959), pl. 3.

The scoring indications 'cho', 'solus' and 'vers 4 voc' are a little more Purcellian and do not include any letter forms that are not found somewhere in his autographs. But it is difficult to to draw firm conclusions from such a small sample, and in general the writing is less rounded and more sloping than the titles and headings in Purcell's other autographs. It is difficult to avoid the conclusion that none of the text is in Purcell's hand, though how many other individuals were involved is hard to say. Occasionally, as in the tenor part in the right-hand bottom corner of the recto, the hand seems to vary because the same copyist is using a different nib, though the words 'turn us' and 'turn' in the third, fourth and fifth bars of the treble part two lines above could possibly be in a third hand.

There is little doubt, however, that most if not all the text was added by the composer himself, Daniel Roseingrave. The same hand also appears in a large oblong quarto organ book now in the music library of the University of California at Berkeley, Mus. 751. Now bound in two volumes (A and B), this was originally a single book with full anthems at the front and verse anthems at the back; each section is paginated separately. The hand in question copied only a few pieces at the end of the front section, including Roseingrave's *Haste thee O God* (pp. 156–7), but added a long sequence of anthems towards the end of the back section, including Roseingrave's *Lord, thou art become gracious* (pp. 141–2), *Bow down thine ear O Lord* (p. 142), *The voice of my beloved* (p. 145), a Service in F major (pp. 162–9, 172–4) and *O clap your hands* (pp. 178–9).

A glance at the text hand of these pieces confirms that it is the same as that of the Christ Church sheet (ill. 5.3). The signature is unmistakable, especially the 'D' formed with one looping stroke, the archaic 'R', virtually in secretary form, and the 's' with a superscript 'e'. The archaic form of 'e', seen most clearly at the end of the word 'become' in the title of the Christ Church sheet, is common in the Berkeley manuscript, as is the archaic sloping 'T' of 'Turn us' at the beginning of the last system of the recto, the ampersand and the unusual indication 'solus'. Also, the hand of the fragments of music copied upside-down in the right-hand corner of the verso, with its 'arrowhead' C clefs, is clearly the same as in the 'Roseingrave' section of the Berkeley manuscript.

The music fragments on the verso appear to consist of two unrelated items, neither of which come from *Lord, thou art become gracious*. The first, apparently a wordless score for two tenors and bass, seems to be the end of a verse passage from an anthem, with a typical repeated final phrase (Ex. 5.1). The fragment was clearly added to the manuscript after the anthem was copied: the last bar of the bass had to be crammed onto the tenor part to avoid becoming entangled with Purcell's terminal flourish. Not much can be

Ex. 5.1

said about the other fragment, except that it seems to need a treble clef; it does not make much sense as music.

There is no proof that the section of the Berkeley organ book with the Daniel Roseingrave anthems is in his autograph, but it seems extremely likely in view of the fact that he is the only composer not given the title 'Mr' or 'Dr'. The same can be said of the hand that started the manuscript and copied most of the rest: it is almost certainly the John Reading who was organist of Winchester Cathedral from 1675 to 1681, and of Winchester College from 1681 to 1692. Like Roseingrave, he nearly always gave other composers formal titles, but signed his own pieces 'John Reading' in a signature-like form. The same feature is found in another manuscript in the same hand, British Library R.M. 20.h.9. In it, a score with church music at the front and consort music at the back, a 'Cannon of 4: in: 2: Arsin and Thesin' on fols. 6v–7 by 'John Reading' is the only piece not ascribed to a composer with a formal title. Moreover, the manuscript contains the only other known copy of *Lord, thou art become gracious* on fols. 18–20v. R.M. 20.h.9 certainly has a Winchester provenance, for it has the bookplate of James Kent, organist of the Cathedral and the College 1738–74. The same must be true of the Berkeley organ book, since it was mostly written by two Winchester organists – Daniel Roseingrave succeeded Reading at the Cathedral in 1681 and remained there until 1692 – and it contains some items by other

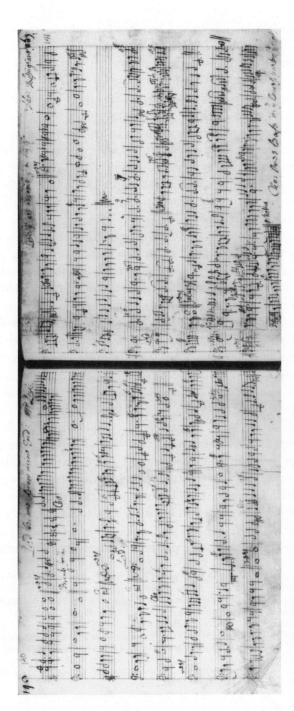

5.3 University of California at Berkeley, Mus. 751, vol. B, p. 141

local composers such as John Silver and Vaughan Richardson, organists of the Cathedral 1661–6 and 1692–1729.[6]

At this point we need to review the relevant portion of Daniel Roseingrave's life. It is not known where or when he was born, but Burney and Hawkins both state that he was a chorister with Purcell in the Chapel Royal.[7] No contemporary record of his service there seems to survive, but in fact there is no complete list of the boys of the Restoration chapel before 1685 – Francis Sandford published their names in *The History of the Coronation of the Most High, Most Mighty, and Excellent Monarch, James II* (London, 1687), p. 69 – and comparatively few of those who served in the 1660s and 1670s can be identified for certain. Burney may have got his information from Daniel's son Thomas, whom he knew in London in the 1740s.

It has often been said that the Roseingrave family was Irish in origin. Daniel may have obtained his posts at the two Dublin cathedrals in 1698 through family connections, and his sons Daniel and Ralph made their careers in Dublin, while Thomas returned there in mid-career. The name Roseingrave (with its variants Rosengrave, Rossengrave, Rosingrave and Rossingrave) is extremely rare: there are none recorded in most English counties in the records of *The International Genealogical Index*, produced on microfiche by the Church of Jesus Christ of Latter-Day Saints. Therefore, it must be significant that a Ralph Rossengrave, a maltster of St Thomas Court, died intestate in Dublin in 1667.[8] If this is Daniel's father (Ralph was clearly a family name), then one must ask how he came to be chosen for the Chapel Royal in London. Again, the answer may be a family connection: *The International Genealogical Index* records several families of London Roseingraves, including one in St Martins-in-the-Fields (Edward Rosingrave married Margeria Paget on 22 April 1640) and one in St Margaret's, Westminster (Justinian and Sarah, son and daughter of Edward and Sarah Rosingrave, christened on 29 July 1641 and 13 December 1642). These parishes, convenient for Whitehall, were the two most favoured by seventeenth-century court musicians, who might have supplied the necessary introductions.

---

6 H. Watkins Shaw, *The Succession of Organists of the Chapel Royal and the Cathedrals of England and Wales from c. 1538* (Oxford, 1991), pp. 297–9; a typed statement on a flyleaf of Mus. 751A suggests that the manuscript came from Chichester, though no evidence is offered for this assertion beyond the opinion of Franklin B. Zimmerman that the initials 'T.C.' may refer to Thomas Capell, organist of Chichester Cathedral 1744–76; see Shaw, *The Succession of Organists*, pp. 78–9.

7 Charles Burney, *A General History of Music*, 1776–89; ed. F. Mercer (London, 1935; repr. 1957), vol. II, 703–4; Sir John Hawkins, *A General History of the Science and Practice of Music*, 1776 (rev. edn London, 1853), vol. II, 771.

8 *Appendix to the Twenty-Sixth Report of the Deputy Keeper of the Public Records and Keeper of the State Papers in Ireland* (Dublin, 1895), p. 41.

We move from speculation to fact with Daniel's appointment as Master of the Choristers at Gloucester Cathedral in the year 1678–9, and as Organist in 1679.[9] On 10 April 1679 he was admonished for 'beating and wounding of John Payn one of the singingmen of this Church', and in 1681 he married Anne Washborne, daughter of the Prebendary; a licence was issued in London on 23 April.[10] He moved to Winchester that autumn: he was appointed by a chapter on 25 November, and took up his post on St Thomas's day, 21 December, though John Reading was still living in the Close on 27 April 1682, when he was told to leave because of 'his lewde and scandalous behaviour on ye night of X^s Passion last past'.[11] Reading seem to have been dismissed from the Cathedral because of his violent behaviour: on 9 September 1678 he was found 'guilty of giving undue and oversevere correction to some of the Choristers', and was warned 'to forbear all such undue correction for the time to come, & to take greater care & diligence in the improvem^t. of the Choristers in Musick then hitherto he hath done'.[12]

Roseingrave's period at Winchester seems to have been uneventful. We know from details they gave when entering Trinity College Dublin that his sons Daniel and Thomas were born there: Daniel was said to be aged 17 on 15 March 1701/2, which means that he was born in 1684 or the spring of 1685, while Thomas was said to be aged 17 on 1 February 1706/7, which means that he was born in 1690 or the spring of 1691 (rather than 1688, as is usually said).[13] Records of their christening do not seem to survive in the Winchester parish registers; the only Roseingrave in the Cathedral register is his daughter Anne, baptized on 13 November 1682 and buried on 24 July 1684.[14]

Daniel Roseingrave did not lose touch with Gloucester: he was paid £5 14s. by the Gloucester authorities in September 1687 'for his iorny about ye Organ', and he sent his son Daniel to the College School in 1700.[15] He

9   Shaw, *The Succession of Organists*, pp. 121–2.
10 S. Eward, *No Fine but a Glass of Wine: Cathedral Life at Gloucester in Stuart Times* (Wilton, 1985), p. 134; *Calendar of Marriage Licences Issued by the Faculty Office 1632–1714*, ed. G. E. Cokayne and E. A. Fry (London, 1905; repr. 1968), p. 78.
11 Winchester Cathedral Library (WCL), Chapter Book 1660–95, fol. 387; Chapter Orders Book, W39/6/32, p. 55; see A. Parker, 'The Cathedral Choir and its Music, 1660–1800', *Winchester Cathedral: Nine Hundred Years*, ed. J. Cook (Chichester, 1993), pp. 305–14; I am grateful to Andrew Parker for providing me with copies of his unpublished transcriptions of material in WCL, and for assisting me on a visit to Winchester.
12 WCL, Chapter Book 1660–95, fol. 336.
13 *Alumni Dublinenses: A Register of the Students, Graduates, Professors and Provosts of Trinity College in the University of Dublin (1593–1860)*, ed. G. D. Burtchaell and T. U. Sadleir (Dublin, 1935), p. 716.
14 WCL, W50/7/1.
15 Eward, *No Fine*, pp. 179, 247.

moved to Salisbury in 1692: he was appointed organist, instructor of the choristers and lay vicar on 19 April, and Vaughan Richardson was appointed in his place at Winchester on 7 December.[16] Roseingrave's career in Salisbury and Dublin need not be rehearsed here, but his fiery temperament did not desert him. He was fined twice for fighting in 1699 and 1700; the second occasion caused the authorities at Christ Church to order 'that from henceforth no vicar or stipendary of this church do wear a sword, under penalty of expulsion'.[17] He died in Dublin in 1727.

It is not easy to understand under what circumstances Purcell and Roseingrave copied the Christ Church sheet. The anthem is interesting and unusual, with some attractive galliard-like cross rhythms in the first section and some remarkable chromatic harmonies at the end of the four-part verse. But it is short-winded and rather aimless in places. That Purcell would have bothered to score it up for study purposes in the early 1680s is unlikely. Harder still to explain is how Roseingrave came to add the text. Perhaps Purcell made the score for performance, to accompany it on the organ or to check its text before copying parts – as he seems to have done with the pre-Civil War anthems in Fitzwilliam MS 88, which he scored up from John Barnard's *First Book of Selected Church Musick* (1641).[18] But had Purcell wanted to make an organ part he surely would have laid it out on two staves or would have just copied a continuo part as Roseingrave did in the Berkeley manuscript. Furthermore, Purcell did not make any corrections to the text. The one change – the f added above the penultimate bar of the alto part – seems to be in Roseingrave's hand; the reading is confirmed by the score in R.M. 20.h.9. And we still need to explain how Purcell and Roseingrave come to be working together when one was in London and the other in Winchester.

One possibility is that the sheet was copied by Purcell in London and posted to Roseingrave, hence the double fold; alternatively, Purcell might have taken it with him on one of the occasions when the court went to Winchester in the early 1680s. At this period Charles II was much concerned with his unrealized plan to build a palace in Winchester; he stayed there in the summers of 1682, 1683 and 1684. There is no evidence that Purcell was in attendance on these occasions, but a list of those who went to Winchester in 1683 includes the Serjeant Trumpeter and a group of unspecified musicians; Nicholas Staggins, the Master of the Music, was paid travel expenses that

---

[16] Shaw, *The Succession*, p. 264; WCL, Chapter Book 1660–95, fol. 434.
[17] W. H. Grindle, *Irish Cathedral Music* (Belfast, 1989), p. 28.
[18] See chap. 2, above.

year for a visit to Winchester between 29 August and 25 September.[19]
Purcell's 1683 ode *Fly, bold rebellion* could have been performed there during
that time, for the text is concerned with the Rye House plot, which had come
to light that spring. An obvious occasion would have been 9 September, the
day appointed to celebrate deliverance from the plot, though it must be said
that the work is headed 'Welcome Song' in the autograph score in British
Library R.M. 20.h.8, fol. 197v, so it may have greeted the king on his return
to Whitehall later that month.

Why would Roseingrave have needed Purcell to copy out his own anthem?
A possible explanation is that he composed the work before he left London
for Gloucester and found himself without a copy at some stage, perhaps after
his move to Winchester. He might have asked his former Chapel Royal colleague to copy it from a London source, now lost, perhaps for some special
occasion. This would explain why Purcell evidently copied it in haste, without
bothering to rule the staves or add the text. On receiving it Roseingrave
might have added enough words to make it possible for a copyist who knew
the text (Psalm 85, v.1) to prepare a set of parts. At some point Roseingrave
(who could of course have been that copyist)[20] added the continuo part of
the anthem to what is now the Berkeley organ book, and John Reading
copied it in score into R.M. 20.h.9. Eventually, having fulfilled its purpose,
the sheet was used by Roseingrave to sketch ideas for other compositions.
How it ended up at Christ Church is, for the moment, a mystery.

[19] A. Ashbee, *Records of English Court Music*, vol. I: *1660–1685* (Snodland, 1986), 206, 207–8; vol. V,
    1625–1714 (Aldershot, 1991), 165.
[20] There are a number of payments to him at Winchester for 'pricking' or supplying music books.
    See WCL, Chapter Orders I, 46; Treasurer's Book 1683-4, fols. 10, 11; Treasurer's Book 1684-5,
    fols. 9, 10.

6

'Only Purcell e're shall equal Blow'

BRUCE WOOD

'The relationship between Blow and Purcell is one of the most important in English music; it is also one of the least well defined. Little is known about the personal relationship, and even less in respect of direct influences on the musical side.' Thus Anthony Lewis, writing over thirty years ago.[1] Since then, parts of the picture have become clearer.[2] Important areas of it still await the restorer's hand, but it is apparent that from the mid-1670s until Purcell's death the two men were engaged in a constant traffic in musical ideas: a traffic which casts light incidentally on their professional relationship as well as directly on their music, for it must surely imply that they were on the best of terms.

By no means all this light is perfectly focused. Even where obvious affinities can be found in the music, it is not always possible to establish who was borrowing from whom. But there can be little doubt that their constant mutual indebtedness was one of the factors which led their contemporaries to place them side by side in the musical pantheon: 'Hail, mighty Pair! of Jubal's art / The greatest glory.'[3] Not everyone echoed these sentiments. One of the panegyrics which followed Purcell's untimely death told a very different story:

> So ceas'd the rival Crew when *Purcell* came,
> They sung no more, or only Sung his Fame.
> Struck dumb they all admir'd the God-like Man.

These lines were penned by Dryden,[4] whose coolness towards English musicians during the 1680s had given way to boundless admiration for

---

[1] 'Purcell and Blow's "Venus and Adonis"', *Music & Letters* 44 (1963), 266.
[2] See Rosamond McGuinness, *English Court Odes 1660–1820* (Oxford, 1971), pp. 88–140, and 'The Ground Bass in the English Court Ode', *Music & Letters* 51 (1970), 118–40, 265–78.
[3] Henry Sacheverell, dedicatory poem prefacing *Harmonia Sacra*, vol. II (London, 1693). The poem is quoted in full in Franklin B. Zimmerman, *Henry Purcell, 1659–1695: His Life and Times* , rev, edn (Philadelphia, 1983), pp. 314–15.
[4] *Ode on the Death of Mr Henry Purcell* (London, 1696). In Blow's setting of these lines the word 'matchless' was substituted for 'God-like'.

Purcell; even so, they were perhaps intended more conventionally than literally. Another posthumous eulogy pointed firmly to the equality of two otherwise peerless men. It was written not only with greater detachment, over two years after Purcell's death, but also, unusually, from the viewpoint of a fellow musician – Henry Hall, organist of Hereford Cathedral, who had been a Chapel Royal chorister with Purcell under the tutelage of Blow:

> Hail! and forever hail Harmonious Shade!
> I lov'd thee Living, and admire thee Dead.
> *Apollo*'s Harp at once our souls did strike,
> We learnt together, but not learnt alike:
> Though equal care our Master might bestow,
> Yet only *Purcell* e're shall equal *Blow*.

True, the same poem described Purcell as 'the Pride and Wonder of the Age', but this is scarcely surprising given its context: the collection of poems which prefaced *Orpheus Britannicus*.[5] Two years later Hall returned to his theme of equality in a prefatory poem for Blow's *Amphion Anglicus* – this time acclaiming the composer in the same breath not only as Purcell but as Corelli too.[6] Three centuries on, with the English Amphion almost totally overshadowed by the British Orpheus, it is high time to clarify their musical relationship.

The most valuable musical sources for a study of that relationship are their church music and odes, along with *Venus and Adonis* and *Dido and Aeneas*. Their keyboard music and their solo songs, despite many points of contact, are less illuminating, for want of sufficiently precise chronological evidence; the same applies to instrumental chamber music, of which Blow anyway wrote little. Even with the odes and anthems it is often impossible to be certain which work is the precursor and which the derivative. All of Purcell's odes, and most of Blow's, being occasional pieces, can be dated exactly, but with many of their anthems the best that can be managed is a *terminus ad quem*.

It is the anthems of the teenaged Purcell which show the first signs of Blow's influence – overlying that of Humfrey, whose declamatory eloquence and harmonic expressiveness nevertheless lived on in the music of his successors long after his death. But Humfrey was no contrapuntist, whereas Blow was already, by the mid-1670s, composing works which continued and refreshed the old English tradition of the polyphonic full anthem. These works display formidable skill at manipulating as many as eight parts to create coherent and impressively varied textures; but they have other qualities besides – notably

---

5 From '*To the Memory of my Dear Friend Mr. Henry Purcell*', in *Orpheus Britannicus* (London, 1698), p. vi.
6 '*To his Esteemed Friend, Dr. Blow, upon Publishing his Book of Songs*', in *Amphion Anglicus* (London, 1700), p. ii.

their carefully balanced structures, which often insert contrasting verse ensembles between the massive outer choruses, and their intensity, created by harmony which is often acutely dissonant and at times decidedly complex.

The clearest evidence of Purcell's borrowing from Blow in this distinctive style is to be found in his early scorebook, now Fitzwilliam MS 88, which contains fair copies of music he composed up to about 1683; the collection also includes his models for many of these works. His *O Lord God of hosts*, which appears on fols. 92–89v of the volume reversed, strikingly resembles Blow's *God is our hope and strength*, which is on fols. 141–138. In between come over two dozen other pieces by Byrd, Tallis, Orlando Gibbons, William Mundy, Tomkins, Giles and Child as well as Blow and Purcell himself: it seems clear that the young composer was much preoccupied with the polyphonic style, though perhaps not for the sole purpose of private study.[7]

God is our hope and strength is certainly the earlier of the two anthems: it was copied into the Chapel Royal books before midsummer 1676, while *O Lord God of hosts* followed between 1677 and the end of 1680.[8] Both pieces are in the unusual key of A major which, as Peter Holman points out, 'would have produced some piquant effects whenever the music moved outside the limited cycle of keys encompassed by mean-tone organ tuning'.[9] Both anthems do indeed contain bold excursions – Blow, at the words 'though the waters rage and swell', encompasses the chords of B major and G minor within a single phrase, while Purcell ventures briefly onto a triad of A♯ minor – and display other notable similarities besides. Purcell appropriated from the Blow not only its variety in the rhythmic placing of imitative ideas – crustic in the opening chorus, anacrustic and syncopated in the closing one – but even the layout of the first verse passage, a dialogue between upper and lower voices (SSA and ATB). He outstripped his teacher, however, in two respects: the poignant expressiveness created by more extensive chromaticism, and the greater variety he lent to dense polyphonic textures, both by juxtaposing contrasting ideas and, in the opening chorus, by seemingly effortless inversion of both the points of imitation.

Two other anthems in Fitzwilliam MS 88 invite detailed examination: Blow's *O Lord God of my salvation*, which Purcell transcribed on fols. 99–96, and his own *Hear my prayer, O Lord*, whose opening chorus – all that is extant – occupies fols. 83v–82v, only seven anthems later, and was almost certainly modelled on that of the Blow although, since Purcell's transcription

---

[7] Robert Thompson has suggested that Purcell may have undertaken the task of clarifying confused underlay in the works he copied, taking as his starting-point the versions given in the Barnard printed partbooks. See chap. 1, above.

[8] Andrew Ashbee, *Records of English Court Music*, vol. I: *1660–1685* (Snodland, 1986), 163, 194.

[9] *The Music of Henry Purcell* (Oxford, 1994), p. 124.

of the latter is its earliest surviving source, the opposite may be true. The two pieces are in different keys – the Blow is in G minor, the Purcell in C minor – but are identical in length, and the layout of the imitative entries, beginning with the inner voices and employing all eight together only in a powerful climax reached in the last few bars, is remarkably similar. But Purcell again outshines Blow, and in the same manner as before: the apex of *Hear my prayer, O Lord* is almost excruciating in its intensity, and this imposing musical edifice (the grandeur of whose effect in performance belies its mere thirty-four bars) is built not upon a single point of imitation but with consummate double counterpoint. Both composers employ inversion, but Purcell does so far more consistently and purposefully.

Purcell's Service in B♭, similar in style and layout to his full-with-verse anthems, is a close cousin to that of Blow in G, with which he must surely have been familiar, though it may have been later that he copied two of its movements into a Chapel Royal organ-book.[10] His most obvious borrowing is the canonic writing which forms a prominent feature of the B♭ Service: its three-part, four-part and double canons are all anticipated in Blow's setting, though he avoided slavishness by employing them at different places in the Service. Only that in the doxology of the Magnificat follows Blow's lead directly, and here Purcell achieves greater intensity, cunningly turning the screw of modulation where Blow's canon remains tonally static. He further outdoes his former teacher by introducing inversion canon – a device which from 1680 onwards he handled with astonishing ease. Both services also employ a head-motif. This feature was not uncommon in Restoration services and had more distant precedents in innumerable Renaissance mass settings, but it was probably Blow's G major Service which prompted Purcell to experiment with motivic unity as well as canons. (His experiments went beyond the head-motif, however, and also beyond purely liturgical confines, for he integrated the material of the evening canticles with that of his full-with-verse anthem *O God, thou art my God*, much as a parody mass is integrated with its parent motet or chanson.)[11]

At the opposite stylistic pole from the utilitarian service stood the glamorous symphony anthem. In this genre too Purcell's early efforts were closely linked

---

[10] See H. Watkins Shaw, 'A Cambridge Manuscript from the English Chapel Royal', *Music & Letters* 42 (1961), 263–7. Blow's Service was certainly composed by 1677, for it is attributed to 'Mr' Blow in the Westminster Abbey Triforium Books, copied by Stephen Bing. Blow's doctorate, which he received in December 1677, was the first Lambeth doctorate ever granted, a signal recognition of his services to church music. Manuscripts copied within the institution of which he was organist would certainly have taken immediate account of his new style.

[11] See Franklin B, Zimmerman, 'Purcell's "Service Anthem" "O God, thou art my God" and the B-Flat Major Service', *The Musical Quarterly* 50 (1964), 207–14.

to those of Blow. Probably as early as 1676, certainly by the end of 1677, Purcell had composed *My beloved spake*, his first extant symphony anthem. In style and structure it is indebted to Humfrey as well as Blow, but it also has plenty of individuality. One of its most engaging passages is the tenor solo 'The fig-tree putteth forth her green figs', in which an obbligato violin deftly imitates the vocal line. Such an accompaniment was beyond Humfrey – as witness his only obbligato violin part, in *O give thanks unto the Lord*;[12] and Blow's efforts too had been tentative, at any rate in anthems known to have been composed before *My beloved spake*. But in *Cry aloud, and spare not*[13] all the solo verses have an obbligato violin part which is shapely and eloquent from first note to last. Unfortunately there is only an approximate *terminus ad quem* for this anthem: it was the first piece which Purcell transcribed into Fitzwilliam MS 88, his earliest fair-copy album, on acquiring it from its previous owner, who had dated its table of contents 1677. It remains unclear whether *Cry aloud, and spare not* was indebted to *My beloved spake* or vice versa.

In applying integrative techniques to the symphony anthem, Blow was unquestionably the pioneer. His works of this type represent a notable advance over those of Humfrey and were to offer Purcell a stimulus to further effort. In Blow's *The Lord is my shepherd*, for instance, material from the triple-time section of the imposing opening symphony is repeated as an accompaniment to the first verse, though after a couple of instrumental phrases this ingenious pattern collapses into rhapsodic ruin. Blow's anthem was in the repertory by 1677.[14] Three years later Purcell fully realized the scheme at which his teacher had balked. In his anthem *O praise God in his holiness* the outer parts of the triple-time section of the symphony are repeated in their entirety as accompaniment to the opening verse. The same scheme is employed in *Welcome, Vicegerent*, his first welcome song for Charles II, composed during the summer of 1680; here, however, he went further, repeating not merely the outside parts but the complete texture of the triple-time section of the symphony, neatly superimposed on the four-part opening chorus.

That *Welcome, Vicegerent* begins with a chorus is unusual but not unprecedented: Blow had done the same in *Great Janus, though the festival be thine*, composed for New Year 1679.[15] In *Welcome, Vicegerent* Purcell appropriated

---

12 Musica Britannica, vol. XXXV, 1–19; see bars 155–75.
13 Musica Britannica, vol. LXIV, 23–35.
14 It is attributed to 'Mr' Blow in British Library Add. MS 50,860 and Tokyo, Nanki Library N-5/10 – two Chapel Royal bass books – in the handwriting of William Tucker, a junior priest at the Chapel and a minor canon of Westminster Abbey, who died in February 1679. The anthem is included in Musica Britannica, vol. VII.
15 For evidence of dating see McGuinness, *English Court Odes*, pp. 16, 46.

this feature, gilding the lily with the elaborate accompaniment. And the triple-time movement of the symphony which it repeated was no mere homophonic dance but imitative in texture, at least in its opening bars. This feature, contrasting sharply with the invariable homophony of the triple-time movements in Humfrey's symphonies, was not in itself a new departure in England: Blow had again anticipated Purcell – initially in his anthem *Cry aloud, and spare not* and later in *Great Janus*. And whereas Purcell's movement soon made the easy descent into homophony, both of those by Blow remained doggedly contrapuntal almost throughout. In the anthem he works two related points in turn, with a thoroughness and ingenuity Purcell was not yet able to match. The symphony of *Cry aloud, and spare not* broke new ground in another respect. Blow lent symmetry to its ternary grouping of common- and triple-time movements by making the closing section a truncated repeat of the first (whereas in the few earlier English examples, such as Humfrey's *Lift up your heads, O ye gates,*[16] the common-time coda was both very brief and thematically unrelated to the opening). Purcell soon followed suit in *Awake, awake, put on thy strength*, composed probably in 1683, and found the same plan still serviceable, four years later, for the much more Italianate symphony of *Behold, I bring you glad tidings*.

After his initial experiment with a fugal second strain in the symphony of *Welcome, Vicegerent*, Purcell favoured this pattern in his odes and symphony songs (though never again as an obbligato accompaniment to the opening vocal movement); but, curiously, he employed it much more rarely in his anthems. Blow made no such distinction between sacred and secular. But, again in the overture of a symphony anthem, he introduced an important technique which has come to be associated less with his name than with Purcell's: the ground bass.

Blow had been composing grounds since the mid-1670s. Among the pieces in his earliest surviving fair-copy album, completed by about 1675, is a vigorous two-voice motet, *Cantate domino*, entirely constructed on a ground.[17] The bass is a commonplace, beginning with a chromatic descent – exactly like Dido's Lament – but its treatment is already ingenious, with upper parts whose overlapping imitative phrases deftly conceal several of the cadential seams in the bass. By the end of the decade Blow had further honed his technique. His *O give thanks unto the Lord, and call upon his Name* was composed no later than 1680, to judge from the palaeographic style of the

---

[16] Musica Britannica, vol. XXXIV, 99–106.
[17] Oxford, Christ Church MS 14; see H. Watkins Shaw, 'The Autographs of John Blow', *The Music Review* 25 (1964), 88–9. *Cantate domino* is found on fols. 109v–111.

autograph fair-copy (another surviving version is less polished and obviously the earlier of the two).[18] The ground bass which underpins its opening symphony and links it to the first verse is boldly asymmetrical, and the whole movement is remarkably assured and more sophisticated than any earlier English exemplar.[19]

Purcell's response was direct. His anthem *In thee, O Lord, do I put my trust,* composed a year or more after *O give thanks,*[20] begins with a movement which is strikingly similar, even to the asymmetry of the ground – five bars long, as against Blow's even more unusual seven. Purcell's movement is perhaps the finer of the two, though by no great margin; it is a little more closely argued, thanks to the ease with which the ground and its inversion infect the upper parts. But several of its most engaging features are lifted straight from Blow's symphony: the crotchet-based rhythmic patterns, later breaking into sprightly trochees; the imitative first entry of the upper parts over a dominant bass; the cunning mismatch between the phrase lengths of the melody and those of the bass; and the rhetorical syncopated minims preceded by rests. (Blow subsequently used a rather similar ground in an air for countertenor and recorders near the beginning of his 1688 New Year ode *Ye Sons of Phoebus, now appear,* but this can scarcely be considered a borrowing: the bar-long repose on the tonic which Purcell uses so effectively is omitted, the ground is transposed to various keys as well as broken, and the treatment of the upper parts is quite different.)

Purcell's anthem ends with another ground, which unifies a verse, ritornello and chorus all in dancing quavers. The movement is not one of his best efforts – Westrup's dismissive description of its 'unfruitful stodginess' hits the mark[21] – but it appears to have prompted one of Blow's best by way of response. His *Blessed is the man*[22] cannot be dated with certainty, though it was composed by 1683. But the ground-bass movement with which it ends, a substantial affair embracing three verse passages (one of them accompanied by all the upper strings), three choruses and a ritornello, forms a conclusion

18 Musica Britannica, vol LXIV, 53–72, 178; see also Watkins Shaw, 'Autographs', pp. 85–95.
19 It may have been modelled on a continental work: by the time it was composed the Italians had been employing ostinato basses for many decades. Sophisticated examples were also current in France, though many of them – especially those of Lully – treat the bass more freely, and none of those that I have been able to find resembles the present movement even remotely.
20 The anthem is usually dated about 1681 or 1682 on the evidence of its position in the chronologically ordered autograph score-book, British Library MS R.M. 20.h.8; but its text, considered in conjunction with those of the two anthems which precede and follow it there, *Awake, awake put on thy strength* and *The Lord is my light,* suggests that all three pieces may have been associated with the uncovering of the Rye House Plot in 1683.
21 J. A. Westrup, *Purcell* (London, 1936), p. 214.
22 Musica Britannica, vol. L, 1–17.

so much more accomplished than that of *In thee, O Lord* that it seems most unlikely that Purcell's anthem was composed later, a mere pale reflection of an existing movement. More probably this was what Anthony Lewis (discussing another instance of interaction between Blow and Purcell which also, co-incidentally, involved ground basses) termed 'a gentle but glorious protest' by one composer against the other's poaching.[23] Blow's bass follows a common-place pattern – a stepwise descent that turns back upwards to the cadential dominant. Three or four years earlier Purcell himself had employed a minor-key version of it in his motet *Beati omnes qui timent dominum* (a piece which may itself have been composed in response to Blow's *Cantate domino* and which Blow had copied at the very end of his next fair-copy album, some thirty pages after his own *O give thanks unto the Lord*);[24] and in the major mode it subsequently served Purcell well in triple-time guise for the song 'Let each gallant heart', published in 1683, and for the lengthy chaconne in his 1686 welcome song *Sound the trumpet, beat the drum*. In *Blessed is the man* Blow transforms this cliché with exuberant inventiveness, far outshining his model.

The two movements are very similar in rhythmic character and even share some melodic detail. Blow's bass, however, is more shapely than Purcell's and more varied in its harmonic implications. It is treated more flexibly and resourcefully, modulating freely where Purcell's sticks fast in the tonic; and the movement gains further variety from kaleidoscopic changes of scoring, which Purcell eschewed (though he showed his characteristic deftness at 'covering the seams' by contradicting the phrase structure of the bass with that of the upper parts). Blow has been criticized, with some justice, for taking the line of least resistance by breaking the bass and changing the scoring of ground-bass movements,[25] but here these expedients are made a virtue. The movement is notable also for its internal symmetries. The opening and closing sections, which are the biggest, are of balanced length; the remainder is divided by its clear tonal plan into two groups of sections – the first modulating, the second static – each of which contains three smaller blocks, respectively of two, two and four bars, demarcated by changes in scoring. It is not, however, such self-effacing subtleties which lend the movement conviction, but its resolute rhythmic momentum, attractive melodic detail and sturdily independent inner voices.

Blow was also first to experiment with the ground-bass technique in a court ode. His offering for New Year 1681, *Great Sir, the joy of all our hearts*,[26]

---

[23] 'Purcell and Blow's "Venus and Adonis"', p. 269.
[24] Christ Church MS 628, pp. 143–6, copied by Blow *c.* 1680: see Shaw, 'Autographs', p. 89.
[25] McGuinness, 'The Ground Bass', p. 266.
[26] Barber Institute MS 5001, pp. 71–91 (autograph).

contains an extended movement built over a running bass line which is not always literally repeated – the type of movement for which Peter Holman has coined the useful term 'pseudo-ground'.[27] The piece supplied Purcell with a model, soundly crafted if not particularly imaginative, for what came to be one of his favourite types of ground-bass composition – the solo air, rounded off with a ritornello which repeats or develops its material – though Blow's air is instead punctuated with two related ritornellos making a neat cyclic structure.

Purcell's first opportunity for a riposte was his welcome song for the king's return to Whitehall after the summer remove that same year: *Swifter Isis, swifter flow* duly contains a full-blown ground-bass air. But it is disappointing. Its bass, imitated by the upper parts in the two ritornellos which frame the air, employs a curiously ponderous crotchet arpeggio, hinting at a trumpet fanfare but possibly suggested rather by the 'lab'ring oars' of the text. Elsewhere in the same welcome song – in the fluent Italianate duet for trebles, 'The king whose absence like the sun' – there is a running bass line not unlike that in Blow's ode; Purcell develops it freely, however, instead of employing it as a ground. His next autumn welcome song, *The summer's absence unconcerned we bear*, contains a true ground, but a thoroughly undistinguished one: 'And when late from your throne' consists of a lengthy air, a short chorus and a ritornello, all underpinned by that baldest of clichés, the descending tetrachord – repeated no fewer than twenty times.

It was not until 1683 that the ground-bass movements in Purcell's welcome songs and odes attained characteristic fluency and inventiveness, though in that year he wrote three: one each in *From hardy climes*, *Fly, bold rebellion* and *Welcome to all the pleasures*. All three of these grounds, with their striding energy and innate harmonic tensions, bear the unmistakable stamp of his authorship; but in fact these features were anticipated in Blow's 1683 New Year ode *Dread Sir, Father Janus*. The countertenor air 'All due, great Prince, is yours' (Ex. 6.1) differs in three respects from what became the Purcellian archetype. Internal repetition of the vocal line falls into a ternary pattern, whereas Purcell's airs, if they contained such repeats, were invariably binary; the ritornello which rounds off the movement is content to repeat its material verbatim, whereas Purcell usually subjected his ideas to further development; and the ground itself is treated more freely, so as to accommodate a modulation to the dominant and back (offering welcome relief from its tendency to harp on the tonic). But the movement is very similar in style to those in the three Purcell odes, and the ritornello contains much the same kind of attractive harmonic detail, even if its part-writing is not quite so intricate or imaginative as theirs.

[27]   *Henry Purcell*.

After 1683 Purcell included at least one ground-bass air in nearly every one of his odes, though neither he nor Blow, who was less fond of the device, repeated the experiment of beginning or ending an ode or an anthem with a movement constructed over a ground. But in several of his anthems from the mid-1670s onwards Blow adopted another structural innovation in the opening symphony. This was ternary form, to which, as we have just seen, Blow was also attracted elsewhere. Humfrey and Locke had confined themselves to binary form in their symphonies, and there seems to be no English precedent for the ternary plan which Blow first employed in *And I heard a great voice* (1674).[28] In three further anthems – *When Israel came out of Egypt*,[29] dating from the same year, and *I beheld, and lo, a great multitude*[30] and *The Lord is my shepherd*,[31] both composed by 1677 – the second strain and the reprise of the opening are repeated together to form a ternary/binary hybrid.

During the 1680s Blow returned to this form, or variants thereof, in *Blessed is the man that hath not walked, Hear my voice, O God*[32] and the A minor version of *The Lord is King*.[33] Purcell never followed this lead directly, but in two anthems – *I was glad* and *Rejoice in the Lord*, both composed during 1683 or 1684 – the second strain of a binary symphony ends with a clear reminder of the opening material. Curiously, these are the only such movements in Purcell's output, despite the potential of the device for shaping attractively rounded instrumental movements.

Neither composer showed much interest in structural innovation in the symphonies of their odes. Style, however, was another matter. Blow's ode for New Year 1683, *Dread Sir, Father Janus*,[34] has an imposing if conventional opening in common time, but its second movement is a lively confection of dancing quavers in compound time (Ex. 6.2a). It was only a matter of weeks before Purcell followed suit in the second movement of the symphony in *From hardy climes* – composed in the late spring for the wedding of Princess Anne to Prince George of Denmark (Ex. 6.2b). But this is no mere flattering imitation. The phrase structure and pattern of entries are more disciplined than those of its model; its vivacity is enhanced by the addition of nimble

[28] Musica Britannica, vol. VII, 62–77.
[29] This anthem (Musica Britannica, vol. LXIV, 125–45) begins with a short prelude; the symphony concerned is at bars 30–60.
[30] Ed. H. Watkins Shaw (Oxford, 1969).
[31] Musica Britannica, vol. VII, 93–108.
[32] King's College Cambridge Rowe MS 22, fols. 88v–99; ed. Bruce Wood in 'John Blow's Anthems with Orchestra', Ph. D. thesis, Cambridge (1976), vol. I, 228–57.
[33] Barber Institute MS 5001, pp. 210–23; ed. Wood in 'John Blow's Anthems', IV, 1–32.
[34] Barber Institute MS 5001, pp. 31–51 (autograph).

Ex. 6.1

semiquavers to the quaver movement; its melodic outline is clarified by shapely sequential patterns; and its climax is firmly underpinned by a dominant pedal, a device which Blow hardly ever used. The symphony of Purcell's autumn welcome song, *Fly, bold rebellion*, has a similarly fleet-footed second movement, though in 9/8 instead of 6/8; and its opening strain (Ex. 6.3a), in which swaggering dotted rhythms make their way through all the parts, owes even more to that of *Dread Sir, Father Janus* (Ex. 6.3b).

The royal odes of 1683 share yet another feature: solos written for the redoubtable bass John Gostling. Blow's *Dread Sir, Father Janus* provided Purcell with two models. Its first vocal movement (Ex. 6.4a) is a bipartite solo pairing a declamatory opening with a triple-time dance song. This pattern – Italian in origin, but long familiar in England – might seem an

Ex. 6.2a

Ex. 6.2b

Ex. 6.3a

Ex. 6.3b

Ex. 6.4a

obvious opening gambit for royal odes but was in fact almost untried in such a context.[35] The example by Blow, if delivered with Gostling's customary panache, must have been arresting enough, but that by Purcell is an altogether grander affair: the air modulates freely while the declamatory section

---

[35] The first vocal movement of Cooke's *Good morrow to the Year* (1666) (Barber Institute MS 5001, pp. 1–9) is an exiguous declamatory passage for bass, followed by an equally tiny triple-time air for treble; that of Humfrey's *See, mighty Sir* (1670?) (British Library Add. MS 33,287, fols. 69v–71v) is a

contains some telling details – the unexpected C♮ on 'dangerous', the vividly pictorial moment of stasis on 'gaze' (Ex. 6.4b).

Later in *Dread Sir, Father Janus* comes a solo of a kind which Gostling must have particularly relished: the rumbustious triple-time air 'The sons of the earth' (Ex. 6.5a), full of wide-leaping phrases and abrupt plunges into the vocal depths, as the text proclaims the infernal origins of the king's enemies.

Ex. 6.5a

tenor solo, with a declamatory opening successively in quadruple and duple time, followed by a triple-time air. There is no other English example before 1683 of a bipartite solo serving as the opening vocal number in an ode, or for that matter in a symphony anthem. (Locke's *I will hear what the Lord God will say*, printed in Musica Britannica, vol. XXXVIII, 82–8, which begins with such a movement, is not a complete anthem but forms the concluding portion of *Lord, thou hast been gracious*, which survives – severed from it, and misattributed to Blow – only in British Library Add. MS 31,444, fols. 184–188v: see Wood, 'John Blow's Anthems', IV, 242–56, 273, and V, 432–3.)

Prophetic words: within the year their downfall was being celebrated in Purcell's autumn welcome song – most specifically in the rousing air 'The plot is display'd' (Ex. 6.5b), whose debt to 'The sons of the earth' is obvious. That Purcell's air is the more memorable is thanks to superior organization, in particular to repetition of ideas, rather than to better material as such.

Ex. 6.5b

All three of these solos exploit Gostling's remarkable compass with an assurance that is particularly impressive, considering that it was apparently only a year previously that either composer had begun to write for 'that stupendious Base'.[36] Blow had led the way, not with an air but with a declamatory solo, in the New Year ode, *Arise, great Monarch*[37] (Ex. 6.6a);

[36] McGuinness suggests in *English Court Odes*, p. 16, that Blow's *Up, shepherds* was composed in 1681, but the evidence she adduces is not conclusive.
[37] Barber Institute MS 5001, pp. 53–70 (autograph).

Purcell had responded in similar vein, at the opening of his autumn welcome song *The summer's absence unconcerned we bear* (Ex. 6.6b). The contrast is instructive. Blow wastes the first of Gostling's sensational bottom Ds on a weak and unimportant final syllable, whereas Purcell tellingly reserves all of them for focal points in the text; he also gives this magisterial piece of writing pride of place at the beginning of his ode, whereas Blow buries his innovative effort in the middle. More surprising than Blow's fumbling is the fact that both composers waited so long to exploit Gostling's prowess below the stave, which had been recognised even before he became a Gentleman of the Chapel Royal in February 1679.[38]

The 1670s had brought other conspicuous newcomers to the Chapel. The arrival in London of woodwind players from France, with their new-fangled oboes and three-piece recorders, had made it possible for Blow and Purcell to write for these exotic instruments in their odes and anthems: from 1678 onwards, the Frenchmen were supernumerary court musicians.[39] It is not clear which composer was the pioneer: of what seem to be the first four works to include independent parts for oboe and recorder, only two –

Ex. 6.6a

[38] Westrup, *Henry Purcell,* pp. 305–6.   [39] Ashbee, *Records of English Court Music,* vol. I, 179.

Ex. 6.6b

The sum - mer's ab - sence un - con - cern'd we bear,

Since you, since you,___ great___ Sir, great___

Sir, more charm - ing fair ap - pear,

welcome songs by Purcell – can be dated with certainty, while of the others, both anthems by Blow, only one has even a definite *terminus ad quem.*

The earlier of the two welcome songs is *Swifter Isis*, composed in 1681. Purcell's use of the woodwind here is decidedly limited: one bass solo is accompanied by recorders, and one brief instrumental passage – the ritornello that concludes the ground-bass air described earlier – is scored for oboe as well as four-part strings. His next welcome song, *What shall be done in behalf of the man*, composed the following spring for the Duke of York's return from Scotland, again includes parts for recorders, which are similarly confined to two movements: the opening solo and one recurring ritornello (Ex. 6.7a). The latter is strongly reminiscent of Lully; but it has a closer and homelier relative in Blow's symphony anthem *Sing unto the Lord, O ye saints*[40] (Ex. 6.7b), which was composed by 1683, though whether before or after Purcell's ode is unknown. Purcell's treatment of the woodwind, though more assured than in *Swifter Isis*, is far less imaginative than that of Blow, who fully exploited the unusual combination of two recorders doubling on tenor oboes, both in instrumental and in vocal movements. He displayed equal

[40]   Musica Britannica, vol. L, 124–47.

resource in another anthem, *Lord, who shall dwell in thy tabernacle*,[41] whose
opening symphony not only contrasts the recorders and strings antiphonally
but also combines them in rich five-part polyphony. Whether or not Blow
was the first to write for the new woodwind instruments, in these works
belonging to the early 1680s he did so a good deal more boldly than Purcell.

The younger man certainly borrowed from *Sing unto the Lord, O ye saints*
one feature which has nothing to do with the woodwind instruments. In the
summer of 1683, the French players apparently returned to Paris, and for the
next few years court odes and symphony anthems were scored for strings
alone. Purcell's 1684 welcome song *From those serene and rapturous joys* (his

Ex. 6.7a

41 Both the Blow anthems are included in Musica Britannica, vol. L.

Ex. 6.7b

last for Charles II) makes more extensive use than any of his previous odes of the upper strings to accompany the voices rather than to alternate with them. The most striking of the movements concerned is the chorus 'Welcome home', which follows the opening verse and is later repeated, with adjustments, in the subdominant. The textures of this chorus – voices in block chords, accompanying violin parts formed of stepwise running quavers in parallel thirds – strongly suggest direct Italian influence; but the movement has an obvious antecedent in the tantalizing four-bar fragment which is all that survives of the concluding chorus of Blow's *Sing unto the Lord, O ye saints* (Exx. 6.8a and b).

The links between *Venus and Adonis* and *Dido and Aeneas* are among the closest of any two works by Blow and Purcell. These have all been rehearsed elsewhere, but their extent is worth reiterating. Several of the connections fall within the province not of composer but of librettist: both employ cupids, initially in conventional contexts but subsequently as mourners or weepers;[42]

---

[42] In Act 1 of *Dido*, Cupids are mentioned not in the stage directions but in the text. From the Prologue:

VENUS.   These are all my Guards ye View,
                What can these blind Archers do.
PHOE[BUS].   Blind they are, but strike the Heart.
And from the end of Act 1:
CHO[RUS].   Go Revel ye *Cupids*, the day is your own.

both treat the chorus as shepherds and shepherdesses, and subsequently as huntsmen; in both a boar plays an important part – and the bearing onstage in *Dido* of the dead beast's head occasions an explicit comparison with the inferior specimen that killed Adonis. But the purely musical debts which *Dido* owes to *Venus* are even more significant: a prologue and three acts; tonal planning – a journey from C (major in *Venus*, minor in *Dido*) at the beginning of the first act to G minor at the end of the third, with the second opening in F (again, major in *Venus*, minor in *Dido*) and ending in D minor;[43] the tragic

Ex. 6.8a

43 Although the end of Act 2 in *Dido* is lost, most commentators agree that it must have concluded in D minor. See *Dido and Aeneas*, ed. A. Margaret Laurie and Thurston Dart (London, 1961), pp. 104–6; and the Norton Critical Score of *Dido*, pp. 183–87, 239–52.

Ex. 6.8b

Al - le - lu - ia, Al - le - lu - ia,

Al - le - lu - ia, Al - le - lu - ia,

intensity of the final act, culminating in a choral threnody; the importance of the dance movements; the preponderance and style of the declamatory writing; the use of very similar running bass lines in the second act of each work; and even the vocal forces required. The recent controversial argument that *Dido* may have been composed as early as 1683 or 1684 does not directly affect the question of its debt to *Venus*.[44] But a short lapse of time between two works so closely linked would certainly be consistent with most of the other borrowings discussed here.

The anthems which Blow and Purcell composed for the coronation of James II in 1685 show equally close connections; but this is almost certainly the result of collaboration rather than of mutual influence. Blow's *Behold, O God our defender*,[45] sung at the Anointing, and Purcell's introit *I was glad*, besides being identical in vocal scoring (SSATB), have similar designs: a vigorous triple-time opening followed by a shift into common time and a preponderance of forthright music in block chords, with counterpoint confined to the closing bars. But Purcell, working of necessity on a much larger scale, was able to secure far bolder contrasts, while the dazzling contrapuntal display which ends his introit, involving not only inversion but also single and double augmentation of the point of imitation, could not have been matched by Blow or any other composer of the period.

---

44 See Bruce Wood and Andrew Pinnock, '"Unscarr'd by turning times"?: The Dating of *Dido and Aeneas*', *Early Music* 20 (1992), 372–90; letters to the editor of *Early Music* from John Buttrey (20, 701) and from Martin Adams (21, (1993), 510); Curtis Price, '*Dido and Aeneas*: Questions of Style and Evidence', *Early Music* 22 (1994), 115–24; letter from Wood and Pinnock, *Early Music* 22, 365–7.

45 *Musica Britannica*, vol. VII, 48–50.

More striking than the kinship between these two pieces, however, is that between the two symphony anthems, Blow's *God spake sometime in visions*[46] and Purcell's *My heart is inditing*. Both pieces are for eight-part full choir, with verses in as many as seven parts, and their combination of clefs is otherwise unique, at least in English music: treble, soprano, mezzo-soprano, alto, tenor, baritone and two basses. Structurally too they show strong affinities. The most obvious of these – the repetition (slightly curtailed in Blow's anthem) of the opening symphony as a buttress, half or two-thirds of the way through – is a common feature of both men's Chapel Royal anthems, and thus perhaps to be expected, but the ordering of verses, choruses and ritornellos, and thematic relationships and contrasts unifying and separating lengthy musical paragraphs, is too similar to be explained away by coincidence or by the constraints of text or liturgical function. Differences between the two pieces may also have been planned. Blow's anthem, sung after the crowning of the king, is strongly assertive in musical character, especially in its sturdy duple-time opening movement and its two vigorously declaimed choruses in common time, 'My hand shall hold him fast' and 'And in my Name shall his horn be exalted'. In contrast, Purcell's, which accompanied the crowning of the queen, is much more sensuous – even the big opening chorus has a dancing grace – and much of it is delicately expressive. This characteristic, achieved largely by sensitively manipulated dissonance, is enhanced by Purcell's consistent predilection for instrumental doubling of voices at the octave or fifteenth, producing an effect of far greater brilliance than the solid unison doubling which Blow preferred.

During the 1680s the interest in Italian music which both composers had long shared was increasingly reflected in their own compositions, especially their instrumental writing. The remarkable synthesis of Italian and English features achieved by Purcell in his *Sonnata's of Three Parts* (1683) was not lost on Blow, who about this time began scoring his Chapel Royal anthems for three-part in preference to four-part strings. *The Lord is King* exists in two versions. The earlier, composed by 1683,[47] was extensively re-worked: Blow transposed it up a tone (re-allocating the topmost verse part from tenor to countertenor, and modifying the highest reaches of the chorus treble line), excised the tenor violin part (re-casting the second violin part as necessary), and re-modelled some of the instrumental movements. He prefaced the opening symphony with a completely new slow introduction (Ex. 6.9a) which strikingly resembles that of the symphony in Purcell's 1685 welcome song *Why are all the Muses mute?*, though the latter is scored not for three-

[46] *Ibid.*, 1–45.   [47] Musica Britannica, vol. LXIV, 103–24.

part but for four-part strings (Ex. 6.9b). Although the date of the second version of Blow's anthem is unknown, its new opening may well have served as the model for the passage in Purcell's ode. It is certainly inferior: the bass part drops out disappointingly soon after its first entry, and the tonal scheme is weak, with the first three cadences in the relative major or its dominant and the last two in the tonic. In Purcell's movement, by contrast, the textures are perfectly controlled, while the four intermediate cadences fall successively in the tonic, subdominant, dominant and relative major. Another difference is that the upper parts in Blow's movement are too often yoked together rhythmically, whereas Purcell deftly contrasts both slower-moving and more active voices against the main theme.

Ex. 6.9a

Ex. 6.9b

Vocal movements too increasingly show the influence of Italian models. Both composers began to favour a vigorous canzona-like style for verse passages; one of the earliest examples, in Purcell's 1686 welcome song *Ye tuneful Muses* (Ex. 6.10a), is remarkably similar in style and construction to one in the New Year ode Blow had composed some nine months earlier, *Hail, Monarch, sprung of race divine*[48] – even the vocal scoring being identical – and contains a brazenly direct crib from it (Ex. 6.10b). Both composers show a firm grasp of the style; almost the only important difference between the two passages is that Purcell's is on a larger scale, the material quoted being further developed in a short concluding ritornello.

Blow's and Purcell's long-standing interest in Italianate musical idioms must have received a powerful stimulus towards the end of 1687 from G. B. Draghi's Cecilian ode *From harmony*,[49] a setting of Dryden's splendid poem. The work undeniably has its *longueurs*, but three aspects of it seem to have made a deep impression: the five-part strings, not the three-viola French scoring but the two-viola Italian one, with the addition of trumpets as well as recorders; brilliant vocal writing and obbligato accompaniments; and its spacious Italian overture, opening with fanfare-like figures stated over a tonic pedal before the rhythmic texture becomes busier (Ex. 6.11a). This last feature elicited an immediate response. We shall probably never know whether Purcell's *Behold, I bring you glad tidings* (Ex. 6.11b), his anthem for Christmas Day 1687, or Blow's ode *Ye sons of Phoebus, now appear*[50] (Ex. 6.11c), composed for the celebrations of New Year just seven days later, came first; but Purcell clearly built the short initial paragraph of his opening symphony on this idea, continuing with a canzona based on fresh fanfare figures before making a truncated reprise of the opening, whilst Blow preferred to create a more heterogeneous single movement in which a triadic and homophonic opening statement gave way to contrapuntal discussion of other material.

Purcell returned to fanfare patterns, more explicitly trumpet-like in character, in *Now does the glorious day appear*, the first of his birthday odes for Queen Mary, performed in April 1689. Here he outdid Blow by treating the opening fanfare contrapuntally: a dozen bars into the movement, a statement in an inner part is deftly if unobtrusively answered by the bass in augmentation. The same work also followed a purely structural lead Blow had given in *Ye sons of Phoebus*, by repeating the opening chorus after intervening verse material, thus framing a lengthy and imposing musical paragraph. In a matter of months the court heard Blow's riposte, in his 1690

---

[48] Royal College of Music MS 1097, fols. 135–150 (autograph).
[49] Transcribed by Blow in *ibid.*, fols. 85–112.   [50] *Ibid.*, fols. 159–178v (autograph).

Ex. 6.10a

Till then make bright your war - rior s shield,

Till then make bright your war - rior s

His shi - ning arms and helm pre - pare,

shield, Till then make

Ex. 6.10b

fright, And blest you with his joy - ful

fright, And blest you with his joy - ful ray, And

ray, And blest you with his joy - ful, joy - ful, joy - ful ray.

blest you with his joy - ful, joy - ful, joy - ful ray.

135

Ex. 6.11a

Ex. 6.11b

Ex. 6.11c

New Year ode *With cheerful hearts let all appear.*[51] Here he added a new element: internal antiphonal exchanges in the opening symphony (Ex. 6.12a). Purcell promptly responded in his next birthday ode for the Queen, *Arise, my Muse* – trumping Blow's ace by scoring the movement for brass as well as strings (Ex. 6.12b), an anticipation of the stately exchanges which two years later would so arrestingly open *Hail, bright Cecilia* (Ex. 6.12c).

[51]   *Ibid.*, fols. 179–194v (autograph).

Despite the affinities among these opening gestures, the most obvious musical traffic between Blow and Purcell from the late 1680s onwards is in orchestral technique. Here Purcell was much the bolder pioneer. The Queen's birthday ode in 1689, *Now does the glorious day appear*, gave him the first opportunity to try out the five-part string scoring he had heard in Draghi's

Ex. 6.12a

Ex. 6.12b

Ex. 6.12c

1687 ode, since in the politically unsettled autumn of 1688 neither James II's birthday nor the Cecilian festival had apparently been celebrated with music. The use of trumpets in the birthday ode was evidently not possible in 1689: Purcell had to wait a further year.

Blow had a longer wait before he could write even for five-part strings. Work on his 1688 New Year ode was probably well in hand by the time he heard Draghi's ode even though, as we have seen, he must have added the opening symphony after doing so. Not until New Year 1690 could he respond to its instrumentation, in his ode *With cheerful hearts*, but the work shows less resource than Purcell's in combining the richer sonorities of five-part strings with choral voices. Whereas the younger man had kept all five string parts fully independent whenever they accompanied the full choir, Blow was content to add a single obbligato violin line while the other strings merely doubled the voices.

By the time *With cheerful hearts* was heard, Purcell was busy on *The Yorkshire Feast Song*, the first English score for full Baroque orchestra. He took Draghi's trumpets a step further, by making them fully independent instead of inserting their parts, as Draghi had confusingly done on staves belonging to the violins; besides recorders, he added oboes, which are nowhere independent of the violins and serve chiefly to add colour, though in places they are apparently intended to alternate with the violins (whose staves they share, with the same consequent ambiguities as those affecting Draghi's trumpet writing). Somewhat surprisingly, Purcell wrote for strings in only four parts.

The performance of *The Yorkshire Feast Song* on 27 March was followed on the Queen's birthday, a month later, by that of *Arise, my Muse*, which not only included oboes, recorders and trumpets but returned to the five-part string scoring as well – thus for the only time matching Draghi's orchestra exactly though far outshining it in effect. (Purcell seems, however, to have finished *Arise, my Muse* in extreme haste, leaving part of Durfey's poem unset and omitting the trumpets and oboes, whose inclusion might have been supposed *de rigueur*, from the rather perfunctory final chorus.)[52] The two odes were surely invaluable as studies in orchestral technique for *Dioclesian*, Purcell's most ambitious score so far, first performed some six weeks after the Queen's birthday. The treatment of trumpets and oboes in the opera shows an important advance: a complete four-part family of oboes, tenor oboe and bassoon. In two of the fully scored movements, Purcell gives them parts which are, for the first time, independent of both trumpets and strings, all three groups being both contrasted and combined to create the widest possible range of colour. There is even one ritornello for trumpets and oboes without strings, though here their parts merely double each other.

How Blow may have responded to these pyrotechnics is unknown. The ode for William III's birthday in November 1690, which may have fallen to his lot, and that for the following New Year, which almost certainly did so, are both lost; not even their texts have survived.[53] In any event Purcell's 1691

---

[52] See *The Works of Henry Purcell*, vol. XI, ed. B. Wood (1993), xxi.

[53] No other composer is known to have set a New Year ode between 1678 and 1700. Matthew Prior's ode *Light of the World*, written for New Year 1694, was 'set by Dr. [sic] *PURCELL*, And Sung before their MAJESTIES *On New-Years-Day*, 1694', or so the author claimed in an edition of his collected poems published long afterwards, in 1718. A broadsheet print of the ode alone, however, issued in January 1694, described it only as 'Intended to be Sung before their Majesties': information repeated in the unauthorized 1708 edition of Prior's poems. The ode actually sung on New Year's Day 1694 was Peter Motteux's *Sound, sound the trumpet*, set to music by Blow; the words and music for one of its verses were published in *The Gentleman's Journal*, January and February 1694, pp. 29–32, and the complete text in the same issue, pp. 5–7. Purcell's 'lost' setting of Prior's ode probably never existed: it seems highly unlikely that he composed *Light of the World*, or even planned to do so, given Blow's long-standing responsibility for New Year odes.

ode for Queen Mary, *Welcome, welcome, glorious morn,* shows no real advance in orchestral technique over *Dioclesian,* save in one ritornello laid out for trumpets and oboes without strings. And in *King Arthur,* first performed not long after the Queen's birthday, Purcell drew back from complex scoring: here the oboes are never used independently (a few non-harmonic notes apart) in movements which include trumpets.

One important orchestral component still remained to be put in place: the kettledrums. Blow, rather than Purcell, first added a notated part for them, in his 1691 Cecilian ode *The glorious day is come,*[54] which also allows oboes and trumpets the same independence as they enjoy in *Welcome, welcome, glorious morn.* Perhaps even more striking than either of these features, however, is the imposing scale of the work. As grand as any English ode thus far, it has a duration of nearly thirty-five minutes, as long as *The Yorkshire Feast Song* or *Welcome, welcome, glorious morn.* Purcell responded swiftly. Within six months he had included kettledrums in *The Fairy Queen,* making them far more conspicuous than Blow had done by the simple expedient of placing their first entry right at the beginning of an act, and for good measure making it a solo passage – the earliest such in orchestral history. A further striking orchestral novelty was the use of mutes in one of the numbers accompanied by strings. The spacious proportions of Blow's Cecilian ode were not merely matched but exceeded in Purcell's offering the following year, *Hail, bright Cecilia,* which is also superior in musical invention. The variety of colour is kaleidoscopic. No two of the thirteen movements share the same vocal and instrumental scoring, and the treatment of the orchestra is consummate, with oboes, trumpets, recorders and strings used both separately and in every practicable combination.

Blow's reply to *Hail, bright Cecilia,* if he dared venture one, remains a matter for conjecture for, of the various odes he composed during the last three years of Purcell's life, only one has been preserved intact, while the surviving fragments of others cast no useful light on the question. Other genres offer virtually no points of contact during these years: Purcell was composing almost exclusively for the theatre, Blow for the Chapel Royal. Blow's one extant ode, *Great Quire of Heaven,* was composed for St Cecilia's Day 1695.[55] Its first performance, the day after Purcell's death, must have been given in a

---

[54] Ed. Maurice Bevan (London, 1981).

[55] London, Guildhall Library MS G.Mus. 452, pp. 1–62. W.H. Husk, in *An Account of the Musical Celebrations on St. Cecilia's Day* (London, 1857), was unable to date this ode. Recently, however, a broadsheet print of its text, dated 1695, has come to light in Chetham's Library, Manchester. I am most grateful to Dr David Hopkins for drawing my attention to the discovery of this apparently unique copy.

memorial atmosphere. In such circumstances the compendium of Purcellisms which it unfolds would have seemed sadly appropriate: a rousing air for counter-tenor with obbligato trumpet (pioneered five years earlier in *Dioclesian*, and by now a favourite ingredient in odes as well as operas), a florid obbligato oboe part[56] (strongly resembling that in 'Bid the Virtues' in the 1694 Queen Mary ode *Come ye sons of art*), the liberal use of recorders and violins to accompany other verses (following the example of *Hail, bright Cecilia*), the virtuosic nature of some of the soprano writing (recalling 'Ye gentle spirits of the air' in *The Fairy Queen* and 'Let sullen Discord smile' in the 1693 Queen Mary ode *Celebrate this festival*), and colourful independent use of oboes and trumpets in purely orchestral passages.

If the ode resembled a review of techniques pioneered by Purcell, Blow's setting of the Te Deum and Jubilate,[57] first heard a few hours earlier at the Cecilian service, must have sounded like an even more specific tribute; for from beginning to end it is a flattering imitation of the setting Purcell had composed for the previous year's festival. Blow had followed his erstwhile pupil not merely in providing an opulent accompaniment scored for trumpets and strings (the innovation which had caused such a sensation in 1694) but also in the general layout of both canticles. There are striking similarities in the division of the text into verses and choruses, in the instrumentation of individual movements, in the greater than usual freedom with which Blow used instruments to double voices at the octave (a technique which may be observed also in *Great Quire of Heaven*), and in some of the musical ideas themselves. Even the passage in Purcell's Te Deum which earned especial plaudits[58] – his evocation of Cherubim and Seraphim (Ex. 6.13a) – was unblushingly appropriated by Blow (Ex. 6.13b).

Despite all these similarities, the features of Blow's setting which probably attracted most attention in 1695 – the trumpet writing and the treatment of the full choir – are less effective than Purcell's. The trumpet parts often consist of slow-moving descants, unrelated to the vocal lines, rather than incisive imitative entries which could dominate the densest choral *tutti*. The brilliance of the instruments' topmost register is never exploited: Purcell's trumpet parts extend to d''', Blow's only to b''. And whereas, especially in

---

56 The instrumental part is undesignated in all sources. But its character and articulation marks are clearly appropriate to the oboe, not the violin; and in the earliest source of all, Guildhall Library MS G. Mus. 452, in the hand of William Isaack, the obbligato parts in the verse immediately ensuing are labelled 'violins' – a designation which, if the preceding obbligato part were for violin, would be superfluous (contrary to the copyist's habits).

57 British Library Add. MS 31,457, fols. 45–74v; transcribed in Wood, 'John Blow's Anthems', vol. IV, 156–241.

58 British Library MS Harl. 7342, fol. 12.

Ex. 6.13a

Ex. 6.13b

Ex. 6.14

contrapuntal passages, Purcell uses the trumpets rather sparingly, often holding them back until the climax, Blow is much less concerned to husband his resources. As for the choral passages, those in Blow's setting are less colourful than Purcell's – more generally contrapuntal, and lacking variety in the treatment of the counterpoint itself.

Blow's setting, however, is something more than a pallid copy of Purcell's. In some respects it is superior. The section in the Te Deum beginning 'The glorious company of the Apostles', for instance, presented by Purcell as a succession of short-winded contrasting verses, is set by Blow as a single broad movement, a dignified and well-constructed air for bass. And in the closing pages of the same canticle Blow achieved a harmonic master-stroke (Ex. 6.14) of which Purcell would surely have been proud. Nevertheless, the extent of Blow's poaching is surprising. It far exceeds that in any of his other works – or in those where Purcell returned the compliment – and it shows an unusual lack of discrimination, for he purloined from the weaker as well as the stronger passages of his model, a decidedly uneven piece. That he should have borrowed at all from so innovatory a composition, which had made such an impression at its first hearing, and that he should have brazenly done so for the same occasion only a year later, is less surprising. The numerous examples given earlier show that the two had long found it an irresistible challenge to emulate any notable musical success scored by the other.

This friendly rivalry followed two distinct patterns. First, the two composers borrowed almost exclusively from each other's *recent* music, allowing a lapse of only a few months at most. Secondly, although the traffic was reciprocal, throughout most of the 1680s it was usually Blow who initiated, Purcell who emulated – as often as not producing musical results that were superior to the pioneering efforts of his old teacher. From about 1690 onwards, however, Purcell established himself as the bolder innovator. Henry Hall's judgement, that Purcell alone had been the equal of Blow, does somewhat less than justice to the younger composer, especially in the last six years of his life; but it shrewdly and perceptively sums up their musical relationship during the preceding decade.

7

Purcell's odes: propaganda and panegyric

IAN SPINK

Purcell's twenty-four odes span the years 1680 to 1695 and represent a conspectus of his development as a composer from the age of twenty-one until his death. They contain some of his best music, for too long unperformed, largely because their stilted and bombastic verse is no longer to our taste and the secular rituals which they represent cannot be taken seriously — other than perhaps the celebration of St Cecilia's Day. Some of the poetry is doggerel, but the music itself is of a high order, rarely showing signs of perfunctory routine. In many respects, indeed, the odes epitomize Purcell's genius and, with their bold gestures and elaborate conceits, represent a high-water mark of the English Baroque, nowhere more spectacularly than in *Hail, bright Cecilia.*

My purpose is not, however, to trace the stylistic development of these odes or to discuss technical advances from one to another. It would not be possible to do so in the space available, though by way of introduction some general observations may be made. All but one of these works conform to the general scheme of instrumental overture followed by varied series of solos, duets and trios, interspersed and ending with choruses. Certain broad trends are discernible, most obviously increasing length, wider tonal range and, from 1690, a more ostentatious manner typified by the use of trumpets. Vocal pieces on ground basses, which occur in virtually all of them, become freer, whilst the almost equally ubiquitous florid declamatory movements (usually for bass, sometimes for countertenor) become even more extravagant. Such features reflect the growing virtuosity and self-confidence of the composer and are paralleled in his church and theatre music. But in some respects the court ode allowed more scope for Purcell's particular gifts, and in turn encouraged their development. It offered a large scale on which to work, the full resources of the court's musical establishment, including the best singers and instrumentalists; above all, a form which provided both opportunity and challenge to a composer who 'thought big' and had a technique to match. Whether he believed in what he was expected to do is hardly the point – he was a thorough professional.

Most of Purcell's odes are 'welcome songs' for Charles II and James II and birthday odes for Queen Mary. Welcome songs were used to celebrate the king's return to Whitehall from his summer residence at Windsor or an autumn visit to Newmarket. So far as one can tell, they were normally performed on the actual day in question (unless it was a Sunday); the one specific date inscribed on a score – 21 October 1682 for *The summer's absence unconcerned we bear* – coincides exactly with the day the king returned from Newmarket. Once back in town the 'season' could get under way; theatre-going picked up, the Michaelmas law term commenced, the Lord Mayor began his period of office and parliament reassembled (if it had been called). Welcome songs fell away during the reign of William and Mary, partly because the king was usually campaigning abroad during the summer and autumn and was liable to return to London unpredictably. The progress of his armies against Louis XIV and the weather in the channel might each delay him. He was more likely to return in time for his birthday (4 November), and thus welcome songs were abandoned as a regular feature. In fact, Purcell wrote no birthday songs for King William, but he wrote five for Queen Mary – who ruled jointly with her husband rather than as consort between 1689 and her death in 1694. Odes for other occasions include *The Yorkshire Feast Song*, written for what was to become the annual meeting of the Yorkshire Society of London (1690), a commemoration ode for the centenary of Trinity College, Dublin (1694), a birthday ode for the Duke of Gloucester (1695) and three odes for St Cecilia's Day (not counting *Laudate Ceciliam*).

The composition of the verse for court odes was frequently undertaken by the Poet Laureate, though it was not until the eighteenth century that collaboration between Laureate and Master of the King's Musick became regular. Indeed, before 1684 the poet's name is usually not known.[1] In that year Thomas Flatman wrote both the New Year and Welcome Ode for Charles II, set respectively by John Blow and Henry Purcell. At the time Dryden was Laureate, but it would be unkind to ascribe the anonymous court odes of James II's reign to him, though his great ode to St Cecilia was written in 1687. When Dryden was deprived of his office in 1689 on account of his conversion to Roman catholicism, the bays passed to the 'true-blue protestant poet' Thomas Shadwell, who wrote a birthday ode for Queen

---

[1] A chronological list of odes is in Rosamond McGuinness, *English Court Odes 1660–1820* (Oxford, 1971), pp. 13–43.

Mary that year and a New Year and birthday ode for the king in 1692. Nahum Tate then succeeded to the position on Shadwell's death, and thereafter produced odes regularly throughout his life in collaboration with Blow, Purcell, Nicholas Staggins and John Eccles – the last two being Masters of the King's (or Queen's) Musick. Nevertheless, during this period other poets also wrote odes, among them Thomas Durfey, Sir Charles Sedley and Peter Motteux.

The literary models for these works were the 'Pindarique Odes' of Abraham Cowley. Their irregular verse structure and high-flown language were in turn imitations of Pindar, and the resulting mixture of short and long lines, varied rhythms, and regular and irregular rhymes was well suited to the florid discourse and outrageous metaphor that made these occasions something special. Not that such verse was without its large- and small-scale symmetries, but the effect was nevertheless free and richly varied, an epitome of the Baroque style and an ideal vehicle for Purcell's own extravagant gestures.

A good example of the poetic techniques of these odes is provided by the opening stanzas of Flatman's welcome song for 1684, *From those serene and rapturous joys*. For once, the quality of the verse is respectable. Unusually, it begins quietly and without bombast, welcoming the king back to London after the rural pleasures of a summer spent at Windsor (including, no doubt, a certain amount of fishing), but striking a more heroic posture in the second stanza:

> From those serene and rapturous joys
>   A Country life alone can give,
>   Exempt from tumult and from noise,
> Where Kings forget the troubles of their reigns,
> And are almost as happy as their humble Swains,
>   By feeling that they live,
>   Behold th'indulgent Prince is come
> To view the Conquests of His mercy shown
> To the new Proselytes of His mighty Town,
> And men and Angels bid him welcome Home.
>
> Not with an Helmet or a glitt'ring Spear
>   Does he appear;
> He boasts no Trophies of a cruel Conqueror,
> Brought back in triumph from a bloody War,
>   But with an Olive branch adorn'd
> As once the long expected Dove return'd.

Here we have verses of four, six, eight, ten and twelve syllables, and rhymes that come in pairs, alternate or skip a few lines. The poetry is always on the move, never complacent – that is until the final stanza:

> With trumpets and shouts we receive the World's Wonder,
> And let the Clouds echo His welcome with thunder,
> Such a thunder as applauded what mortals had done,
> When they fixt on his Brows his Imperial Crown.

Final choruses often resort to triple rhythm in this way, which, of course, does not sound so banal when sung.

Classical, and especially musical, allusions were part and parcel of the convention:

> As when Apollo with his sacred lyre
> Did in the Theban stones a harmony inspire.
> (*Welcome, Vicegerent*, 1680)

Harmony and discord, after all, can be both musical and political, and the one was intended to bolster the other. Moreover, the use of musical imagery was highly appropriate, since odes were conceived as essentially musical utterances. What else was to be expected when one invoked the muses? And once (in 1685), when it seemed they remained silent, the ode began without an overture, until the king himself had roused them.

> Why, why are all the Muses mute?
> Why sleeps the viol and the lute?
> Why hangs untuned the idle lyre?
> Awake, 'tis Caesar does inspire
> And animates the vocal choir.

(In fact, he animates the instruments, since they represent the muses.) *Sound the trumpet, beat the drum* (1687) typified the rhetoric even before trumpets became a regular part of the instrumentation, and sometimes a court ode seems about to become one for St Cecilia. Thus, *Come ye sons of art* (1694) contains the stanza

> Sound the trumpet till around
> You make the list'ning shores rebound;
> On the sprightly hautboy play,
> All the instruments of joy
> That skillful numbers can employ,
> To celebrate the glories of this day.

and continues with an almost verbatim quotation of the opening couplet from Tate's Cecilia ode of 1685 set originally by William Turner:

> Strike the viol, touch the lute,
> Wake the harp, inspire the flute,
> Sing your patronness's praise,
> In cheerful and harmonious lays.

148

(Tate's ode begins 'Tune the viol, touch the lute / Wake the harp, inspire the flute'. In view of the fact that the author of *Come ye sons of art* is not known, one wonders whether Tate was quoting himself.

WELCOME SONGS

The political dimension of these welcome songs and birthday odes is their *raison d'être*. The early ones (1680–3) must be seen against the background of the Exclusion Bill and Popish Plot, which aimed to bar the king's brother, the catholic James, Duke of York, from the succession, presenting a challenge to the king's authority and ultimately a threat to the throne. Titus Oates's allegations of a plot to murder the king and massacre the protestants were first made in 1678. During the ensuing period of anti-catholic hysteria, the Earl of Shaftesbury, President of the Council and leader of what was becoming known as the 'whig' party, advanced the claim of Charles's protestant (but illegitimate) son, the Duke of Monmouth, to the throne in preference to the Duke of York. The king was forced to protect his brother's position but could not prevent many catholics and suspected catholics (like Pepys) from being imprisoned – often on perjured evidence – and sometimes executed. Charles resisted these pressures as best he could and from what had undoubtedly become a dire situation by the beginning of 1681 managed to turn it round so that by the end of the year he held the initiative – thanks largely to financial support from Louis XIV which made him independent of parliament. The following year Shaftesbury was arrested but fled to Holland and the king's victory became more or less complete. That was not the end of the trouble, however, for in March 1683 the king and the duke might have been murdered on the road back to London from Newmarket, had they not returned a few days early. The existence of the so-called Rye House plot later leaked out; it was kept quiet for a while, but those implicated were executed before the end of the year.

Public demonstrations of loyalty during this period were therefore encouraged, and court odes were a propaganda tool to this end, advocating Divine Right and the subject's obligation of Passive Obedience. Purcell's first welcome song, *Welcome, Vicegerent*, is described as 'A Song to Welcome home his Majesty from Windsor 1680' in British Library Add. MS 22,100. A later source, Add. MS 31,447, calls it 'A Welcome Song at yᵉ Princ of Denmarks Comeing home', but this would suggest a date about mid-August 1687. Not only is such a date too late for the style of the piece, the address is surely to Charles (not his nephew-in-law) ruling by Divine Right: 'Welcome, Vicegerent of the Mighty King / That made and governs everything.' Other evidence confirms this. The fact that the work was not entered into Purcell's autograph manuscript (British Library R.M. MS 20.h.8) suggests a date prior to the commencement of that manuscript (1681) though Vaughan Williams, who edited it for the Purcell Society in 1905, thought that Purcell might have left it out 'as an early work not worthy of preservation'.[2] If 1680 was the year, then a suitable date would have been 9 September when, according to Luttrell, 'his majestie and the whole court returned from Windsor'.[3] The text certainly implies the onset of autumn:

> Now decrepid Winter's coming,
>   Yet the presence of a King
> Makes him young and still a-blooming,
>   Turns his Autumn into Spring.

But the return of the king from Newmarket a month later on 9 October is another and perhaps more likely possibility, given the deepening autumnal season.[4]

The occasion for *Swifter Isis, swifter flow* is difficult to pin-point more precisely than Purcell himself does in the title: 'A Welcome Song in ye year 1681, For ye King'. For some reason Vaughan Williams thought that 'this Ode was probably written to welcome Charles II on his return from Newmarket to London, 12 October, 1681', but there seems little to support this in the text.[5] A straightforward reading suggests a celebration for the return of the king from Oxford. He is returning downstream to London ('Augusta') by barge:

> Swifter, Isis, swifter flow,
> Muster all your streams together,
> Then in a full body go,
> And guard great Britain's monarch hither.
>
> Welcome, dread Sir, to town,
> Thrice welcome to this your chief seat,
>   Pensive at your retreat,
>   As joyful at your return.

and it is spring,

---

2 *The Works of Henry Purcell*, vol. XV, ed. R. Vaughan Williams (London, 1905), ii.
3 Narcissus Luttrell, *A Brief Relation of State Affairs from September 1678 to April 1714*, 6 vols. (Oxford, 1857), vol. I, 54.
4 *Ibid.*, p. 56.
5 *The Works of Henry Purcell*, vol. XV, iv.

Land him safely on her shore,
Who his long absence does deplore,
He with joy her walls does fill,
As high spring tides your channels swell,

An obvious occasion for this would have been Charles's return to Whitehall following the Oxford parliament, which he called for 21 March 1681 in the hope of finally settling the exclusion crisis to his advantage. The intention was probably to return to London via Windsor and Hampton Court once the business had been concluded, completing the last stage of the journey by barge and making a triumphal entry into London to be greeted by the welcome song and accompanying celebrations.

Hark, hark! just now my listening ears
Are struck with the repeated sound
Of labouring oars, and it appears,
By growing strong, they're this way bound,
See, see, it is the royal barge,
Oh, how she does my eyes delight,
Let bells ring, and great guns discharge,
Whilst numerous bonfires banish night.

As it happened, however, parliament proved less docile than Charles had hoped. On Monday, 28 March, he suddenly dissolved the sitting and 'departed forthwith for Windsor, and lay there that night, and arrived at Whitehall the next morning'.[6] The king's sudden and unpremeditated return to London must have thrown into confusion whatever plans had been made for a musical welcome. Almost certainly the original schedule would have had to be abandoned and either the performance hurriedly brought forward to that very evening (assuming it was in an adequate state of rehearsal), or to within the next few days (despite it being holy week) – if not cancelled. In any case, 'the repeated sound / Of labouring oars' and all the other descriptive aspects would have lost their immediacy, though they must always have been to some extent figments of the poet's imagination.

If not on 29 March or soon after, when might the ode have been performed? The greater the delay the more inappropriate the words would have become. Admittedly, the phrase 'high spring tides' might have applied to any monthly high tide, but reference to the Isis must surely imply a return from Oxford: for the poet to address 'Isis' instead of 'Thamesis' would otherwise have been an odd conceit. The Oxford connection therefore seems

[6]   Luttrell, *A Brief Relation of State Affairs*, vol. I, 72.

151

inescapable, and no other purpose than celebrating the king's intended return seems more likely.

Inappropriate though the text would have been for any delayed performance, it is just conceivable that *Swifter Isis, swifter flow* may have been given later in the year. The court went to Windsor on 28 April and stayed there most of the summer. On 17 August Luttrell records that the king 'past by Whitehall from Windsor in his barge, and went on board the ship Tyger, lord Berkely commander . . . and did his lordship the honour to dine with him on board'.[7] Reference to 'land him safely on her shore', among other things, makes this unlikely to have been the event. Ten days later 'the king returned to London from Windsor, dineing at Hampton Court',[8] and it is possible that the king continued to London by barge for a welcome then, or, more formally, four days later, when the Lord Mayor and Aldermen of London paid their official respects to the king 'on his return to town from Windsor'.[9] The references in the ode to Augusta's particular rejoicing (including 'the best of your subjects') give some support to this occasion. But out of all these possibilities the most likely scenario is that the ode was written to welcome the king back to London following the Oxford parliament in the spring of 1681, but because of his early return performed either hastily (making a nonsense of parts of the text) or not at all at that time. A later performance on 27 August (or soon after) is not impossible, but the absence of allusions to summer or rural pleasures suggests that this was not the original intention.

Nowhere is the link between the subject of an ode and affairs of state more obvious than in *What shall be done in behalf of the man* (1682), celebrating the return of the Duke of York from Scotland in 1682. For much of the exclusion crisis Charles had thought it best to keep his brother out of the way by appointing him High Commissioner in Scotland. Now that the whigs were in retreat, James was recalled. His ship landed at Yarmouth on 10 March 1682 and, following a splendid entertainment by the mayor and aldermen of Norwich that evening, he left the following morning for Newmarket to join his brother.[10] However, this is unlikely to have been the occasion of the ode. Quite apart from the fact that it was still officially 1681 (whereas the manuscript says 1682), a more likely date for the performance would have been 27 May, when there were great rejoicings at the duke's official entry into the capital. Luttrell reports:

> The 27th, their majesties came in the morning in their coaches to Putney, and went down the river in their barges to meet their royall highnesses; but

7 *Ibid.*, p. 117.   8 *Ibid.*, p. 118.   9 *Ibid.*, p. 119.   10 *Ibid.*, p. 171.

they stayeing longer then was expected, his majestie did not meet them, but returned to Whitehall . . . but about three in the afternoon their royall highnesses, with the lady Ann, arrived safe at Whitehall . . . thence their majesties went to Windsor, and their royall highnesses to St. James's; and at night were ringing of bells, and bonefires in severall places, and other publick expressions of joy.[11]

The text of the ode is full of references to the exclusion crisis; the duke's sojourn in the low countries and Scotland, the reunion of the two brothers (*Albion and Albanius* as Dryden was soon to apotheosize them), the duke's right of succession and his loyalty to the king – with a dig at the Duke of Monmouth:

> Such forward duty in a brother lies
>   As has outdone
> And ought to shame even a son.

Later that year, on 21 October, there was an ode for the king's return from Newmarket (*The summer's absence unconcerned we bear*) expressing the hope that when the moment came, the succession would be both legitimate and peaceful: 'And when late from your throne Heaven's call you attend, / In peace let your crown on the next head descend.'

This was what the exclusionists had sought to avoid and what the fanatics may even then have been plotting to prevent, as the king and his brother were returning to London. The plan was to assassinate them when they took that road again the following March, at Rye House, near Hoddesdon. But luckily a fire at Newmarket caused them to return early, thus frustrating the plan. That there had been a plot was not discovered until early June, whereupon those implicated (and who had not already fled abroad, like Monmouth) were arrested – the Earl of Essex, Lord William Russell, Algernon Sidney, among others. Justice was swift, and a day of thanksgiving was proclaimed for 9 September. This, however, was probably not the occasion for which *Fly, bold rebellion* was written, since the text makes clear that, once again, it is the king's return to London that is being celebrated: 'Fly, bold Rebellion, make haste and be gone! / Victorious in counsel great Charles is returned.' Either it was Charles's return to London from Winchester on 25 September that was being marked, or (less likely because the court was in mourning for the King of Portugal, the queen's brother) his return from Newmarket on 17 October.[12] In so far as the text tells us anything, the former seems more probable, since a longer absence than two week at the races seems implied. As ever, loyalty and the Divine Right of Kings was the order of the day:

11   *Ibid.*, p. 189.   12   *Ibid.*, p. 281, 284.

> Then with heart and with voice, prepare to rejoice
> All you that are loyal and true:
> They nobly contend, who maintain to the end
> Those Honours to Majesty due.

But the populace was warned not to meddle. Triple time might suggest good humour, but a change from F major to the horror key of F minor imparts a sinister threat:

> Come then, change your notes, disloyal crowd,
> You that already have been too loud
> With importunate follies and clamours;
> 'Tis no business of yours
> To dispute the high powers,
> As if you were the government framers.

Rebellion having flown, the last welcome song of Charles II's reign – *From those serene and rapturous joys* – was performed on his return from Winchester on 25 September 1684.[13] Its uncharacteristic air of quiet contentment seems almost valedictory. Now, perhaps, there would be no more arguments about the succession and all would be well. Charles died the following February, and James was crowned king on St George's day 1685.

Like his brother, James II spent his summers at Windsor but did not return to London until October. (Unlike his brother he did not visit Newmarket later in the month.) His birthday was 14 October, and this was marked by public observance and celebrations – bells, bonfires and balls. But Purcell's odes for James are not birthday odes, despite those for 1686 and 1687 sometimes being called so. The words 'birthday' or 'anniversary' are never mentioned or even implied, and the texts clearly suggest that they are welcome songs. It is therefore very unlikely they played any part in birthday celebrations at court, even though the events were close together. Thus, when Evelyn observed that on 14 October 1685 there was 'a solemn Ball at Court: And Musique of Instruments & Voices before the Ball', the allusion was probably not to *Why, why are all the muses mute?*[14] The occasion for this would have been the week before, when on 'the 6th their majesties returned to Whitehal from Windsor'.[15]

The defeat of Monmouth's rebellion in the west during the summer is clearly referred to, and from then on imperial triumph is a major, if – as things turned out – ironic theme. Each of the three odes refers to James as Caesar; for example, in 1685:

13   *Ibid.*, p. 316.
14   *The Diary of John Evelyn*, ed. E. S. de Beer, 6 vols. (Oxford, 1955), vol. IV, 480.
15   Luttrell, *A Brief Relation of State Affairs*, vol. I, 359.

> Great Caesar's reign with conquest did begin,
> And with triumphant shouts was ushered in.
> Accurs'd rebellion reared his head,
> And his proud banners vainly spread.

The following year the king and queen were welcomed back with *Ye tuneful muses, raise your heads*. It refers, almost innocently, to the new and enlarged standing army with which James intended to maintain his position.

> From the rattling of drums and the trumpet's loud sounds
> Wherein Caesar's safety and his fame abounds,
>   The best protectors of his royal right
>   'Gainst fanatical fury and sanctified spite,
>   By which he glory first did gain,
>   And may they still preserve his reign.

This was the ode in which Purcell introduced a ballad tune at the words 'Be lively then and gay' – first (and last) in the bass, and in the middle as a descant for the violins. The ballad ('Hey, boys, up go we') had political overtones, with both whig and tory words that went to it – the latter beginning 'Down with the whigs, we'll now grow wise'.[16] No doubt the audience was amused; likewise a few moments later in a passage for violins where all four open strings are sounded at the words 'tune all your strings'.

In 1687 the king and queen (otherwise Caesar and Urania) arrived back from Windsor on 11 October, to a particularly splendid ode, *Sound the trumpet, beat the drum*. It carried the same message: 'Jove is Heaven's Caesar, Caesar Jove below', but unfortunately its promise of 'No more alarms of rebel war' was to prove false. James had so antagonized parliament, the church and most of the population with his romanizing policies that the country had become virtually ungovernable. By October 1688 he was in the midst of the crisis; the following month he escaped to France, and exile.

BIRTHDAY ODES

Just as welcome odes for Charles II and James II may be seen as propaganda on their behalf during a period of political unrest and eventually rebellion, so birthday odes for William (4 November) and Mary (30 April) served to bolster the legitimacy of their joint monarchy. While Nicholas Staggins and John Blow supplied a series of birthday odes for the king, Purcell wrote one a year from 1689 to 1694 for the queen.

---

[16] Claude M. Simpson, *The British Broadside Ballad and its Music* (New Brunswick, 1966), pp. 304–8; William Chappell, *The Ballad Literature and Popular Music of the Olden Time*, 2 vols. (London, 1859), vol. II, 425–9.

Luttrell continues to tell us something about these celebrations. In November 1690 he wrote:

> The 4th, being his majesties birth day, was observed here very strictly, by shutting up the shops, firing the great guns at the Tower, ringing of bells, and bonefires at night; their majesties dined publickly at Whitehall, where was a great resort of nobility and gentry, and at night was a consort of musick, and a play afterwards.[17]

And, on 30 April 1692:

> This being the queens birth day, a new ode was sung before her upon the occasion: the nobility and gentry, with the lord mayor and aldermen of this citty, attended to compliment thereon.[18]

The 'new ode' was *Love's goddess sure was blind.*

It is not clear from such accounts where in Whitehall these celebrations were held – the court theatre is one possibility, the Banqueting House another. The performers (to judge from the names of singers written in the score) were from the Chapel Royal and theatre, with instruments provided by the King's Musick. For the king's birthday in 1693, Blow, as Master of the Children of the Chapel Royal, was ordered to 'direct such of Their Ma^ts singing boys as Dr Staggins shall desire to practize and sing the song upon his Ma^ts Birthday'.[19] On this occasion the work was Staggins's *Sound a call, the Tritons sing*, though the performance was probably at Kensington Palace. Luttrell records: 'This being his majesties birth day a great concourse of nobility and gentry appeared at Whitehal to congratulate him thereon; and at night will be a great ball at Kensington.'[20]

Balls, indeed, seem to have been essential to royal birthday celebrations. Ode followed by dancing thus becomes the equivalent of the court masque earlier in the century, and the frequent yoking together of the poets laureate, Thomas Shadwell and Nahum Tate, with the Master of the King's Musick, Nicholas Staggins, underlines the similarity. Fortunately, Staggins was not left to compose all these birthday odes by himself; three are known to have been set by him, and one by Blow in 1692. (Blow continued to set the New Year odes, however.) For some reason Purcell never wrote a birthday ode for King William – nor a New Year's ode, unless Matthew Prior's *Light of the world* 'Set by Dr [*sic*] Purcell and Sung before their Majesties' is more than a ghost. The 1709 edition of Prior's works appended the note 'intended to be Sung

---

17 Luttrell, *A Brief Relation of State Affairs*, vol. II, 125.   18 *Ibid.*, p. 437.
19 Andrew Ashbee, *Records of English Court Music*, vol. II (Snodland, 1987), 50.
20 Luttrell, *A Brief Relation of State Affairs*, vol. III, 220.

before their Majesties' but, in fact, it was Blow's *Sound, sound the trumpet* that was performed that year. Peter Motteux, who wrote the words, complained that 'I had so little time allowed me to write it' and gives the impression that the ode was a stop-gap.[21] Perhaps pressure of work on the ode for Trinity College, Dublin, due for 9 January, prevented Purcell from getting down to setting Prior's verses. Whether there was some personal reason why Purcell never wrote an ode for King William is a matter for speculation. He lacked official status compared with Staggins and Blow, but he may also have preferred to set birthday odes for the queen, thus leaving uncompromised (or less compromised) any Stuart sympathies he may have felt.

There is no need to go into great detail with regard to the content of these birthday odes. They are typical examples of the pindaric style, euphuistic and naively patriotic. The queen's virtue and beauty are constant themes, as are the manifold blessings of her reign. According to Shadwell in *Now does the glorious day appear* (1689), she is another Gloriana, a second Queen Elizabeth: 'No more shall we the great *Eliza* boast, / For her Great Name in Greater *Mary's* will be lost.'

As a counterpoise to this, and to provide an opportunity to broaden the musical content, her husband's success in arms is an ever present refrain, and this opened the way for trumpets. As it happens, the 1689 ode does not include a trumpet part (though the first of its three violin parts is brimfull of trumpet idioms); nor, despite its title, did *Sound the trumpet, beat the drum* (1687) in the original version.[22] But from 1690 onwards trumpet parts are a frequent ingredient in the instrumentation of these odes, as they are in the operas.[23] Whether this is to be seen as pandering to the king's unsophisticated militaristic taste, indulging a foreign fashion, or following the natural inclination of his own musical development, can hardly be determined; somehow they all came together at that time. In fact, Purcell's earliest odes with trumpets are *The Yorkshire Feast Song* of 27 March 1690 and the birthday ode *Arise, my muse*, performed a month later. Both also have oboes for the first time (flutes had been used sporadically since 1682).

As already mentioned, the use of trumpets inaugurates a new phase in Purcell's stylistic development. Yet, despite William's martial triumphs, the

---

[21] *The Gentleman's Journal* (January–February 1694), p. 5; McGuinness, *English Court Odes*, p. 52; Zimmerman, *Henry Purcell, 1659–1695: His Life and Times*, rev. edn (Philadelphia, 1983), p. 223.

[22] A later version of this ode (British Library R.M. MS 24.e.7) does have trumpets and drums. Conceivably it may be a relic of a version with new words 'performed as a Welcome Song on King William's return from Flanders' after Purcell's death.

[23] Don Smithers, *The Music and History of the Baroque Trumpet before 1721* (London, 1973), pp. 205–10. Draghi's setting of Dryden's *Song for St Cecilia's Day* (1687) had used trumpets.

convention demanded that he yield to Mary's 'victorious charms'. Shadwell, who really believed in the Glorious Revolution, put it thus in *Now does the glorious day appear* (1689):

By beauteous softness mixt with Majesty,
   An Empire over every Heart she gains,
And from her awfull Power none could be free,
   She with such Sweetness and such Justice Reigns:
Her Hero, too, whose Conduct and whose Arms
   The trembling Papal World their Force must yield,
Must bend himself to her victorious Charms,
   And give up all the Trophies of each Field.

There was some unfinished business, however. James II was in Ireland and in the spring of 1690 William set sail

To hunt the Savages from Dens:
To teach 'em Loyalty and Sence:
And sordid Souls of the true Faith Convince.
   (Durfey, *Arise, my muse*, 1690)

Such an enterprise may not have been difficult to sell to the whigs. The tories, however, might well have had reservations about taking up arms against their erstwhile king, unless to defend their beloved Church of England. Thus Durfey imagines the church as '*Eusebia* drown'd in tears', turning to William as its champion, and crying, 'Ah wretched me, must *Caesar* for my sake, / These fatal dangers undertake'.

William, like James before him, appears again and again as Caesar, and the term 'hero' is freely bandied about. He gets less prominent billing in Sir Charles Sedley's *Love's goddess sure* (1692) – largely taken up with extolling the queen's beauty, sweetness of nature, wit and goodness – but, even so, his role is alluded to in 'May her blest example chase':

May her Hero bring home Peace
Won with Honour in the Field,
And all home-bred factions cease;
He our Sword, and she our Shield.

This was the song which Purcell wrote as a compliment to the queen using the ballad tune 'Cold and raw' as the bass. Sir John Hawkins tells how one day after listening to Arabella Hunt and John Gostling singing some of Purcell's songs to his own accompaniment, the queen – no doubt rather bored – asked Mrs Hunt to sing 'Cold and raw', which she did, accompanying herself on the lute.

Purcell was all the while sitting at the harpsichord unemployed, and not a little nettled at the queen's preference of a vulgar ballad to his music; but seeing her majesty delighted with this tune, he determined that she should hear it upon another occasion: and accordingly in the next birthday song, viz., that for the year 1692, he composed an air to the words 'May her bright example chace Vice in troops out of the land', the bass whereof is the tune to Cold and Raw.[24]

But the main source of poetic inspiration in these odes is the fact that Queen Mary's birthday was in spring, which enabled the optimistic associations of the season to be exploited. Thus, the anonymous 1691 ode begins:

> Welcome, welcome, glorious Morn,
> Nature smiles at thy return.
> At thy return the joyful Earth
> Renews the Blessings of Maria's Birth.
> The busy Sun prolongs his Race
> The youthful year his earliest Tribute pays
> And Frost forsake his head and Tears his face.

Indeed, Tate's *Celebrate this festival* (1693) is a festival of spring. Warlike trumpets cease (though only for a while), sullen discord smiles, the altar is crowned, the shrine bedecked and spring arrives at last:

> April, who till now, has mourn'd
> Claps for Joy his Sable Wing,
> To see within his Orb return'd
> The choicest Blessings he could bring,
> Maria's Birth-Day, and the Spring.

In addition to the six birthday odes Purcell wrote for the queen, there is one (*Who can from joy refrain?*) written for the queen's nephew, William, Duke of Gloucester, and performed on 24 July 1695 to mark his sixth birthday. The performance was probably at Windsor, since *The Post Boy* of the following day contained this report:

> Yesterday being the Anniversary of the Birth of His Highness the Duke of Gloucester, the same was observed in this City by ringing of Bells, and other Demonstrations of Joy suitable to the occasion, and there was last night a fine Ball at Windsor, upon the same subject.[25]

24   Hawkins, *A General History of the Science and Practice of Music*, 1776 (rev. edn London, 1853), vol. II, 564; see also Simpson, *The British Broadside Ballad*, pp. 687–92.
25   Olive Baldwin and Thelma Wilson, '"Who can from joy refraine?": Purcell's Birthday Song for the Duke of Gloucester', *The Musical Times* 122 (1981), 596–9.

Sole survivor of Princess (later Queen) Anne's many children, the hopes of the protestant Stuart succession rested on him. Unhappily, he suffered from hydrocephalus and lived only until he was eleven, in every respect an object of pity – made worse, as it now seems, by the bombast and appalling hyperbole of the text. A sad irony was the lad's passion for playing at soldiers despite the fact that he could hardly walk unaided:

> Sound yᵉ Trumpet, and beat yᵉ Warlike Drumms;
> The Prince will be wᵗʰ Laurells Crown'd,
> Before his Manhood Comes.
> Ah! how pleased he is and Gay,
> When yᵉ Trumpet strikes His ear
> His Hands like shakeing Lillies play,
> And catch at ev'ry Spear
>
> If now he burns wᵗʰ noble Flame,
> When grown, what will he doe?
> From Pole to Pole he'l stretch his Fame
> And all the World subdue.

ST CECILIA ODES

There is a well-known account by Peter Motteux published in the first issue of *The Gentleman's Journal* (January, 1691/2) that describes the way St Cecilia's day was observed at the end of the seventeenth century.

> On that day or the next when it falls on a *Sunday* . . . most of the Lovers of Music, whereof many are persons of the first Rank, meet at *Stationers Hall* in *London*, not thro a Principle of Superstition, but to propagate the advancement of that divine Science. A splendid Entertainment is provided, and before it is always a performance of Music by the best Voices and Hands in Town; the Words, which are always in the Patronesses praise, are set by some of the greatest Masters in Town . . . 6 Stewards are chosen for each ensuing year, four of which are either Persons of Quality or Gentlemen of Note, and the two last, either Gentlemen of their majesties Music, or some of the chief Masters in Town . . . This Feast is one of the genteelest in the world; there are no formalities nor gatherings like as at others, and the appearance there is always very splendid. Whilst the Company is at Table, the Hautboys and Trumpets play successively. Mr. *Showers* hath taught the latter of late years to sound with all the softness imaginable, they plaid us some flat Tunes, made by Mr. *Finger*, with a general applause, it being a thing formerly thought impossible upon an Instrument design'd for a sharp Key.[26]

---

[26] *The Gentleman's Journal* (January 1691/2), pp. 4–5.

More details are provided by an admission ticket for the 1696 celebration, preserved in the British Museum.[27] Proceedings began at 9 o'clock in the morning at St Bride's Church, Fleet Street, '*where will be a Sermon & Anthem, & afterwards to dine at Stationers Hall near Ludgate, where before Dinner there will be a Performance* of *MUSICK*' – the ode for that year was by Nicola Matteis, who was also one of the stewards. Tickets cost ten shillings, and no servants were to be admitted.

How this tradition started is far from clear. Virtually nothing is known about any regular musical celebration before Purcell's *Welcome to all the pleasures*, performed in 1683 and published with a dedication 'To the Gentlemen of the Musical Society'.[28] The title-page, however, seems to imply that the tradition had already been established, since the work was described as 'A Musical Entertainment perform'd on November XXII, 1683. It being the Festival of St Cecilia . . . whose memory is annually honour'd by a public Feast made on that Day by the Masters and Lovers of Music, as well in England as in Foreign Parts'. On the other hand, the ode for the following year, Blow's *Begin the song*, was described on its title-page as 'A Second Musical Entertainment', thus tending to confirm 1683 as the inaugural year. (Or perhaps Blow's ode was only the second to be published?) On balance, however, the evidence seems to point to 1683 as the year when St Cecilia concerts became a regular event organized by the Musical Society. They had probably grown up informally as part of the burgeoning concert life that developed after John Banister's concerts started in 1672. Certainly, what seems like a new tradition begins in 1683, continuing annually with a few gaps until 1703, and more sporadically thereafter.

This is not the place to go into the organization of these festivals, or even to offer a year-by-year account except briefly to put Purcell's contributions in perspective.[29] Following Blow's ode in 1684, it fell to William Turner to provide the ode for 1685, a setting of Tate's *Tune the viol, touch the lyre*. Nothing is known of any festival in 1686, but 1687 was marked by Dryden's great ode *From harmony, from heavenly harmony*, set by Giovanni Battista Draghi. National upheaval may have caused the cancellation of the 1688 celebration (William of Orange landed at Torbay on 5 November and a civil war looked likely), and it was not until 1690 that the series recommenced with Shadwell's *O sacred harmony, prepare our lays*, set to music by Robert King. Each of 'the

27 Zimmerman, *Henry Purcell*, p. 205.
28 *The Works of Henry Purcell*, vol. X, rev. B. Wood (London, 1990), ix.
29 What follows is largely indebted to W. H. Husk, *An Account of the Annual Celebration on St Cecilia's Day* (London, 1857), pp. 13–50, 143–93.

greatest masters' having been thus called on, it was Blow's turn again in 1691 with *The glorious day is come* (Durfey), and Purcell's in 1692, with *Hail, bright Cecilia* (Nicholas Brady).

The following year the ode was set by Gottfried Finger (*Cecilia look, look down and see*), complemented by a sermon by Ralph Battell, Sub-dean of the Chapel Royal, preached in St Bride's Church, on 'The Lawfulness and Expediency of Church Music'. From then on a sermon in praise or justification of music was a regular feature of the celebrations. This more religious emphasis was followed up by Purcell's Te Deum and Jubilate in D, written for the 1694 festival, overshadowing any ode there may have been, and Blow's in 1695. (Purcell himself died on the eve of St Cecilia's day that year.) There seems to have been a return to composing odes in 1696 when Nicola Matteis was chosen, while in 1697 Jeremiah Clarke set Dryden's *Alexander's Feast*. The following year it was the turn of Daniel Purcell, and again in 1699. Blow composed the ode for 1700, and John Eccles for 1701 – setting Congreve's *O harmony, to thee we sing*.

Provincial centres also began to observe the occasion, and some surviving odes were probably written for local celebrations; Daniel Purcell's *Begin and strike th'harmonious lyre!*, for example, seems to have been given at Oxford in 1693, and Vaughan Richardson's *Ye tuneful and harmonious choir* at Winchester in 1704.[30] But in London, the observations became less frequent after 1703, though Maurice Greene and William Boyce were among later composers to contribute to the tradition.

There is thus a well documented history of St Cecilia celebrations over a period of roughly twenty years. The text of the first, Purcell's *Welcome to all the pleasures* (1683), was by Christopher Fishburn, a nephew of Sir Christopher Wren, who had served in the brief Flanders campaign of 1678 and was described in 1698 as 'an Inns of Court Gentleman'.[31] He was also an amateur composer, and Playford published some of his songs in *Choice Ayres* (1684). One of these, 'Beneath a dark and melancholy grove', shows certain resemblances to Purcell's setting, though the words differ after the opening lines.[32] So far as the ode was concerned, it was certainly a fruitful collaboration, resulting in one of Purcell's most confident and successful early works. Having published his first set of trio sonatas the year before (1683), he

---

[30] Michael Tilmouth, 'A Calendar of References to Music in Newspapers Published in London and the Provinces, 1660–1719', *R.M.A. Research Chronicle* 1 (1961), 57.

[31] Rodney M. Baine, 'Rochester or Fishbourne: a Question of Authorship', *Review of English Studies* 22 (1946), 203–5.

[32] Ian Spink, *English Song: Dowland to Purcell* (London, 1974), pp. 180–2.

probably felt that to have this specimen of his vocal music in print would do no harm to his reputation.

Two further Cecilia odes have also been dated 1683 though one of them is probably later. There is no reason, however, to question the date of *Laudate Ceciliam*, 'A Latine Song made upon St Cecilia . . . in ye year 1683', according to Purcell's autograph. Why he should have composed a second Cecilia ode that year is not known. It has been suggested that it was, in effect, a motet written in honour of St Cecilia for the queen's catholic chapel.[33] Its strong Italian influence, especially that of Carissimi, would have made it particularly appropriate for such a purpose. Less likely perhaps is a performance at the Oxford Music School, where 'Latine would not have been out of place, though the Italianate style may have been.[34] The 'song' certainly lies well outside the tradition that we are concerned with here.

The 'third' Cecilia ode of 1683 is *Raise the voice*, whose date is problematic. One of its sources carries the note 'perform'd Novr. 22. 1683', but this is a late addition to what, in any case, is a late manuscript,[35] and it seems highly unlikely that Purcell would have composed three such odes in the same year. Taken in sequence with the rest, it fits uncomfortably at that date – or, it has to be admitted, any date. At first sight, its modest vocal and instrumental requirements appear to link it with *Laudate Ceciliam* but, whereas one can accept the peculiarities of that piece because of its Latin text and sacred character, no such explanation can account for the anomalies in *Raise the voice*. For one thing, it is not present in British Library R.M. MS 20.h.8 which contains autographs of all but one of the odes written between 1681 and 1687 in chronological order, the exception being *Welcome to all the pleasures* (probably not there because it was published). Most of the indicators point to a date no later than 1689, when the ode's instrumental minuet appeared in *The Second Part of Musick's Hand-maid* arranged for keyboard. Stylistic pointers to a date about 1687–8 include the common-time fugal movement of the opening symphony not otherwise known in Purcell before 1687 and the more advanced handling of the ground 'Mark, how readily', in which some of the vocal solo is accompanied by violins, and not just followed by a resetting of the voice part for strings.[36] Yet one remains

---

33 *The Works of Henry Purcell*, vol. X, rev. B. Wood, ix; Franklin B. Zimmerman, *Henry Purcell, 1659–1695: An Analytical Catalogue of His Music* (New York, 1963), p. 150.

34 Martin Adams suggests the possibility of a performance at Magdalen College, Oxford, through the offices of Charles Morgan and Daniel Purcell; see 'Purcell's *Laudate Ceciliam*: An Essay in Stylistic Experimentation', *Irish Musical Studies*, vol. I, ed. G. Gillen and H. White (Dublin, 1990), 240.

35 *The Works of Henry Purcell*, vol. X, ix–x.

36 Adams, 'Purcell's *Laudate Ceciliam*', p. 246.

Ex. 7.1　　(a)　*Raise the voice*

(b)　*Behold, I bring you glad tidings* (Christmas, 1687)

Ex. 7.2　　(a)　*Raise the voice*

(b)　*Behold, I bring you glad tidings*

uneasy, largely because the work as a whole seems rather jejune for such a date. In this connection comparison with *Behold, I bring you glad tidings*, an anthem dating from Christmas 1687, may be revealing. Rather unusually, both have symphonies with bustling quaver fugue subjects (Ex. 7.1), and their opening vocal gestures are somewhat similar (Ex. 7.2). If one can overlook the artistic gulf between the two, the resemblances may indeed suggest that they were composed about the same time.

One piece of evidence, however, does not support such a date. The name 'Bowen' written above the treble solo 'The god himself says he'll be present here' (bar 112) refers, presumably, to Jemmey Bowen, well known as a soloist in the last years of Purcell's life. This implies a performance between 1692 and 1695 but, though the ode may have been performed then, it is hardly possible stylistically that it can have been written in the 1690s. Bruce Wood has suggested that it could have been written for a projected performance in 1688: 'a performance which, after the hasty abdication of James II earlier that very month, never took place'.[37] Alternatively, a performance in 1686 or 1687 outside London – at Oxford, for example – is another possibility.

Purcell's last ode in praise of St Cecilia was *Hail, bright Cecilia*, performed at Stationers' Hall on 22 November 1692. Motteux reported in *The Gentleman's Journal* the same month:

> In my first Journal I gave you a large account of the Musick Feast on St. *Cecilia's* day; So, to avoid repetitions, I shall onely tell you that the last was no ways inferiour to the former . . . The following Ode was admirably set to Music by Mr. *Henry Purcell*, and perform'd twice with universal applause, particularly the second Stanza, which was sung with incredible Graces by Mr. *Purcell* himself.[38]

The second stanza was, of course, "'Tis nature's voice', and Motteux's remarks have usually been taken as indicating that the singer was Purcell.[39] A single sheet engraving of the song by Thomas Cross, probably of the following year, also mentions that it was 'set by Mr. Henry Purcell and sung by himself at St Cæcilia's Feast'. On the other hand, the autograph score, which includes the names of soloists taking part in what was probably the first performance, indicates Mr Pate as having sung this number. Of course, Pate may have taken part in a later performance, but it is also possible that Motteux's account may be misleading. For Purcell is not known as a singer at all (or, at least, of any particular distinction) and is normally listed among the Gentlemen of the Chapel Royal as one of the organists, though on his death his place in the Chapel was taken by Alexander Damascene, a countertenor. Such replacements were not always for voice, however, and against this is his listing among the basses (but described as 'Organist of Westminster') at the

---

37 *The Works of Henry Purcell*, vol. X, x.
38 *The Gentleman's Journal* (November, 1692), p. 18.
39 Zimmerman, *Henry Purcell*, pp. 206–7; J. A. Westrup, *Purcell*, rev. edn by Nigel Fortune (London, 1980), p. 193; *The Works of Henry Purcell*, vol. VIII, rev. P. Dennison (London, 1978), x; Jeremy Noble, 'Purcell and the Chapel Royal', in *Henry Purcell (1659–1695): Essays on his Music*, ed. Imogen Holst (London, 1959), pp. 60–2.

coronation of James II.[40] Admittedly, he could have been both bass and countertenor (falsettist), but Motteux's remark apart, there is no evidence that Purcell ever performed as a singer in public – certainly not as a counter-tenor of comparable status to the others who took part in the performance, and in such a taxing number. On balance, therefore, it seems more likely that Pate took the part, and that the correct interpretation of Motteux's report (which Cross also seems to have misunderstood) should be that the song 'was sung with incredible Graces [by Pate, though they had been composed] by Mr. *Purcell* himself'. A further performance was held at York Buildings on 25 January 1694 as part of an entertainment put on for the visit of Prince Lewis of Baden.[41]

MISCELLANEOUS ODES

Purcell's remaining odes include *The Yorkshire Feast Song*, a wedding ode and two 'academic' odes. *From hardy climes* was written for the marriage of Prince George of Denmark to Princess Anne (later Queen Anne), celebrated on 28 July 1683 at St James's. Much is made of the supposed bravery of the prince (also in the birthday song for his son, the young Duke of Gloucester, already mentioned), and the pious – and sadly unfulfilled – hope is expressed that 'So shall the race from your great loins to come / Prove future Kings and Queens of Christendom'.

The Yorkshire Feast Song was intended as a demonstration of loyalty by the Yorkshire gentry in London to William of Orange on his acceptance of the crown, 13 February 1690. The performance was originally to have been given at Merchant Taylors' Hall the day after, but because 'several of the Stewards were Members of the late Parliament, who are now obliged to go to the country', it was postponed until 27 March.[42] Durfey, who wrote the words, described it as 'An Ode on the Assembly of the Nobility and Gentry of the City and County of York, at the Anniversary Feast', adding that it was one of Purcell's finest compositions and cost £100 to perform.[43] Whatever Purcell's political views may have been, this was the most overtly pro-William and anti-catholic text he set:

---

[40]   Edward F. Rimbault, *The Old Cheque-Book . . . of the Chapel Royal*, Camden Society, n. s., vol. III (London, 1872), 21; Francis Sandford, *The History of the Coronation of the Most High, Most Mighty and Most Excellent Monarch James II* (London, 1687), p. 65.
[41]   Tilmouth, 'A Calendar', p. 14.
[42]   *The Works of Henry Purcell*, vol. I, ed. W. H. Cummings (London, 1878), ii.
[43]   Thomas D'Urfey, *Wit and Mirth; or Pills to purge Melancholy* (London, 1719), vol. I, 114.

Sound Trumpets sound, beat every Drum,
Till it be known through *Christendom*,
This is the Knell of falling *Rome*,
To him that our Mighty Defender has been,
Sound all,
And to all the Heroes invited him in,
Sound all,
And as the chief Agents of the Royal Work,
Long flourish the City and County of *York*.

Celestial Music was 'perform'd at Mr Maidwell's, a schoolmaster, on the 5th of August, 1689, the words by one of his scholars'. The scholar's identity is unknown, but his text forsakes the pindaric style for simple heroic couplets in praise of music. Lewis Maidwell kept a school in King Street, Westminster, and was the author of a play called *The Loving Enemies* put on at the Dorset Garden theatre in January 1680 and published later that year. He was also the author of *An Essay upon the Necessity and Excellency of Education* (1705). Any further connection between Purcell and Maidwell is unknown.[44]

It was no doubt through Nahum Tate that the commission came to set *Great parent, hail!* for the centenary of Trinity College, Dublin. The performance took place on 9 January 1694 in Christ Church Cathedral, Dublin and, according to the *London Gazette*, 'The afternoon was taken up with speeches, verses, and music, both vocal and instrumental, in praise of their foundress [Queen Elizabeth] and benefactors, of their majesties King William and Queen Mary'.[45] Another account speaks of 'an Ode made by Mr Tate (the Poet Laureate) who was bred up in this College . . . sung by the principal Gentlemen of the Kingdom [Ireland]'.[46]

CHRONOLOGICAL LIST OF PURCELL'S ODES

Note: Titles from Purcell's autograph manuscript (British Library R.M. MS 20.h.8) have been given, together with those from other early sources which provide additional (or contradictory) information. Singers mentioned in these sources have been listed with an indication of the clefs their parts are written in. For arguments relating to dates of performance see above. 'Z' references are to Zimmerman, *Henry*

---

44   Zimmerman, *Henry Purcell*, pp. 414–15, notes 3–4; *The London Stage 1660–1800*, Part 1: *1660–1700*, ed. William van Lennep (Carbondale, 1965), p. 283.

45   Zimmerman, *Henry Purcell*, pp. 232–4, points out that the actual centenary of the foundation should have been 16 March 1692; other authorities give 3 March as the anniversary of its incorporation.

46   John Dunton, *Some Account of my Conversation in Ireland* (1699); see *The Works of Henry Purcell*, vol. XXVII, ed. Arnold Goldsborough, Dennis Arundell, Anthony Lewis and Thurston Dart (London, 1966), xvi.

Purcell, 1659–1685: An Analytical Catalogue of His Music (New York, 1963), followed by the relevant volume and page number of *The Works of Henry Purcell.*

1680   *Welcome, Vicegerent of the mighty king* (anon)
'A Song to Welcome home his Majesty from Windsor 1680' (Add. MS 22,100)
'A Welcome Song at yᵉ Princ of Denmarks comeing home' (Add. MS 31,447)
9 September, or 9 October
Z 340, XV, 1

1681   *Swifter Isis, swifter flow* (anon)
'A Welcome Song in yᵉ Year 1681 For yᵉ King' (R.M. MS 20.h.8)
29 March or soon after; or 27 August or soon after. It may not have been performed at all.
Z 336; XV, 24

1682   *What shall be done in behalf of the man* (anon)
'A Welcome Song for his Royall Highness at his return from Scotland in yᵉ Yeare 1682' (R.M. MS 20.h .8)
27 May
Z 341; XV, 52

   The summer's absence unconcerned we bear (anon)
'A Welcome Song for his Majesty at his return from New Market October yᵉ 21 – 1682' (R.M. MS 20.h.8)
Z 337; XV, 83

1683   *From hardy climes* (anon)
'A Song yᵗ was perform'd to Prince George upon his Marriage with yᵉ Lady Ann' (R.M. MS 20.h.8)
28 July 1683
Z 325, XXVII, 1

   Fly, bold rebellion (anon)
'yᵉ Welcome Song perform'd to his Majesty in yᵉ Year 1683' (R.M. MS 20.h.8)
25 September
Z 324; XV, 116

   Welcome to all the pleasures (Christopher Fishburn)
'A Musical Entertainment perform'd on November XXII. 1683. It being the Festival of St Cecilia . . .' (pub. London, 1694)
Z 339; X (rev.), 1

   Raise, raise the voice (anon)
'perform'd Novr. 22, 1683' – possibly 1687, or unperformed
Z 334; X (rev.), 36

1684   *From those serene and rapturous joys* (Thomas Flatman)
        'The Welcome Song perform'd to his Majesty in yᵉ year 1684' (R.M. MS
        20.h.8)
        'On the King's Return to White-hall, after his Summer's Progress, 1684'
        (Flatman, *Poems and Songs*, 1686)
        25 September
        Z 326; XVIII, 1

1685   *Why, why are all the muses mute?* (anon)
        'Welcome Song 1685 being yᵉ first Song performd to King James yᵉ 2d'
        (R.M. MS 20.h.8)
        6 October
        Singer: Turner (C3)
        Z 343; XVIII, 37

1686   *Ye tuneful muses, raise your heads* (anon)
        'Welcome Song 1686' (R.M. MS 20.h.8)
        1 October
        Singer: Turner (C3)
        Z 334; XVIII, 80

1687   *Sound the trumpet, beat the drum* (anon)
        'Welcome Song 1687' (R.M. MS 20.h.8)
        'Ode for King James 2ⁿᵈ's Birthday 1687' (R.M. MS 24.e.7)
        11 October
        Singers: Abell (C3), Bowman (F4), Marsh (C4), Robert (C4), Turner (C3)
        Z 335; XVIII, 121

        [Raise, raise the voice, see 1683]

1689   *Now does the glorious day appear* (Thomas Shadwell)
        '*An* Ode *on the Queens Birth-Day Sang before their Majesties at* Whitehal.
        By Tho. Shadwell' (*Poems on Affairs of State*, vol. II, 1697)
        30 April
        Z 332; XI, 1

        Celestial music did the gods inspire (anon)
        'A Song that was perform'd at Mʳ Maidwells a school master on yᵉ 5th of
        August 1689 yᵉ Words by one of his scholars' (R.M. MS 20.h.8 – not
        autograph)
        5 August
        Z 322; XXVII, 29

1690   *Of old when heroes thought it base* (Thomas Durfey)
        'An *Ode* on the Assembly of the Nobility and Gentry of the City and
        County of *York*, at the Anniversary Feast, *March* the 27th, 1690' (Durfey,

Wit and Mirth, vol. I, 1719)
27 March 1690
Z 333; I

Arise, my muse (Thomas Durfey)
'*An* Ode on *the Anniversary of the* Queens-Birth. *Set to Musick by Mr.* Henry Purcell, *April 30th,* 1690' (*Poems on Affairs of State,* vol. III, 1698)
Singers: Bourchier (C3), Damascene (C3), Robert (C3), Turner (C3),
30 April
Z 320; XI, 36

1691   *Welcome, welcome, glorious morn* (anon)
'Queen's Birth-day Song 1691' (British Library Add. MS 31,447)
30 April
Z 338; XI, 72

1692   *Love's goddess sure was blind* (Sir Charles Sedley)
'Queen's Birth-Days-Song 1692' (British Library Add. MS 31,447)
'An Anniversary Ode sung before Her Majesty the 29th of *April:* the Words by *Sir Charles Sidley*' (*Gentleman's Journal,* May, 1692)
29 April
Z 331; XXIV, 1

Hail, bright Cecilia (Nicholas Brady)
'An Ode on St Cecilia's Day 1692'
Singers: Ayliff (G2), Bouchier (C3), 'Solo Boy' (G2) Bowman (F4), Damascene (C3), Edwards (F4), Freeman (C3), Hart (F4), Howell (C2, C3), Pate (C3, C4) , Snow (C4), Turner (C3), Williams (F4), Woodson (F4)
22 November
Z 328; VIII

1693   *Celebrate this festival* (Nahum Tate)
'The Queens Birthday Song being yᵉ [April] 1692 [sic]'
(R.M. MS 24.e.4)
'An Ode upon Her Majesty's Birth-day, *April* the 30th, by N. Tate Esq'
(*Gentleman's Journal,* April, 1693)
Singers: Ayliff (G2), Bowman (F4), 'the Boy' (G2), Damascene (C3), Edwards (F4), Howell (C2), Robert (C3), Snow (C4), Turner (C3), Woodson (F4)
Z 321; XXIV, 36

1694   *Light of the world* (Matthew Prior)
'Hymn to the Sun Set by Dr. Purcell and sung before Their Majesties on New-Years Day, 1693/4'
(almost certainly not performed; music lost or not written)

Great parent, hail! (Nahum Tate)
'Commemoration Ode performed at Christ-Church in Dublin, Jany. 9, 1693/4' (British Library Add. MS 22,100)
Z 327; XXVII, 59

Come ye sons of art (anon)
30 April
Singers: Damascene (C3)
Z 323; XXIV, 87

1695   *Who can from joy refrain?* (anon)
'A Song for yᵉ Duke of Glosters Birth day July yᵉ 24th 1695' (Oxford, Bodleian MS Mus. c. 27*)
Singers: Damascene (C3), Freeman (C3), Howell (C3), Robert (C3), Woodson (F4)
Z342; IV

8

Purcell, Blow and the English court ode

MARTIN ADAMS

The various relationships between the music of Blow and Purcell are more extensive than one might expect of a teacher and pupil. Some of the reasons for this are unrecoverable and must lie in the composers' personalities. Circumstances would have played a part: Blow was just ten years older than his famous pupil; their backgrounds in the Chapel Royal and as court composers were almost identical; and, after some eighteen years of disruption caused by the Civil War and the Protectorate, the Restoration of the monarchy in 1660 began a period of unusually robust musical innovation, circumstances especially suited to two naturally adventurous composers. Nowhere in their output does mutual influence emerge more profitably than in the court ode.

Precedents for the court ode have been discussed elsewhere, along with many of the ways in which, early in the period, composers, notably Henry Cooke, Master of the Children of the Chapel Royal, responded to the Parliamentary decree that 29 May – Charles II's birthday and the date of his landing in England – should be an annual festival.[1] There also was a tradition of performing welcome songs after a royal journey, and a much more consistent, long-established custom of a musical offering to the king at the new year, usually a masque. In the early 1660s the latter continued the practice common under Charles I; but by 1666 the celebrations had become associated with a distinctive type of piece for choral, solo vocal and instrumental forces, and the masque suffered a corresponding decline.

In that year Cooke produced *Good morrow to the year* (Barber Institute MS 5001, fol. 6), the earliest surviving example of the Restoration court ode.[2] It was perhaps natural that for this new secular panegyric Cooke should

---

[1] Rosamond McGuinness, *English Court Odes 1660–1820* (Oxford, 1971), chap. 1, from which most datings in this article are taken. See also chap. 7, above.

[2] Sources cited are not necessarily the primary ones but those used in researching this chapter. A microfiche copy of this manuscript accompanies the *Catalogue of the Printed Music and Music*

string together sections for verse, chorus and instruments, similar to the methods of the more established sacred equivalent, the verse anthem with strings, in which he had already proved a notable innovator.[3] Certainly the methods displayed in this ode are more radical than those of Locke's from the same year, *All things their certain periods have* (British Library Add. MS 33,234, fol. 35).

There are masque-like features too, notably in the functional, dance-based proportions of the opening symphony for two violins and continuo – a two-bar fanfare on a G major chord and in ₵ time, followed by a section in **3i** time, this a dance-like binary structure of 16 + 17 bars (assuming notation in 3/4 time). Whether or not a dance actually took place is not known, but masque fingerprints never entirely disappeared from the seventeenth-century court ode and, as late as 1687 during the chaconne from Purcell's *Sound the trumpet* (Z 335/7), dances almost certainly did take place.

Cooke's later odes show some increase of scale over his first effort, and this continued when Pelham Humfrey was appointed to Cooke's place, after the latter's death in 1672.[4] Humfrey was the much better composer, and his birthday song from that year, *When from his throne the Persian god displays* (Add. MS 33,287, fol. 72) – just two other odes by him survive – shows the same attention to declamatory detail which distinguishes his better anthems. Also characteristic is his sense for large-scale structure, shown in repeating the opening symphony to mark a main division of the text, and in linking movements via a resourceful range of head-motif techniques. In this and his other odes, the link to the anthem is also underlined by abandoning the short opening symphony characteristic of most of Cooke's odes and anthems, and using instead the type which predominates in his and others' verse anthems with strings until the mid-1680s: an opening section in duple time featuring dotted rhythms and a binary-form, dance-like second section in **3i** time, all with four-part strings instead of the three favoured by Cooke.[5]

Manuscripts before 1801 in the Music Library of the University of Birmingham Barber Institute of Fine Arts, ed. Iain Fenlon (London, 1976). For a full list of sources see McGuinness, *English Court Odes*, chap. 2; also David R. Evans, 'Blow's Court Odes: A New Discovery', *The Musical Times* 125 (1984), 567–9.

3   Ian Cheverton, 'Captain Henry Cooke (c. 1616–1672), the Beginnings of a Reappraisal', *Soundings* 9 (1982), 74–86; Robert Manning, 'Purcell's Anthems: An Analytical Study of the Music and its Content', Ph.D. thesis, University of Birmingham (1979), p. 23. The link between welcome songs and the verse anthem goes back at least to the second decade of the century. Cf. Orlando Gibbons (?), *Do Not Repine, Fair Sun*, ed. Philip Brett (London, 1961).

4   Andrew Ashbee, *Records of English Court Music*, vol. I: *1660–1685* (Snodland, 1986), 117–18.

5   For discussions of the background to this type of symphony, and of other issues raised in this chapter, see Martin Adams, *Henry Purcell: The Origins and Development of his Musical Style* (Cambridge, 1995).

On Humfrey's death in 1674, it became John Blow's duty to provide the music for the new year and birthday odes.[6] If he wrote any earlier than *Dread Sir, the prince of light* (British Library Add. MS 33,237, fol. 75), which is most likely to have been for the new-year celebration of 1678,[7] they have not been discovered, a regrettable lacuna, for such odes might show more of how he progressed from anthem-based methods. Blow above all established the general direction for the future and Purcell, responding competitively to many of his innovations, produced the works which give the genre its enduring interest.

Most anthem texts consist of a series of Biblical verses, typically from the Psalms, and the characteristically trenchant, distinctive expression of each verse lent itself to a multi-sectional structure of one verse per section. Running a series of contrasted verses together facilitated the articulation of larger structural units, concerned generally with praise, penitence or the goodness of God, for example. In the verse anthem with strings such units might be defined by ending with a chorus or, more frequently, a string symphony, often based on material immediately preceding. Blow's anthems, including some from the mid-1670s, show adept recycling of material and an interest in experimental structure which he soon applied to the ode.

By the 1660s, the ode was a recognized poetic genre in England – like its ostensible Greek precedents by Pindar, Horace and others, conceived as public address, full of exalted imagery.[8] Its English origins lay partly in Cowley's widely read *Pindaric Odes* (1656), which featured bold imagery and forceful rhetoric drawing freely on Classical allusion. They were irregular in metre, line length and in the number of lines per strophe; indeed, in *The Lives of the English Poets* (1779–81) Samuel Johnson deplored Cowley's 'lax and lawless versification'.[9] Freedom can be a dangerous thing, and in the seventeenth-century court ode served only to emphasize the mediocrity of the largely anonymous authors, even though most of their texts were more regular than Cowley's. Indeed, of the many types of ode set to music during the period, only two have any literary strength, Sedley's *Love's goddess sure*, which Purcell set in 1692, and Dryden's *A Song for St Cecilia's Day, 1687*, set in that year by Draghi and in 1739 by Handel – a text which stands far above anything else, though not written for court.

---

6   *The Old Cheque Book . . . of the Chapel Royal*, ed. Edward F. Rimbault (London, 1872; reprint, New York, 1966), pp. 15–16; Ashbee, *Records of English Court Music*, vol. I, 165, vol. V, 67.

7   McGuinness, *English Court Odes*, p. 45, n.10.

8   For a more detailed examination and critique of Restoration ode texts, see McGuinness, *English Court Odes*, chap. 3.

9   For a general history and critique of the genre see John D. Jump, *The Ode*, in *The Critical Idiom*, 45 vols. (London, 1969–85), vol. XXX (1974).

The application of anthem-based methods to texts much longer than those of most verse anthems left little room for musical or textual repetition, except perhaps in the main choruses and at the ends of sections. Various types of triple time predominated, partly because of the ease with which they fit the natural rhythms of English, and various verse sections followed on from one another, more or less without a break. In *Dread Sir, the prince of light*, Blow shows the path away from this expedient towards music with the potential to match the high-flown poetic gestures. Though not significantly longer than Humfrey's odes,[10] its adventurous deployment of forces and formal types reveals an innovative, courageous musical mind.

Like many odes and anthems by Humfrey and Cooke, *Dread Sir, the prince of light* is arranged into two large units, each ending with a re-working for chorus of a preceding verse. After the opening symphony, the first unit is mainly in ₵ and 𝄵 time and includes vocal and instrumental pieces closer in style to dance and theatre song than to anything in Blow's own anthems (Ex. 8.1).[11] Like most earlier odes, each section begins and ends in the same key; but Blow treads some genuinely new ground in his efforts to expand scale, to increase the musical substance of the ode and to heighten textual emphasis. The second unit has three sections:

1. Verse *a* – Chorus – Ritornello, 'This message we bring' (3i time) (Ex. 8.2)

   In 'headmotif' style, the verse draws on the second section of the opening symphony. The chorus is a repetition of the end of the verse and the ritornello an extended, polyphonic reworking of material from the verse.

2. Verse *b* – Ritornello, 'This happy omen' (₵ time)

   The ritornello is a development of the end of the verse.

3. Verse *atb* with Chorus SATB, 'This message we bring' (3i time)

   This repeats 1 above, with alternate lines for verse and chorus. The last line, declaring the king 'ever shall reign', is greatly extended by polyphonic development and follows Cooke's example by ending with a few bars in ₵ time.

While some verse anthems of this time, such as Purcell's *My beloved spake*, include reworkings and repetitions of sections, it was largely in the ode that Blow and then Purcell began to amplify these principles and strike out in

---

10   McGuinness, *English Court Odes*, p. 45, n. 10.
11   Cf. examples from the 1670s in Ian Spink, *English Song, Dowland to Purcell* (London, 1974), pp. 151–200, especially Staggins (pp. 160 and 189) and Banister (p. 164).

Ex. 8.1 Blow, *Dread Sir, the prince of light*

Let   no   dis - loy - al   cares   his   peace de - stroy

Ex. 8.2 Blow, *Dread Sir, the prince of light*

This   mes - sage we   bring   to the   joy   of   our King, from this

wise and the   learn - ed A - pol - lo.

new directions. Some so-far-unidentified foreign music may have had some influence; Blow was particularly interested in Italian vocal music and copied out a considerable quantity of it.[12] Although French music was by this time becoming less fashionable, he was certainly familiar with it. *Dread Sir, the prince of light* seems to be the first court ode to use fugal imitation in the second section of the opening symphony, a step closer to the later methods of Lully.

Like most experimental composers, Blow occasionally made a sally which produced interesting results but of limited scope. *Awake, awake, my lyre!*, almost certainly written for the Oxford Music School in the late 1670s,[13] is notable as an early example of an ode produced outside the court. The triple time which had dominated odes thus far is here modified by extensive hemiola rhythms, not only at the ends of lines, but at any point where such rhythms might more faithfully accommodate the rhythms of the text. The music is organized into three units, plus an opening symphony. Each of the first two consists of a solo, a symphony, a chorus (a four-part setting of the

[12] H. Watkins Shaw, 'The Autographs of John Blow', *The Music Review* 25 (1964), 85–95.
[13] See preface to Hinrichsen edition (1968), ed. H. Watkins Shaw. Cf. McGuinness, *English Court Odes*, p. 46, n. 13.

solo) and a repetition of the symphony. Each section of the unit is derived from the second part of the opening symphony (*A*), mostly by similarities in melodic outline, though some sections also follow similar harmonic patterns. The last unit is inaugurated by a recitative and a symphony, both of which are more distantly related to *A*. By contrast the final solo, 'Sleep again, my lyre', brings the music full circle, like Cowley's poem, with the closest relationship to *A* since the first solo, 'Awake, awake my lyre', and explicitly in the subsequent re-statement of *A*. The concluding chorus is a four-part rendering of the last solo.

Few court ode texts are so balanced and tranquil as *Awake, awake my lyre!* Blow's 1678 birthday ode, *The Birth of Jove*, and his new year offering for 1680, *The New Year is begun* (British Library Add. MS 33,287, fols. 58 and 93), use similar stylistic methods but are much less successful. Future odes paid less attention to minute textual inflection and cross-referencing of text and music and more to dramatic contrasts. This direction is implicit in *Dread Sir, the prince of light*, with its repeated and reworked sections, and forcefully confirmed in Blow's 1679 new year ode *Great Janus, though the festival be thine* (Add. MS 33,287, fol. 53), the longest and most ambitious yet in deployment of resources and stylistic variety. For the first time, the second section of the symphony is a fully worked fugue; the choruses have independent string parts; and one structural unit moves to another key.

Table 8.1 Sections in *Great Janus, though the festival be thine*

Units		Time signature	Harmonic area
1	Symphony	₵ – 3i	d
	Chorus with Strings*a*	3i	d
	Verse *ssatb* with Strings		d – a
	Chorus SSATB		V of d – d
2	Verse *atb* + Ritornello (from verse)	6/4	d – g
	Verse + Chorus: *ssb* + SSATB + *atb* + SSATB	₵	g
	Symphony (2 vlns + cont.)*b*		g – V of d
		3i	d
3	Verse *a* + Ritornello (from verse)		d
	Chorus SSATB		d
4	Verse *t* + Chorus of whole verse + Ritornello		
	from same	3i	d
	Chorus SSATB with Strings		d

a This description indicates one or more independent parts, in this case the first violin. In most choruses without independent string parts, the strings probably doubled.
b Not directly derived from the preceding material.

The verse and chorus in $\mathbf{\phi}$ time, 'Then since peace affords us leisure' (unit 2 above), develops the methods first seen in 'This message we bring', but in a different key and metre from the earlier part of the ode. An eight-bar phrase for *ssb* verse (Ex. 8.3) is repeated by SSATB chorus, and an eight-bar consequent phrase for *atb* verse is followed by a repetition of the chorus, altered to end in G minor. Repetitive structures of this kind were to prove amenable to sophisticated elaboration, especially in Purcell's hands, as in the massive rondeaus 'From the rattling of drums' from the 1686 birthday ode *Ye tuneful Muses* and 'Happy realm' from the 1693 ode *Celebrate this festival.*

Purcell's first ode, *Welcome, Vicegerent,* dates from 1680, and from this beginning, Purcell is far less indebted to the verse anthem than was Blow.[14] He shows virtually no interest in the elaborate head-motif methods of anthems as late as his own *O sing unto the Lord* of about 1688; he never repeats the opening symphony to articulate main textual divisions, though this is common in anthems up to about 1685. His odes explore a far wider range of keys, structural concepts, and vocal and instrumental styles.

Table 8.2 *Welcome, Vicegerent*

Units		Time signature	Material	Harmonic area
1	Symphony	8/4	*A*	C
		3i	*B1*	
	Chorus		*B2*	
2	Verse *ab* + Rit. (from end of verse)	2 ‖ ϕ	*C*	c
	Chorus	3i	*D*	C
	Ritornello		*E*	
	Verse *t* with Chorus		*F*	
–	continuo link	2		C – G
3	Verse *ss*		*G*	g
	Chorus	ϕ	*H*	G
	Verse *t* with Chorus	3i	*J*	
–	continuo link			G – C
4	Ritornello		*J*	C
	Chorus + Verse *a+b* + Chorus with strings		*K*	

The range of formal types in *Welcome, Vicegerent* is wider than in all earlier odes combined. There are self-contained numbers which, like Blow's 'Then since peace affords us leisure', might conceivably exist independently of the ode. (Indeed, in the 1680s extracts from odes were published, generally as

---

[14] I am very hesitant to accept the existence of *The Address of the Children* (Z D120). See Franklin B. Zimmerman, *Henry Purcell, 1659–1695: His Life and Times*, rev. edn. (Philadelphia, 1983), pp. 29 and 393, n. 31.

Ex. 8.3   Blow, *Great Janus, though the festival be thine*

keyboard transcriptions; this would have been inconceivable with most odes from the 1670s.) Examples include the charming, binary-form *ss* duet (*G*) 'When the summer' (Z 340/8), and the graceful, dance-like setting (*J*) of 'Music the food of love' (Z 340/10), in the same style as 'Hail to the myrtle shade' from that year's play *Theodosius* (Z 606/8), for which Purcell's wrote his earliest stage music. In 'Music the food of love', the simple strophic setting is elaborated through deployment of various forces: a twelve-bar phrase for tenor solo ending in the dominant is repeated for SATB, this followed by the same treatment for the twelve-bar consequent which ends in the tonic. The relationship with Blow's 'This message we bring' (Ex. 8.2) is self-evident.

Even more than Blow, Purcell was walking a tightrope, on which heightened contrasts and a direct, communicative style sometimes sat uneasily with structural integrity. The overall weakness of *Welcome, Vicegerent* is thus perhaps more evident than its occasional successes. Amongst the latter must be counted some of the instrumental music, especially the first section of the opening symphony and the superb ritornello after the chorus 'But your blest presence', not surprising for a composer already accomplished in fantazias, overtures and other instrumental genres. Perhaps the most obvious weakness of *Welcome, Vicegerent* is the crudity of some of the choruses, especially 'But your blest presence' (*D*) and 'All loyalty and honour' (*H*) (see Ex. 8.4). There is nothing quite like them in any anthem, for the aim seems to have been to represent communal acclamation, literally in the choral forces and abstractly in the rhythms and phrase structures of dance. The problem lies less in the music itself than in the syllabic text setting, which sounds like hectoring. Locke had produced better results with a similar style of chorus in his stage

Ex. 8.4   Purcell, *Welcome, Vicegerent*

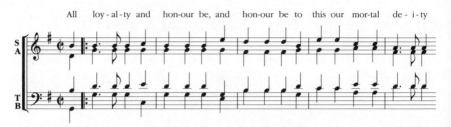

music, and Blow too wrote dance-like choruses, such as ''Tis he has sent us hither' from *Dread Sir, the prince of light*. The extremity of Purcell's results, be they good or ill, stems largely from the extraordinary vigour of his delivery. It is significant that a slightly later melody of similar qualities, the alto solo 'All the grandeur' from Purcell's 1682 ode *What shall be done*, is much more successful when reworked immediately afterwards for four-part strings, good enough indeed to be re-used in that form some nine or ten years later as an air for *The Gordian Knot* (Z 597/2). For both Blow and Purcell, a long-term solution was found in combining periodic dance structures with polyphonic imitation and elaboration to produce a more varied phrase structure and, usually, greater length.

No less problematic are the sometimes less obvious large-scale contrivances with which Purcell attempted to meet the challenges inherent in stringing together extreme stylistic contrasts. These sections of *Welcome, Vicegerent* go further than any earlier ode in using keys for articulation. For the second section of the opening symphony Purcell extracted the string parts of the following chorus, omitting only the *petite reprise*. The concept is engaging but the result unconvincing, for the string material derives its strength largely from being counterpointed against the forceful patterns of the chorus; in particular, the strong, off-beat chords in the middle of the section lose metrical clarity. Then the repetition of the ritornello *J* after the continuo link leading back to C succeeds in blurring rather than in eliding boundaries.

Purcell may have recognized the shortcomings of his first ode, for he did not include it in the autograph which contains all his other odes up to 1690 (British Library R.M. MS 20.h.8). *Welcome, Vicegerent* nevertheless seems to have influenced Blow a few months later when setting the text of the new year ode *Great Sir, the joy of all our hearts* (Barber Institute MS 5001, fol. 41).

With at least five odes now behind him, Blow had established precedents which were to guide him and Purcell for the next fifteen years. *Great Sir, the joy of all our hearts* shows a considerable increase in scale and in the range of

Table 8.3 *Great Sir, the joy of all our hearts*

Units		Time signature	Key
–	Symphony	₵ 3i	C
1	Verse *a*, Chorus with strings, verse *a*, Chorus with strings, verse *b*.		
	Chorus with strings.	₵	
	Ritornello X		
2	Verse *tb*	6/8	a
	Chorus		
	Ritornello		
3	Verse *b* (recit.)	₵	C
	Verse *atb*		
	Ritornello X	₵	
	Chorus	3i	
4	Verse *a* with ritornellos	₵	
	Chorus with strings	3i	

styles and techniques over all his earlier odes. In the first unit, inspired perhaps by Purcell's example in the last chorus of *Welcome, Vicegerent,* he adopts a flexible approach to the disposition of the text, thus emphasizing the opening salutation over the parade of platitudes which follows. The second unit, beginning 'Ye nymphs that around', is distinguished from the first by being in A minor and in 6/8 time, a short continuo introduction providing a transition from C major. Here Blow, rather more convincingly than Purcell in the mechanical and obvious methods of *Welcome, Vicegerent,* creates a whole unit out a single idea. The verse opens with the tenor alone, setting two lines of text to dance-based rhythms and a regular phrase structure which ends on the dominant. The bass then enters with a variant and both voices join in imitation to close the second line in A minor. The continuo returns to preface a second entry from the tenor, which reaches immediately for v; on the close into that key the bass enters to begin some more duetting, which ends in the tonic. This basically binary structure, with each strain about twelve bars long, is reworked for SATB chorus in sixteen bars and at greater length for four-part strings.

Purcell's next few odes suggest that he was profiting from the older man's wider experience. In *Swifter Isis, swifter flow* of 1681, he connects the second section of the opening symphony into the following verse, chorus and ritornello by using the section's opening motif as the basis for a kaleidoscopic series of variations. In the next year's welcome song *The summer's absence*

Purcell follows Blow more closely: a seventeen-bar *atb* verse, 'Shine thus' is reworked with little variation for SATB chorus and then, at slightly greater length and with a more complex texture, for four-part strings. Finally, it is entirely plausible that 'Ye nymphs that around' or one or two similar pieces by Blow inspired Purcell's brilliant treatment of the popular tune 'Hey, boys, up go we' in the verse, chorus and ritornello 'Be lively then' from the 1686 ode *Ye tuneful Muses*.[15]

The third unit of Blow's *Great Sir, the joy of all our hearts* opens with an ample bass recitative underlining the importance of the text and almost certainly conceived for one of the several fine singers then available, if not for John Gostling himself (Ex. 8.5). A similar piece, 'But with as great devotion meet', appears in *Swifter Isis, swifter flow*, a trend which culminates in such virtuoso pieces as the Gostling solo 'While Caesar, like the morning star' from *Sound the trumpet* of 1687.

Perhaps the most interesting piece in Blow's ode is the alto verse at the beginning of the last unit, the first in a long line of modulating ground bass solos in the odes of Blow and Purcell which feature duple or quadruple time and a continuous quaver bass.[16] Blow probably got the idea from the Italians, though precise models have not so far been identified: certainly Stradella, whose music was known in England, was by this time transposing a ground bass into other keys. After one statement of the four-bar ground (Ex. 8.6), the first strain of this binary structure consists of an eight-bar melody over

Ex. 8.5   Blow, *Great Sir, the joy of all our hearts*

---

[15]   See J. A. Westrup, *Purcell*, rev. edn by Nigel Fortune (London, 1980), pp. 178–80.
[16]   These and other ground bass types in the court odes are discussed in detail in Rosamond McGuinness, 'The Ground Bass in the English Court Odes', *Music & Letters* 51 (1970), 118–140 and 265–78.

Ex. 8.6   Blow, *Great Sir, the joy of all our hearts*

two ground statements in C, the whole repeated by four-part strings. The second strain begins with voice and continuo immediately moving away from the tonic. After eight bars of harmonic mobility, ending with a close in the mediant at bar 28, C major returns for two statements of the bass in its original form, the last modified to produce a strong close. Finally, the ritornello from the first strain is repeated with a similarly modified ending.

Blow's and Purcell's different approaches to the running-quaver bass, and to the ostinato techniques which commonly went with it, are revealing. Purcell had an obsessive streak which, in his early days, made him unwilling to engage in anything other than exact repetition of a ground. So, while 'The king, whose presence' from *Swifter Isis, swifter flow*, is evidently indebted to 'Of you, great Sir', this mellifluous duet for sopranos is not a ground but a rondeau-like structure in D minor, beginning with four bars of running quavers in ₵ time, which then constitute the first four bars of duet. The four-bar vocal phrases are organized AABAC¹C²C¹C², with A ending in a half close in the tonic, B a full close in the mediant, and C¹ and C² full closes in C major and D minor respectively. In *The summer's absence* Purcell adopts a still freer approach in the alto solo 'These had by their ill usage drove', which sets a precedent by finishing with a string ritornello, a recasting into four parts of the preceding solo and continuo lines.

'All due, great prince, is yours' from Blow's 1683 new year ode *Dread Sir, Father Janus* (Barber Institute MS 5001, fol. 21) set a pattern, even though it is much shorter than any of Purcell's ground bass songs. To achieve a move into the dominant Blow completely changes the last bar of the ground after just one statement with the voice; repetition of this opening phrase is followed by one statement in the dominant, and the return to the tonic is elided by sustaining the voice on the dominant (see Ex. 6.1, pp. 116–17).

Later that year, in his first true modulating ground, Purcell tried something comparable. 'The sparrow and the gentle dove' from *From hardy climes* is a truly beautiful song, good enough to be selected more than twenty years later for the second book of *Orpheus Britannicus* (1706), though without the concluding ritornello. Like Blow's 'All due, great prince', it is a binary structure with the vocal phrase at the end of the first strain ending on the dominant; but Purcell surpasses Blow's treatment with a half-close in the tonic, the phrasing of the ground perforce overlapping that of the voice, producing a result more mobile than Blow's neat but four-square effort.

'The sparrow and the gentle dove' is the longer and technically more adventurous song. But, while the older composer showed sure judgement in knowing just how far he could stretch invention and technique, Purcell's ambition exceeds his critical powers. The problem lies in the ritornello, especially in Purcell's seeming unwillingness to modify the ground to achieve a smooth key change. The strings begin with the vocal melody in the same key of D minor; at the first half-close, the ground is transposed into the dominant, with C♮ following on from C♯, just one quaver after the close. There is one variation in the new key, ending in a full-close, and the whole of the ritornello is repeated. At the second close in A minor, there is another transposition, producing a variation in F, and the ritornello returns to the tonic. In any context, these transpositions, especially the first, would seem sudden; but following on from the expansive, overlapping phrasing, continuous invention and long-range harmonic direction of the song – all in the tonic yet suggesting other keys in passing – they are an uncomfortable wrench.

It is perhaps significant that in two more songs of this type produced later that same year Purcell did not transpose the ground. 'Here the deities approve' from the Cecilian ode *Welcome to all the pleasures* depends on purely melodic resourcefulness, while the concluding ritornello restates the vocal line exactly, with the inner parts concentrating on that economical motivic elaboration at which Purcell was already peerless. The same technique is used in 'Be welcome then, great sir' from *Fly, bold rebellion* (late 1683), though the ritornello resourcefully explores new motivic derivations in all three upper parts.

Over the next few years Blow wrote further pieces on modulating grounds, such as the duet 'Hark! how the waken'd strings' from the 1684 Cecilian ode *Begin the song* and 'See the pausing lustres stand' from *Hail monarch, sprung of race divine* (Add. MS 33,287, fol. 138v), almost certainly from 1686;[17] all show an interest in finding new formal, motivic and harmonic techniques within the discipline of the ground bass. But, in the long run, Blow's restless curiosity proved less fruitful than Purcell's single-mindedness.

The younger man continued to essay transposition and fragmentation of the ground, for example in 'With him he brings' from the 1686 ode *Ye tuneful Muses*; he was also working at it in other genres and styles, such as 'Cease, anxious world' (Z 362) from late 1684. But all of these suffered from problems similar to those of the ritornello in 'The sparrow and the gentle dove'; indeed, it was not until about 1687 that Purcell achieved complete success in making the boundaries between ground transpositions as fluid as his vocal invention.[18] The 1687 ode *Sound the trumpet* features two solos which achieve consummate results with this technique, 'Crown the year', which uses a different style of bass, and the duet 'Let Caesar and Urania live', an exhilarating piece which clearly anticipates the late masterpieces in the continuous-quaver type of ground, such as 'Sound the trumpet' from *Come ye sons of art.*

The final unit of an ode demanded something special, for the methods of the verse anthem with strings, in which a massive conclusion might be achieved by the chorus remaining silent until the very end of the work, were not generally appropriate. In the early days of the court ode Henry Cooke had rounded off *Good morrow to the year* (1666) with a twenty-bar chorus in five parts, based on the end of the preceding triple-time verse, and much longer and more elaborate than the two earlier choruses. It begins with dense imitation which quickly gives way to more homophonic writing, and ends with a few bars of acclamation in ₵ time, techniques well suited to the rapid dispatch of the text.

Blow often adopted similar methods, as in *Dread Sir, the prince of light* from 1678 and the 1681 birthday ode *Up, shepherds, up* (Bodleian MS Mus.c.26, fol. 121). In a structure built up from accretions of small pieces, length helps create a sense of arrival; but by the early 1680s, Blow had come to realize that if the level of stylistic contrast and the scale of individual units and sections increased, then simply expanding a verse section did not always achieve the required effect.

---

17   For doubts about the date of this ode see McGuinness, *English Court Odes*, p. 49, n. 21.
18   He also achieves this aim in the anthem *Out of the deep* in the short bass solo 'I look for the Lord' possibly composed a year or two earlier.

The crucial issue was large scale context, and the 1679 ode *Great Janus, though the festival be thine* was a turning point for Blow in this respect, as in so many others. The last verse, for tenor, is marked 'soft and slow'. After the vigour and rich scoring of almost all the earlier material, one expects a return to the predominant vein, which comes in the chorus with independent string parts, 'Emperor's name sound loud', not the most elaborate or the longest part of the ode, but an emphatic conclusion nevertheless.

In his first few odes Purcell was inclined to achieve a weighty conclusion through adroit manipulation of contrasts in a quasi-homophonic texture, though much of the energy derives from forcefully independent part-writing. This works handsomely in the clamorous final choruses of *Welcome, Vicegerent* and in the extended conclusion of *Swifter Isis, swifter flow*, which gives the whole of the last verse to the chorus, sandwiching a minor mode setting of 'May no harsher sounds', first in C or ¢ time and then in 3 time, between two more substantial sections in 3 time, the second continuing the minor mode inflections. Here he had perhaps been encouraged by Blow's conclusion to *Great Sir, the joy of all our hearts*, an extended SATB setting in 3i time, brimming with energy and featuring independent string parts and some imitative roulades on 'That you should flourish'. The comparatively simple ending of *From hardy climes*, in which each strain of a binary-form (5 bars + 10 bars) song in 𝄵 time is repeated by SATB chorus, was not pursued in any other court ode by Purcell. Even in late 1683, in *Fly, bold rebellion*, Purcell ended with a fairly short, homophonic chorus, this one achieving its effect through massive SSAATB scoring after an *ssaatbb* verse of extraordinary complexity. Most of his later odes, however, combine the methods Blow had used in *Dread Sir, the prince of light* and *Great Janus, though the festival be thine*, the mixture of polyphonic expansion and homophony being applied usually not to the continuation of a verse, but to a fully independent choral section.

In *The summer's absence* Purcell set the eight-line final verse as a chorus in one section, 'Britannia shall now her large empire bestride'. The first line is spread over twelve bars of sturdy imitation, lines two to four receiving more homophonic treatment with no repetition, and ending with a close into the relative minor. Imitation returns for the fifth line, which lasts eleven bars; and the homophonic treatment of lines six to eight ends with another close into the relative minor. But the last two lines are reworked to close in the tonic, and the chorus ends with a re-setting of the last line, the lower voices elaborating subdominant inflections around the inverted tonic pedal in the sopranos.

Few of Blow's choruses reach this scale, though in this and most other respects he surpassed himself in the 1684 ode *My trembling song awake* (British Library Add. MS 33,287, fol. 118). Many of the verses and choruses follow in the elaborately imitative style of the opening lines. The chorus 'Night and day for ever sing' is much the best ending he had written thus far and, perhaps significantly, it draws heavily on the methods he was already using to great effect in his verse anthems.[19]

Such complex imitation, with more than one piece of text being presented simultaneously, is rare in Blow's odes, and this instance may have been inspired by the example Purcell had set a few months earlier in the opening *aatbb* verse of *Fly, bold rebellion*. This in turn is one of many examples of Purcell's basing a piece drawn directly on material from an earlier ode by Blow; Purcell's debt to his teacher is clearly seen in this, much the finest of his early court odes, which contains more such relationships than any other:[20] compare the second section of the opening symphony with *Dread Sir, Father Janus*; 'But heaven has now dispelled those fears' with 'This message we bring' from Blow's *Dread Sir, the prince of light*; and 'Rivers from their channels turned' with 'Not debauched with traitorous combinations' from *Dread Sir, Father Janus*.[21]

Blow followed the opening symphony of his 1682 ode *Arise, great monarch* (Barber Institute MS 5001, fol. 32) with a vigorous *satb* verse and chorus (Ex. 8.7). Purcell's borrowing of material extends to having a contrasted statement in the dominant (bars 5–7 of Ex. 8.8), but he produces a much more powerful effect by tying parts of text to an economical range of distinct motifs. Every note in this setting of the first line comes from one of the two points x and y – antecedent and consequent phrases which could readily be given to one voice. But splitting them between tenor and bass leads to increasingly complex imitation, with textually apt emphasis on 'be gone!' at the close in the dominant. Elaborate polyphony is combined with forceful harmonic progression, in which tension accumulated through oscillations from the tonic and dominant to subdominant is resolved, locally at least, by the tonicization of the dominant:

$$I - V - I - IV(ii) - V - II$$
$$|$$
$$I - V - I$$

bars   5   8   10   12 13 14

---

[19]   See McGuinness, *English Court Odes*, pp. 90–1, which includes an extract.
[20]   Cf. Westrup, *Purcell*, p. 175.
[21]   The relevant sections of the symphonies are printed in full in McGuinness, *English Court Odes*, pp. 95–7.

Ex. 8.7   Blow, *Arise, great monarch*

Ex. 8.8   Purcell, *Fly, bold rebellion*

Characteristically for Purcell, imitation spans the boundaries articulated by these harmonic changes. This verse encapsulates many of the reasons for Purcell's peerless success in the court ode. The text-sensitive, dramatic flamboyance of the material is sustained and intensified by the extraordinary cogency of the counterpoint, a superlative instance of direct communication – a prerequisite of the ode – being achieved through high art.

The range of Purcell's formal and stylistic types far exceeds Blow's; individual sections tend to be longer, largely because of the former's skill with various kinds of repetition. The structure of *Fly, bold rebellion* impeccably heightens contrasts within and between units and creates an inexorable progression throughout the ode: the third unit, for example, begins with an admonishing bass recitative, 'If then we've found'; the grace of the following tenor air and ritornello 'But kings like the sun' is capped by the extraordinary delicacy of the trio and ritornello 'But heaven has now dispelled those fears'; the call to the 'disloyal crowd' to 'change your notes' does just that with a turn to the minor mode and false relations, though this is but a temporary twist to the prevailing sense of benign disposition, which wins through with the concluding dance-like chorus 'But with heart and with voice'. There is then a new beginning, articulated by the change of tempo, metre and style for the ground bass alto solo 'Be welcome then, great sir', the first item in the last unit.

For the rest of Purcell's life, influences flowed both ways between him and Blow. But with the court ode Purcell had, by 1683, established a decisive lead in stylistic and technical innovation. Blow remained, however, a curious and ingenious solver of the challenges which the ode presented. In *How does the new born infant year rejoice* (British Library Add. MS 33,287, fol. 63) of 1685, he dispatches quickly 'Nay everything great monarch' by writing a rondeau in ¢ time, with the refrain setting a different portion of text except at its last appearance, where the opening lines return. The crude word setting would not have appealed to Purcell, but the same structural concept, with similar melodic outline, surfaces, albeit in triple time, in 'Sound a parley' from *King Arthur*.

In the 1687 new year ode *Is it a dream?* (Royal College of Music MS 1097, fol. 151) Blow wrote another running quaver, ground bass piece – an alto solo with a ritornello for four-part strings, a short bass solo, an *ab* duet and a repetition of the ritornello. The vocal invention is unremarkable, but the idea of a one-bar ground which refuses to close (Ex. 8.9) would have attracted Purcell's interest. This particular feature might have been inspired by 'Muses bring your roses' in Purcell's elegy for John Playford, *Gentle shepherds* (Z 464), or the influence might have been the other way round. But there can be little doubt that Purcell had Blow's piece in mind when, later in the year, he wrote the superlative duet 'Let Caesar and Urania live' for *Sound the trumpet*, in the same key. Purcell had less need to vary his resources to attain length. The vocal part is one of Purcell's typical elaborate binary structures, but the figuration is similar to Blow's; in the ritornello Purcell pursues further melodic variations drawn extensively from the same appoggiatura figures

Ex. 8.9   Blow, *Is it a dream?*

Be- hold,   the   glo- ries of a   migh -ty throne,   be - hold the   glo____

which dominate Blow's ritornello. Now it was the teacher's turn to be inspired by the pupil, and in the 1688 ode *Ye sons of Phoebus* (British Library Add. MS 33,287, fol. 209v), the only one produced in that tumultuous year, he set 'All our songs do claim Caesar' as an *ab* duet over a free ostinato, with vocal figuration plainly indebted to Purcell's duet.

As a last example of Blow offering Purcell an idea which the younger man realized more successfully, we can return to *Is it a dream?* The final chorus has extensive imitations between chorus and strings, using the same figuration and progressions, albeit in D minor rather than major, as Purcell used between groupings of two trumpets and drums, and four-part strings in the opening symphony of *Hail, bright Cecilia.* Purcell produced an extraordinarily subtle, polyphonic use of a basically homophonic idea.

Without Purcell's achievement, the English court ode would be nothing more than a curious backwater, Handel's birthday ode for Queen Anne, *Eternal source of light divine*, notwithstanding. Restoration composers had to invent what was practically a new genre and, while there is no reason to believe Purcell could not have done it from scratch, the music would be inconceivable without the stimulus offered by Blow's technically imaginative search for new methods and styles.

9

Continuity and tempo in Purcell's vocal works

A. MARGARET LAURIE

Works in more than one movement form a large portion of Purcell's vocal output. Over a third of his songs, for example, are cast in more than one section. These different sections vary in thematic material and often in metre and colour, but they are not treated as separate entities; rather Purcell tends to link them together by indicating in a variety of different ways that successive movements should follow one another with little or no break.

The key-notes of two movements are frequently joined by basso continuo runs. These links vary from a single note to a whole bar (or occasionally more) of running quavers. They occur between movements with the same key-note, as, for instance, between 'Pursue thy conquest' and 'To the hills' in Act 1 of *Dido and Aeneas* (in C major) and between the first two sections of 'Let the dreadful engines' in *Don Quixote*, Part I (F major – F minor) but more typically they connect movements in different keys:

Ex. 9.1.   'When a cruel long winter' – 'Hail! great parent' (*The Fairy Queen*, Act 4)

Another fairly common device is to end a movement within a bar. Nearly half of the duple-time movements in *Dido and Aeneas* end thus, two of them finishing on the last beat, the others on the third:

Ex. 9.2.   'See, see, your royal guest appears' (Act 1)

And I'll de-fy   The fee___ ble   stroke   of de-stin-y.

The placing of the time signature of a new movement is also often critical in reducing gaps.[1] Sometimes the new time signature is placed in the middle of a bar:

Ex. 9.3 'From silent shades' (*Bess of Bedlam*, Z 370)

In the majority of such cases, the two parts make up a complete bar in the first tempo, as in Ex. 9.3, though imperfect matching also occurs. More frequently when the new movement starts with an upbeat, the new time signature is placed at the beginning of the first full bar of the new movement so that the upbeat appears in the old tempo:

Ex. 9.4 'Ah, cruel nymph' (Z 352)

Alternatively, the new time signature may be placed before the final strong beat of the previous movement:

Ex. 9.5 'Amidst the shades' (Z 355)

This placing occurs most frequently when the second movement starts in the middle of a bar or at least with an upbeat but is not confined to that context. Sometimes Purcell inserts the time signature of a fast triple movement at the beginning of the last whole bar of a preceding recitative or arioso for purely dramatic effect. A striking instance occurs in Act 1 of *Dido and Aeneas* where the last note of Dido's recitative 'Whence could so much virtue' (in which she admits her love for Aeneas) is written in the triple time of the following

---

[1]   Most of the examples cited in this essay are drawn from autographs, good copies or works whose publication Purcell supervised. The main exception is *Dido and Aeneas*. But the earliest source of the opera (copied after 1760) retains enough seventeenth-century notational features to instil confidence that the time signatures are very likely to be Purcell's originals.

duet, 'Fear no danger', so that this virtually interrupts her, demonstrating Belinda's incomprehension of, and perhaps impatience with, the political considerations that cause Dido's tormenting indecision:

Ex. 9.6

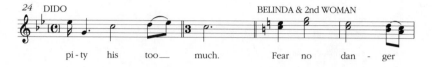

Dido and Aeneas is perhaps the work in which continuity is maintained most consistently, though many of the anthems are also practically seamless. Most of the fast triple movements in Dido and Aeneas end with bar-long notes, but these are of sufficiently short duration not to cause any appreciable break in the music. It is noteworthy, however, that only one internal duple-time movement – 'Oft she visits' in Act 2, scene 2 – ends with an unadorned semibreve; this seems to be a deliberate break to mark the end of a period of repose, albeit uneasy, before catastrophe strikes. In the only other two places in which the voices end with a semibreve ('Pursue thy conquest' in Act 1 and 'Great minds' in Act 3, scene 2) the momentum is kept up by continuo runs. Admittedly the repeat of the first section of the Witches' Dance in Act 3, scene 1 ends with a semibreve also, but this is a character piece in which jerky movement is interspersed with long notes anyway, and the semibreve is there-fore integrated into the texture. Thus, apart from one dramatically significant exception, every scene in Dido and Aeneas is virtually continuous. This con-tinuity is obtained by a combination of all the methods described above coupled with a careful control of tonality. Changes of key are nearly always achieved either by modulation during the course of a movement or by continuo runs linking the two key-notes. Both methods are illustrated in the modulation from C major to E minor and back for 'Cupid only' in Act 1. This is approached by a modulation from C major through G major to E minor in the previous recitative, and is quitted by a modulation through A minor to G major in the following one. The cadence in G major is followed by a continuo run back to C for 'Pursue thy conquest, love'. The only exception to this in the whole work is the abrupt change in Act 2, scene 2 from the D major of 'Haste, haste to town' to the A minor of 'Stay, prince, and hear' in which the Spirit detains Aeneas and commands him to leave. This is clearly designed to underline the shock of the Spirit's appearance, and the feeling of interruption is enhanced by the fact that the previous chorus ends only on the third beat of the bar. Modulation in the course of a movement as a means of maintaining continuity, though not unique to *Dido and Aeneas*, is fairly rare elsewhere in Purcell's work, but his key schemes are always carefully calculated to proceed logically through a succession of keys related to both tonic major and minor.

Many of the movements within the same scene in Purcell's first two semi-operas, *Dioclesian* and *King Arthur*, are also connected – the Sacrifice Scene in the latter, for instance, is continuous – but continuity is not as consistently maintained as in *Dido and Aeneas*; semibreve endings are rather more frequent and do not always seem to be dramatically significant, though, for instance, the climactic high semibreve on 'Drink' in the otherwise conjunct Bacchanals' scene in the masque in *Dioclesian* certainly is. The proportion of unlinked to linked movements in the more masque-like musical scenes in *The Fairy Queen* is considerably higher for, although the music in Acts 1 and 4 is still mainly connected, that in the other three acts is far less so. Although there are no joins in the late works *Timon of Athens* and *Bonduca* (both 1695), there is still a considerable degree of written-in continuity in the last semi-opera, *The Indian Queen*. A similar pattern is observable in the songs and odes; internal endings as long as a semibreve in slow time are rare in earlier works and a majority of movements are deliberately joined, but linkage becomes less prevalent in later works, though it still occurs in the majority of transitions until about 1692 and is never entirely abandoned.

Another possible contributor to continuity is the maintenance of a common pulse throughout a whole work, or considerable part of it. This had been the norm up to the end of the Renaissance period, but by Purcell's time the traditional system was breaking down. It is clear from the discussions of tempo in late seventeenth-century instruction books, brief though they are, that time signatures at this period still carried tempo implications, but little is said about the relationships between different signatures in the same work, so it is difficult to assess to what extent they were still treated as proportions. I believe that the traditional relationships were still accepted, albeit in a somewhat modified, more flexible and not always consistent way. Direct evidence for this is, however, inevitably slight, since for the most part it cannot be notated.

Simpson's *A Compendium of Practical Musick* (1667) contains rather more thorough discussions of time signatures than later English seventeenth-century instruction books (though these draw on Simpson to some extent). In discussing diminution he says:

> Another sign of Diminution is the turning of the Sign of the Mood backward thus ꝰ (being still in use) which requires each Note to be play'd or

sung twice so quick as when it stands the usual way. Also a dash or a stroke through the sign of the Mood thus ₵ is properly a sign of Diminution; though many dash it so without any such Intention. (p. 35)

This reflects the traditional explanation of duple time signatures but acknowledges that the tradition was decaying. The first five editions of Playford's *Introduction to the Skill of Musick* (1654–70) give only ₵ as a time signature for duple time but the sixth edition (1672) adds 'Note, *That when this* Common Mood *is reversed thus* ᗡ *it is to Signifie that the* Time . . . *is . . . as swift again as the usual Measure*'.[2] These instructions were retained until the twelfth edition (1694), 'corrected and amended by Mr Henry Purcell',[3] where the whole discussion of duple time is newly written:

> First I shall speak of *Common-Time*, which may be reckon'd three several sorts; the first and slowest of all is marked thus: C 'Tis measured by a *Semibreve*, which you must divide into four equal Parts, telling *one, two three, four*, distinctly, putting your Hand or Foot down when you tell *one*, and taking it up when you tell *three* . . . Stand by a large Chamber-Clock, and beat your Hand or Foot (as I have before observed) to the slow Motions of the Pendulum . . . The second sort of *Common-Time* is a little faster, which is known by the *Mood*, having a stroak drawn through it, thus ₵. The third sort of *Common-Time* is quickest of all, and then the *Mood* is retorted thus ᗡ; you may well tell *one, two, three, four* in a Bar, almost as fast as the regular Motions of a Watch. The *French Mark* for this retorted *Time*, is a large Figure of 2. (p. 26)

This clearly owes much to Simpson's instructions on beating:

> I would have you pronounce these words (*One, Two, Three, Four*) in an equal length, as you would (leisurely) read them: Then fancy these four words to be four *Crotchets* . . . Some speak of having recourse to the Motion of a lively pulse for the Measure of *Crotchets*; or to the little Minutes of a steddy going Watch for *Quavers* by which to compute the length of other Notes; but this which I have delivered, will (I think) be most useful to you. (p. 18)

It may also be indebted to a similar passage in Thomas Mace, *Musick's Monument* (1676), p. 78, which enjoins the player to put 'the *Foot down and up, Equally* . . . like unto the *Ballance of a good Clock*'.

---

[2] Quoted in Robert Donington, *The Interpretation of Early Music* (London, 1963), p. 344.
[3] According to the title-page, though the next edition (1697) suggests that Purcell was only responsible for rewriting the third section on the art of descant. See Ellen T. Boal, 'Purcell's Clock Tempos and the Fantasias', *Journal of the Viola da Gamba Society of America* 20 (1983), 24.

Ellen TeSelle Boal demonstrates that the 1694 Playford instructions give speeds of ♩ = M.M.120 and ♩ = M.M.240 for 𝐂 and 𝄴 respectively.[4] She then goes on to suggest ♩ = M.M.120 as the basic tempo for 𝐂 or 𝄵 in both the fantazias and trio sonatas and that all the other tempos in the latter can be proportionally derived from it. This is an interesting exercise, but the concept cannot be applied to the rest of Purcell's music, for the variety of rhythmic and harmonic patterns to be found in it require a far greater range of tempos. Moreover ♩ = M.M.240 is too fast to be feasible for any of Purcell's vocal movements with the time-signature 𝄴 (or 2), while ♩ = M.M.120 also seems too fast to be the slowest speed suggested and does not accord with other descriptions of 𝐂 as signifying 'very slow' or 'leisurely'. Indeed, although this speed is possible for the movements which Boal considers, it would not suit most of Purcell's movements in 𝐂; the recitatives, in particular, need to be taken considerably more slowly. Developments in the technology of clock and watch-making in the 1670s had made the accurate measurement of intervals as small as quarter of a second possible for the first time,[5] and fascination with time-keeping may have led Purcell (or whoever wrote the 1694 adaptation of Playford's *Introduction*) to graft clock timings onto the earlier instructions with not altogether tenable results. Half of both speeds would actually be closer to contemporary practice, though somewhat slow. Actually, it seems unlikely that any of the instruction books intended to imply that the same tempo should be adopted in all works with the same time signature; rather they appear to be suggesting a starting point for beginners. Boal indeed admits that 'most of the treatises examined in this study suggest that tempos varied according to the taste of the performer' (p. 199). It would seem, however, that a more or less proportional relationship between the slowest and fastest tempos, though no longer explicit in the 1694 edition of Playford's *Introduction*, was nonetheless still implied. The 'Instructions for Beginners' added to Purcell's *A Choice Collection of Lessons for the Harpsichord or Spinnet* in the 1699 edition contain no such implication, for they simply describe the three time signatures, 𝐂, 𝄵, 𝄴 , as 'ye first is a very slow movement, ye next a little faster, and ye last a brisk & airry time',[6] but as late as 1707 Dean, in his *Complete Tutor for the Violin*, was still saying: 𝐂, 'Very solid or slow movement. 𝄵: Quicker. 𝄴 or 𝟐 as quick again as the first',[7]

4 'Timepieces, Time and Musical Tempo before 1700', Ph.D. thesis, Washington University (1983), p. 119.
5 Boal, 'Timepieces', p. 117.
6 Donington, *The Interpretation of Early Music*, p. 344.
7 *Ibid.*, p. 345.

showing that the principle of proportionality was to some degree still current at the beginning of the eighteenth century.

Purcell's usage of the time signatures $\mathbf{C}$ and $\mathbf{\math-C}$ is not entirely consistent; moreover it changed somewhat in later years. In his earliest vocal works, he uses $\mathbf{C}$ almost entirely for recitative and arioso sections (including declamatory ensembles in anthems) and the slow movements of symphonies, though gradually he came to use it also for more lyrical movements in slow tempos, including some of the grounds on running quaver figures which feature prominently in the odes. In *The Yorkshire Feast Song* (early 1690) $\mathbf{C}$ is used for a greater variety of movements, signifying at least two different moderately fast tempos (while $\mathbf{\mathbb{C}}$ is not used at all) and from then on its use overlaps with that of $\mathbf{\mathbb{C}}$.

Throughout Purcell's career, however, $\mathbf{\mathbb{C}}$ was his most usual signature for duple time, implying a considerable range of tempos. Occasionally it is used for declamatory movements of a vigorous nature, such as 'This poet sings' at the beginning of *Anacreon's defeat* (Z 423) (1687), presumably to indicate that the tempo should be somewhat faster than is normal for recitative. Not surprisingly, it also overlaps with 2 at the upper end of the spectrum, especially in later works. Indeed, there is a small group of movements with the time signature $\mathbf{\mathbb{C}}$ which are definitely fast 2/2 movements; these occur mainly in dramatic music and their time signature usually seems to have been chosen to differentiate their speed from those of nearby movements in 2. Nonetheless, for the most part is $\mathbf{\mathbb{C}}$ used for movements of medium speed with four pulses in a bar.

The relationship between $\mathbf{C}$ and $\mathbf{\mathbb{C}}$ when both are used in the same work is variable. Occasionally Purcell seems to treat them as equivalent, or to change his mind about which he wishes to use. In the song, 'Soft notes' (Z 510) (*c.* 1683), for instance, the opening section of the instrumental prelude has the time signature $\mathbf{\mathbb{C}}$ but the first vocal movement (an arioso) $\mathbf{C}$. Both start, however, with the same phrase, and it seems likely that they were intended to be in the same tempo. The arioso is followed by a lyrical movement with the time signature $\mathbf{\mathbb{C}}$ which is clearly faster; perhaps when Purcell realized that he needed the time signature $\mathbf{\mathbb{C}}$ for the faster section, he altered that of the arioso but forgot about the opening. For the most part, however, where these two time signatures are used together, $\mathbf{\mathbb{C}}$ does seem to signify a faster tempo than $\mathbf{C}$.

When they are directly juxtaposed, $\mathbf{\mathbb{C}}$ may sometimes be double the speed of $\mathbf{C}$. The melancholy opening recitative of 'Gentle shepherds' (Z 464) (1687), for example, has a roulade in dotted semiquavers and demisemiquavers and is therefore very slow; doubling the speed for the following ground in ₵ gives a comfortable speed suited to its mood which relates its dotted quaver roulades back to that of the opening. In *Anacreon's Defeat* the final declamatory passage in C may well be quarter the speed of the preceding very fast 2 and half of the vigorous opening section in ₵. An examination of a wider range of music has demonstrated, however, that this relationship is not found as frequently as I suggested in the preface to the Purcell Society Edition of the solo songs (*The Works of Henry Purcell*, vol. XXV).

In the music for Act 1 of *The Fairy Queen*, the ₵ for 'Enough, enough' immediately following the chorus version of 'Trip it, trip it' (in C) must indicate a change of tempo (presumably a speeding up), since otherwise it would not have been inserted at all. The chorus, 'About him go' (which follows after a contrasting 3/4 movement) has similar rhythms to 'Trip it, trip it' and therefore might be expected to be in the same tempo, but it has the time signature ₵ not C. This probably indicates that it should be taken at the faster tempo of 'Enough, enough'. Given the character of the two pieces, only a small increase in speed would be possible, but this would certainly be dramatically effective. Taking ₵ a little faster than C seems indeed, as the instruction books suggest, to be the most common practice; different equivalences with intervening triple movements can sometimes give them relative speeds of 3 : 2 or 4 : 3.

Unfortunately, as a comparison of autograph with secondary sources shows, most printers and some copyists changed Purcell's C's into ₵'s, though a few C's appear in song books from 1687 onwards. This change can be confusing since it seems to have eliminated distinctions which Purcell intended. For instance, in *Bess of Bedlam* (Z 370) (*c.* 1683), ₵ is used both for the recurring recitative sections and for 'I'll lay me down and die', which clearly should be much faster since it moves mainly in crotchets. The time signature ₵ is repeated, apparently superfluously, at the beginning of the recitative after 'I'll lay me down'. This is unlikely to have occurred unless there really was a change of time signature at this point in Purcell's score. It seems probable that the recitative sections originally bore the time signature C, as in contemporaneous works of this kind which survive in autograph. In *New Songs in the Third Part of . . . Don Quixote* the first and third sections of 'From rosy bow'rs' have the time signature C, while the final section, obviously quicker, has the signature ₵. In *Orpheus Britannicus*, Book I, however, all three sections have the time signature ₵, but the editor, very unusually, has added *Slow* to the third section and *Quick* to the last to retain the distinction which Purcell clearly intended.

Purcell's movements with the time signature 𝄵 are always fast, with a basic harmonic rhythm of two minims in a bar. Although 2 is said to be equivalent to it in the 1694 edition of Playford's *Introduction*, the two time signatures do not always have the same implications for tempo in Purcell's music. Georg Muffat, in the preface to *Florilegium I* (1695) says: 'The measure marked thus 2 [or] ¢ being given in two beats, it is clear that in general it goes as fast again, as this C which is given in four. It is however understood that this measure 2 ought to go very slow in Overtures, Preludes and Symphonies.'[8] The use of the time signature 2 in Purcell's early music is mainly for those introductory symphonies to anthems and odes which have predominantly dotted crotchet – quaver rhythms. It seems that he is adopting continental practice here and that the speed is very moderate (probably in the range ♩ = M.M.50–60). This time signature is also used for a few vocal movements of a similar character and probably similar speed. The signatures 2 and 𝄵 twice appear consecutively in the 1680 *Welcome Song* obviously indicating different tempos; in both instances 𝄵 is the quicker of the two. In the only other work in which these two time signatures both appear (though not juxtaposed), however – the 1684 *Welcome Song* – they do seem to represent very similar, possibly identical, tempos. Purcell's last use of 𝄵 occurs in works dating from early 1685.[9] Thereafter it *is* replaced by 2 which usually signifies a fast movement (in the range ♩ = M.M.72–90), though the 'slow 2' persists, still mainly used for opening sections of the French overture type and dances of similar character such as the Dance for the Followers of Night in *The Fairy Queen*. Perhaps the most remarkable use of this type of movement is for the Sorceress's declamations in Act 2, scene 1 of *Dido and Aeneas*. Here the use of the time signature 2 instead of the normal C indicates that these should be performed appreciably faster than the other declamatory sections in the work with an underlying pulse of two instead of four, imparting to these movements a sense of urgency and implacability. In later works, some fairly moderately paced movements not in the French overture mould, such as 'I am come' and 'See my many coloured fields' in *The Fairy Queen*, bear the time signature 2; in these cases it seems to relate to pulse rather than speed.

When C and 𝄵 (or 2) occur together, a doubling of speed can give comfortable tempos:

---

[8] *Ibid.*, p. 346.
[9] The only later appearance of 𝄵 is in Bodleian MS Mus.c.26, a copy of the 1692 *Ode on St Cecilia's Day*, where it is used for the canzona section of the opening symphony. Although the rest of this manuscript is in Purcell's hand, this movement is not, and the time signature may be inauthentic. It certainly seems inappropriate as this movement is definitely in 4/4, not 2/2.

Ex. 9.7 'Behold the man' (*The Richmond Heiress*)

Doubling of speed may also be implied when ₵ and 𝄵 (or 2) are used together, but often some less extreme relationship will prove to be more tenable.

Purcell's *Choice Collection of Lessons* gives a fairly typical description of triple time:

> Triple time consists of either three or six Crotchets in a barr, and is to be known by this 3/2, this 3i, this 3 or this 6/4 marke, to the first there is three Minims in a barr, and is commonly play'd very slow, the second has three Crotchets in a barr, and they are to be play'd slow, the third has ye same as ye former but is play'd faster, ye last has six Crotchets in a barr & is Commonly to brisk tunes as Jiggs and Paspys [Passepieds].[10]

These instructions, however, are not entirely endorsed by contemporary practice; for example, 3/2 was not always a slow tempo. Alexander Malcolm, in his *Treatise of Musick* (Edinburgh, 1721), more accurately reflects Restoration practice when he says 'the triple 3/2 is ordinarily *adagio*, sometimes *vivace*' (p. 402). There are two main contexts in Purcell's works in which 3/2 movements are fast: for hornpipes, which were written indiscriminately in 3/2 or 3/4 and are clearly very vigorous dances; and in sacred music. Most of the triple-time movements in the early anthems are in 3/2 time, a practice which Purcell continued until about 1685, though 3/4 becomes steadily more common. This practice also spills over occasionally into the early welcome songs. Many of these movements are clearly intended to be quite fast and lively. Nonetheless, when occurring in multi-sectional works with triple-time movements with other signatures, the 3/2 movements are normally the slowest, though *andante* would usually be a better description than *adagio*, for such movements often make much of gentle dotted crotchet – quaver figures and cannot be taken too slowly if they are to flow.

For most of Purcell's career, however, 3/4 was his standard triple time, for which he normally used the time signature 3. Although the instructions quoted above state that 3i is slower than 3, these two time signatures are treated as interchangeable in the 1694 edition of Playford's *Introduction*, and Purcell does not seem to have made any distinction between them. The only appearance in an autograph of 3i as a time signature for 3/4 is in the very

---

[10] p. 351.

early anthem, *My beloved spake.*[11] Here he clearly regards it as equivalent to 3, for the first of the two statements of 'My beloved is mine' has the signature 3, the second 3i. The printed song-books regularly replaced 3 by 3i, and many copyists followed suit. Simpson states 'in all *Tripla's* the Notes are sung or play'd much quicker than they are in Common Time' (p. 34), and there is no doubt that, in general, Purcell's movements in 3 are to be taken fast unless specifically designated *Slow*.

The 1694 edition of Playford's *Introduction* says 'Sometimes you will meet with three *Quavers* in a Bar, which is marked as the *Crotchets,* only Sung as fast again' (p. 27). Purcell uses 3/8 only rarely – there are less than twenty such movements in his entire output – and then always as a section in a larger work. Initially it was an instrumental tempo, used in three of the trio sonatas, but it appears in vocal works from *Dido and Aeneas* onwards. It is always the fastest triple-time movement in a work. In the Cave Scene in *Dido and Aeneas*, for instance, the 'Ho, ho, ho' choruses are in 3/8 to indicate that they are even faster than the already brisk 'Harm's our delight'. There is general agreement that movements in compound time are also fast.

Although for the most part Purcell was content to let his time signatures and the general character of his music convey to his performers the tempos he wanted, he did make some use of time words to increase the available options and to clarify his intentions, probably rather more than is now apparent, since a comparison of autograph and printed sources shows that the latter tend to omit such indications. He explained the meaning of current Italian time words in the preface to his *Sonnata's of Three Parts* (1683) and used them in both sets of trio sonatas and in a few other overtures and symphonies. In vocal works, and indeed in several instrumental works as well, however, he kept to a more limited range of English terms: mainly *Quick, Brisk* (or *Brisk time*) and *Slow* (or *Very Slow*). Boal remarks that in instrumental works 'Purcell appears to have used verbal indications to enhance or supplement but not intensify, the tempo movement suggested by the note values or time signatures'.[12] In many of the fantazias, for instance, the predominant note values in the sections marked *Slow* are minims and crotchets, while those in the sections marked *Brisk* or *Quick* are crotchets and quavers, or even semiquavers; the effect is of a doubling of speed, but the minim beat remains the same. This 'superfluous' use of time words is also found in some overtures and occurs occasionally in vocal movements as well; for instance, 'In vain the am'rous flute' in the *Ode on St Cecilia's Day* (1692) does not

[11]   British Library Add. MS 30,932.   [12]   Boal, 'Timepieces', p. 154.

really need to be marked *Very slow* since it is written in 3/2. But for the most part time words in vocal movements are used to make a genuine distinction in tempo between sections or movements with the same time signature.

There seems to be little, if any, difference between *Quick* and *Brisk*. Both are used mainly in duple time, more often than not to indicate a contrast with a section marked *Slow*. Quite often they seem to imply a return to the tempo of an unmarked section preceding a *Slow* one, as in 'Sing all ye muses' (*Don Quixote*, Part I). *Quick* is also used by itself to indicate a simple increase of speed: *Brisk* is also used in this way at least once: at 'All living things' in 'While thus we bow' in *The Indian Queen*.

Slow is used more frequently than either *Quick* or *Brisk*, both for passages within a movement and for whole movements, though even the latter are to be found within the context of a larger work. Whole movements marked *Slow* or *Very Slow* are nearly always in triple time. As we have seen, movements with a 3 time signature were normally fast and, although 3/2 was available for indicating slow triple movements, even its interpretation was somewhat ambiguous. Purcell seems quite often to have preferred a movement in 3 marked *Slow* instead of a 3/2 one. When he wished to distinguish between the tempos of two movements in 3, he used *Slow* or *Very Slow* over the slower one, even if it comes first. The only time *Quick* is used in a triple movement is in the middle of 'She shall be brought' (at 'With joy and gladness') in *My heart is inditing* to indicate an increase of tempo in an already quite fast movement.

Slow, when applied to triple-time movements, is nearly always relative, that is, it is used for sections within a larger structure which also has sections with the same time signature which are not slow. Since triple-time movements can be very fast, some movements marked *Slow* may not be particularly slow in absolute terms, merely slower than, possibly half the speed of, others with the same time signature in the same work. Thus, for instance, 'Ah Belinda' in Act 1 of *Dido and Aeneas* is marked *Slow* but cannot be taken much slower than ♩ = M.M.84 if the agitated phrases on 'press'd with torment' are to be effective. It is, however, definitely slow in relation to the next movement with this time signature – 'When monarchs unite' – whose crotchet syllabification seems to require one-in-a-bar treatment. In general, time indications in Purcell usually signify a departure from an expected norm or a cancellation, though sometimes they seem, as in the fantazias, merely to emphasize a change of tempo already written in.

Although Purcell did sometimes juxtapose two duple-time and, more rarely, two triple-time movements in different tempos, for the most part his works alternate between duple and triple sections. He was particularly apt to end a predominantly declamatory work with a more lyrical triple movement, especially in early songs such as 'What hope for us remains' (Z 472) (1678) and 'Urge me no more' (Z 426) (c. 1683). Simpson comments in his *A Compendium of Practical Musick* (1667): 'you may sometimes meet with Figures set thus 3/2 called *Sesquialtera* proportion, which signifies a *Tripla* Measure of three Notes to two such like notes of the Common Time' (p. 34). The most commonly used triple time was then 3/2, so it would seem that the traditional *sesquialtera* relationship of 'three-in-the-time-of-two' between the main duple and triple times was still recognized. Although none of the other Restoration instruction books comments upon the relationship between duple and triple tempos beyond saying that triple movements were normally faster than duple ones, it seems likely that the well entrenched *sesquialtera* relationship was to some degree still in use during Purcell's working life and was applied to 3 when this became the usual triple time signature. Certainly it gives comfortable tempos for many of the transitions between Purcell's most frequently used time signatures ¢ and 3 and quite often for those between C and 3/2 (or 'Slow 3'), for example between the second and third sections of 'I came, I saw' (Z 375) and the last two of 'Fly swift ye hours' (Z 369).

Some joins between movements suggest other possibilities. The following example from 'Sing all ye muses' in *Don Quixote*, Part I, for instance, almost certainly implies a constant speed for the crotchet throughout both the 3i and the 2 sections of this duet (with the possible exception of the *Brisk time* episode), and this seems often to be the case when 2 (or 𝄵) and 3 are juxtaposed:

Ex. 9.8

(glo)_____ ry pur - su - ing.

On the other hand, the following passage from 'In vain 'gainst love' in *Henry the Second* suggests that the speed should be doubled in the triple section, for here a quaver in the old tempo is equivalent to a crotchet in the new:

Ex. 9.9

sense I__ thought. Yet love, love, love

Doubling the speed provides a comfortable relationship between many slow ₵ sections, especially declamatory ones, and their lyrical 3 movements, and can also be feasible between moderate ₵ movements and fast triple ones, particularly those of the one-in-a-bar type. It is, however, a fairly extreme relationship and there are some places where the implied doubling of speed is impractical, although a quaver upbeat in the old tempo seems equivalent to a crotchet in the new. The transition to 'When monarchs unite' in *Dido and Aeneas*, Act 1, for instance, is written:

Ex. 9.10

It seems likely that Purcell shortened the upbeat on 'When' to indicate that the crotchets of 'When monarchs unite' should be taken even faster than those of the previous movement, rather than at the same speed, as might be expected between 2 and 3. The tempo of the previous movement is, however, too fast to be doubled, but some quickening would be quite feasible. Whether any equivalence of pulse at all was intended in this instance is, of course, conjectural, but *sesquialtera* would give reasonable speeds for both movements, and the quaver in 2 would be the nearest value to a crotchet in 3 which could be notated. In the similar transition (in reverse) in Act 3 from 'Our next motion' (in 3) to 'Destruction's our delight' (in 2) equating whole bars would give acceptable tempos.

There are certainly times when it is not possible to suggest equivalence between two of Purcell's time signatures. Nonetheless, the speeds within a single work do seem quite frequently to fall naturally into simple relationships, and the use of different equivalences between triple-time movements and their duple neighbours can provide a range of related tempos.

In the songs and in many anthems and odes, especially the earlier ones, the maintenance of a common pulse throughout all, or at least several, sections seems feasible, indeed desirable, particularly when individual sections are short. In *Dido and Aeneas* one can relate the tempos throughout each scene, with the exception of Act 1, where the *Quick* on 'Pursue thy conquest, love' sets a new tempo. It also seems possible to a considerable extent in most of the individual scenes or entries of *Dioclesian* and *King Arthur*. In the Frost Scene (Act 3) of *King Arthur*, for instance, by taking 'Great Love' (in 2) at twice the speed of the prelude (in 𝐂) the semiquaver figure on which the prelude is based is performed at the same speed as the very similar quaver phrase on 'I know thee now' in 'Great Love' (further developed by the violins in the latter part of the song) – a reference that may well have been deliberate – and the intervening movements can be related to these. The pattern has to be broken in the final sequence, however, for here the use of 3/2 for 'Sound a parley' presumably indicates that this movement should be taken at a slower tempo than the flanking chorus ''Tis Love that has warmed us' (in 3), but half speed is far too slow. An unmarked speeding up of the tempo also seems necessary at 'To Woden thanks' in the Sacrifice Scene (Act 1). In *The Fairy Queen* (1692), however, where the individual movements are on the whole longer and more independent, the maintenance of a common pulse becomes much more difficult; indeed it cannot be applied too rigidly in the masque of *King Arthur* either. The use of 𝐂 for several movements which clearly have to be given somewhat different, unrelated tempos in *The Yorkshire Feast Song* (1690) and the *Ode on St Cecilia's Day* (1692) may have been an attempt to get away from rigid equivalences to a more flexible system in works where variety was more important than dramatic continuity, but I think that Purcell instinctively retained some feeling for continuity of pulse even in his latest works, certainly in the songs and to some extent in *The Indian Queen*. Thus, although the choice of speed will vary according to taste and circumstance, I would suggest that the possibility of maintaining a common pulse throughout a work (or at least a considerable stretch of it) should be explored as a potent means of enhancing that continuity which Purcell went to considerable pains to build in in a variety of different ways.

10

Poetic metre, musical metre, and the dance in Purcell's songs

KATHERINE T. ROHRER

When Purcell sat down to set a text, he had first to make some basic decisions about the shape of the music he would produce. As he read through the words and as bits of melody or trenchant rhythmic gestures sprang to mind, he must at least subconsciously have begun to ask questions: single-section or multiple-section? strophic or through-composed? declamatory or lyrical style? fast or slow? duple or triple metre? Those who study relations of text and music in Purcell's work all begin with what Burney identified as the composer's 'exquisite expression of the words'.[1] Many aspects of that expressiveness have been examined: the links between meaning in the texts and various choices of key, melodic motifs, word emphasis and repetition; the shaping of the music to enhance some dramatic value in a stage work; the correspondences between phonological features of the text – stress, rhythm and intonation – and musical organization.

This essay attempts to do something more basic: to postulate the means by which Purcell addressed the question of metre and rhythmic design in the earliest stages of composition. I hope to demonstrate that certain types of poetic metres, and especially certain stress features in the opening line or lines of the text, led the composer to choose particular metrical frameworks for his settings. More of these rhythmic outlines than scholars have previously admitted were based on contemporary French dance models. While this exercise is designed to satisfy an innate longing for identification, categorization and predictability, it will more usefully provide a background of typical practice against which exceptions can be effectively contrasted.

CLASSIFICATION OF POETIC METRES

The musical analyst searching for a powerful means of describing metrical aspects of English verse is in something of a bind these days. The old rules of

---

[1] Charles Burney, *A General History of Music*, vol. II, ed. F. Mercer (London, 1935; repr. 1957), vol. II, 393.

classical scansion as adapted to English accentual-syllabic verse are out of favour, for good reason: the 'foot' is an artificial if not meaningless unit; the vocabulary and symbols that served classical quantitative verse are confusing for those unwilling or unable to make the translations from syllable length to syllable stress. More recent formulations based on linguistic attributes indigenous to the English language represent distinct improvements (for example, those of Chatman, Halle and Keyser, Kiparsky, Attridge, and Roberts);[2] each proposes a new analytical system, however, and while each has its advantages for the literary critic, no one of them seems ideal for the study of texts set to music. (One problem is the repeated conscription of musical terms like 'measure', 'beat' and 'offbeat' into the language of prosodic analysis; another is the failure of systems like Attridge's and Roberts's to distinguish significantly between different types of line-openings.) So, rather than adhering to a single theory, I have borrowed terms and concepts from several.

Poetic metres are abstract schemes that prescribe a pattern of alternating stressed and unstressed syllables within the line of verse and the length of the line as counted in syllables (hence the label 'accentual-syllabic' for the organizational principle of English verse lines). Following Halle and Keyser,[3] one can think of the iambic pentameter line (classically described as a line containing five iambic feet, each iamb consisting of an unstressed syllable followed by a stressed one) as a line of ten positions, each normally holding one syllable but exceptionally holding two or none. The odd-numbered positions are 'weak', that is, expected to hold unstressed syllables; the even-numbered positions are 'strong', expected to hold stressed syllables.

Here is an example of an iambic pentameter line in which word stress corresponds perfectly with the predictions of the poetic metre. Each stressed syllable (marked by a preceding raised vertical) falls in a strong position (marked by its number).[4]

2 Seymour Chatman, *A Theory of Meter, Janua Linguarum*, Series Minor, No. 36 (The Hague, 1965); Morris Halle and Samuel J. Keyser, 'Chaucer and the Study of Prosody', *College English* 28 (1966), 187–219; Paul Kiparsky, 'The Rhythmic Structure of English Verse', *Linguistic Inquiry* 8 (1977), 189–247; Derek Attridge, *The Rhythms of English Poetry* (London, 1982); Philip Davies Roberts, *How Poetry Works: The Elements of English Poetry* (Harmondsworth, 1986).

3 'Chaucer and the Study of Prosody'.

4 See the entry on 'Stress' in David Crystal, *A Dictionary of Linguistics and Phonetics*, 2nd edn (Oxford, 1985), pp. 288–9. Stress is the phonological feature that makes some syllables in polysyllabic words, and some syllables or words in connected speech, sound more prominent than others. Audible cues for stress are pitch, duration and loudness; see Dennis Fry, 'Prosodic Phenomena', from *Manual of Phonetics*, ed. B. Malmberg (Amsterdam, 1968), and Dwight M. Bolinger, 'A Theory of Pitch Accent in English', *Word* 14 (1958), 109–49. Stress in polysyllabic words is determined by the lexicon (the dictionary, which reflects contemporary practice); stress in monosyllabic words is determined by word-class (a more detailed version of 'part of speech'). Word-classes have been divided into two

A [|]midst the [|]shades and [|]cool re[|]freshing [|]streams

  2   4   6   8   10

Many poetic lines, however, contain 'mismatches', in which an unstressed syllable appears in a strong position or a stressed syllable in a weak position.[5] In other words, the expected pattern of alternation between stressed and unstressed syllables is upset by the words that flesh out the abstract scheme. There are two types of mismatches. A stressed word or syllable can occur in a weak position, producing a 'weak-position stress', as in position 1 in the following line:

[|]Great [|]minds a[|]gainst them[|]selves con[|]spire

  2   4   6   8

In a 'strong-position unstress', an unstressed syllable or word fills a strong position, as in position 2 of this line:

Were I to [|]choose the [|]greatest [|]bliss

    2   4   6   8

The 10-position iambic line is called 'pentameter' because it contains five feet; Attridge refers to it as a 'five-beat' line and Roberts as a 'five-stress' or 'five-measure' line.[6] I will usually refer to tetrameter lines as 8-position, to trimeter as 6-position, and so forth, but when encoding line lengths will count the actual numbers of syllables (for example, 7.8. for the lines 'Fear no danger to ensue, / The hero loves as well as you').

Once line lengths have been described, four basic arrangements of stressed and unstressed syllables account for the distinctions between poetic metres.

types: in one category, variously called 'content words' (Gimson, *An Introduction to the Pronunciation of English*, 2nd edn (London, 1980)), 'lexical words' (David Crystal and Derek Davy, *Investigating English Style* (Bloomington, 1969)), and 'open word-classes' (Randolph Quirk et al., *A Comprehensive Grammar of the English Language* (London, 1985)), are those words that have semantic content: roughly, nouns, main verbs, adjectives, most adverbs, demonstrative pronouns and determiners, *wh*-interrogatives and exclamations. The second category, 'form words', 'grammatical words', or 'closed word-classes', includes words that indicate grammatical relationships among those of the first category. Closed word-classes include prepositions, conjunctions, auxiliary and primary verbs (*be, make, do*), personal and reflexive pronouns, and most determiners (articles, possessives, etc.). A complete listing of the word-classes that are normally stressed and normally unstressed appears in Elizabeth Couper-Kuhlen, *An Introduction to English Prosody* (London, 1986), pp. 36–7. That these categories for stressed and unstressed monosyllables are largely translatable to the Modern English of Purcell's time is demonstrated in Katherine T. Rohrer, '"The Energy of English Words": A Linguistic Approach to Henry Purcell's Methods of Setting Texts', Ph.D. thesis, Princeton University (1980), pp. 16–30. Some uncertainty is inevitable, however, and the reader may well disagree with some of the stress markings in the texts used in this essay.

5 These are 'labelling mismatches' in the original conception by Kiparsky in 'Rhythmic Structure of English Verse'.

6 Attridge, *Rhythms of English Poetry*, chap. 5; Roberts, *How Poetry Works*, pp. 27–32.

These four types involve different intersections of two features: whether the line opens with a stressed or an unstressed syllable, and whether each stressed syllable alternates with one unstressed syllable or with two. Following Roberts, one can call the alternation of a stressed syllable with an unstressed one a 'duplet' and the alternation of a stressed syllable with two unstressed ones a 'triplet'.[7] The following matrix demonstrates the four resulting patterns; stressed syllables are symbolized by a vertical, unstressed ones by a dot.

	duplets	triplets
unstress-initial	. I . I (iambic)	. . I . . I (anapaestic)
stress-initial	I . I . (trochaic)	I . . I . . (dactylic)

The alternations here shown with one repetition (the minimum necessary to establish a pattern) can of course be expanded to two, three, four or more repetitions. While one could most accurately refer to the first pattern as 'unstress-initial duplet metre', in the interest of brevity I will use the traditional label 'iambic', despite its theoretical baggage.

The fact that Purcell often responded with great originality and unpredictability to his poetic texts has diverted attention from his reliance on standard metrical solutions for the variety of poetic metres he encountered. These solutions, summarized in Table 10.1, are explained below.

The information in Table 10.1 assumes agreement on two issues of musical organization: the difference between lyrical and declamatory style in Purcell's vocal music, and the interpretation and classification of musical metres. Lyrical style is a song or aria style, one in which musical values are favoured over textual ones. It features relatively regular harmonic rhythm, melodic phrase lengths and pace, that is, the rate at which stressed syllables in the text are unfolded in the rhythmic structure of the music. Musical repetition and repetitive structures such as sequence are hallmarks of the lyrical style. Declamatory style, by contrast, is an expressive recitative that focuses attention on the text; musical repetition is avoided, and harmonic rhythm, pace and phrase lengths are distinctly irregular. In Purcell's music especially, declamatory style involves an effort to mirror speech rhythms, which in turn produces a high level of rhythmic variety in the vocal line. Purcell usually notated declamatory style in the slowest duple metre, ¢ (see below). The opening of a section in declamatory style is usually marked by a static tonic note in the bass that after a bar or two rouses itself to descend, often stepwise, to the fifth degree; in the meantime, the melody may have worked through a complete line or two of verse. In a piece

---

[7] Roberts, *How Poetry Works*, p. 19.

in lyrical style, the bass moves promptly, predictably and sometimes imitatively. Ex. 10.1, 'What hope for us remains now he is gone' (Z 472), is an early declamatory style opening; Ex. 10.15a, the beginning of 'Since the toils and the hazards of war's at an end' from *Dioclesian*, integrates obbligato recorders into vocal declamatory style. All other examples in this paper are in the lyrical style, and an imitative bass line can be seen at the opening of 'Since from my dear Astrea's sight', Ex. 10.8b.

As for metres, the twelfth edition of John Playford's *An Introduction to the Skill of Musick* of 1694 ('corrected and amended by Mr. Henry Purcell') describes two types, common time and tripla time. The three sorts of common time, ranging from slowest to fastest, are marked by $\mathbf{C}$, $\mathbf{¢}$ and the backwards $\mathfrak{D}$ or 2 (the 'French mark for this retorted time'). Each is described as having four counts in a bar. The two sorts of tripla time are one in which the minims receive the count, marked 3/2, and a faster one with three crotchets in a bar, marked 3 or 3i.[8]

With some reservation the author (presumably Purcell) groups compound-duple metres – the 6/4 'always used in *Jigs*' as well as 12/8 – with the common time metres, because rising and falling hand motions are equally timed in each. In a practical sense, however, Purcell's compound-duple pieces (usually in 6/4, less often in 6/8) share more rhythmic similarities with the faster triple-metre pieces than with those in duple metre. The difference between a piece notated in 6/4 and another organized entirely in two-bar units of 3i may be principally one of tempo, while two pieces in $\mathbf{¢}$ and 6/4 could never be mistaken for each other. For this reason I have classified compound-duple metres as essentially triple rather than duple.

Among nine different patterns of versification considered in Table 10.1, the first are four types of iambic openings, differentiated by various stress position mismatches in the first four positions of the line.[9]

'Straight' iambic lines (position 1 weak, position 2 strong: . | . |)

The first type admits no mismatches; weak positions 1 and 3 hold unstressed syllables, and strong positions 2 and 4 hold stressed syllables. The following examples demonstrate ten-, eight- and six-position straight iambic lines.

---

[8] See also discussion in chap. 9, above.
[9] For another approach to the links between poetic metres and music, see Franklin B. Zimmerman, 'Sound and Sense in Purcell's "Single Songs"' in *Words to Music*, ed. Vincent Duckles and Franklin B. Zimmerman (Los Angeles, 1967).

When |first I |saw the |bright Au |relia's |eyes . . .
   2   4   6   8   10

When |Strephon |found his |passions |vain . . .
    2   4   6   8

I |sigh'd and |own'd my |love . . .
2   4   6

The occurrence of a mismatch after the fourth position was apparently irrelevant to Purcell, so that a line such as 'The |soft with |tenderness de |coys' qualifies for this group despite its unstressed syllable in strong position 6.

Purcell's metrical choices for straight iambic lines varied with their length, their position (initial or internal) in a sectional musical structure, and the period of his own compositional development. Throughout his career he usually chose to express straight iambic lines of irregularly mixed lengths, like the 10. 10. 6. 6. 10. of 'What hope for us remains now he is gone' (1678) (see Ex. 10.1) or the 10. 6. 8. 8. of ''Tis nature's voice' (from *Hail, bright Cecilia*, 1693) in the declamatory style – at least in initial sections; in internal sections he frequently turned to lyrical style for contrast. The use of declamatory style for ten-syllable lines is predictable from the fact that these lines fall less easily into symmetrical phrases than those of six or eight syllables; as Attridge says, the five-beat line 'strikes the ear as more faithful to the natural rhythm of speech: it is not that five-beat groups are in any way indigenous to English, but that such groups impose themselves less strongly

Ex. 10.1 'What hope remains for us now he is gone', bars 1–5

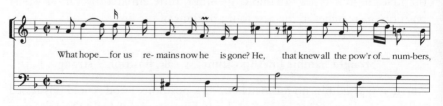

What hope__for us   re- mains now he   is gone? He,   that knew all the pow'r of__ num-bers,

flown, A - las! too__ soon;

212

on the movement of the language'.[10] Declamatory settings of straight ten-syllable iambic lines include the openings of 'From silent shades, and the Elysian groves' (1683), 'They say you're angry and rant mightily' (1685), 'Thy genius, lo! from his sweet bed of rest' (both the 1689 and 1695 settings), 'I look'd and saw within the book of fate' (1691) and 'From rosy bow'rs, where sleeps the god of love' (1695).

At the beginning of a composition, Purcell normally set straight iambic lines of regular lengths – often 8. 8. 8. 8. (the 'long meter' of metrical psalmody, as noted by Attridge)[11] or 8. 6. 8. 6. ('common meter') – in duple-metre lyrical style. Here are examples of each stanza type, set by Purcell in duple metre; they appeared in Books III and V of *Choice Ayres and Songs*, respectively.

Amintor, heedless of his flocks,	(8.)
His flocks which once employ'd his care,	(8.)
Now strays himself among the rocks	(8.)
And to his sorrow adds despair.	(8.)
Beware, poor shepherds! all beware,	(8.)
Beware of Lelia's arts,	(6.)
Whose ev'ry word contains a snare,	(8.)
Her eyes a thousand darts.	(6.)

Throughout his career, Purcell seems to have reserved the application of triple metre to straight iambic lines for contrasting internal sections rather than for initial sections or entire songs. An early exception was the unique occasion of 'She loves and she confesses too', in which Purcell improved upon a composition by Pietro Reggio by replacing the melody but using the same triple metre ground.[12] A couple of later exceptions occur within scene-complexes in the dramatic operas, where individual numbers may serve the same purpose as contrasting sections in a single song: triple metre is used for variety in 'Behold, O mighty'st of gods' in *Dioclesian* (1690) and in 'For folded flocks' in *King Arthur* (1691).

Among the compositions presented as single songs in the third edition of *Orpheus Britannicus*, vol. I[13] are eighty initial or internal sections that begin with straight iambic lines. Twelve of these are 'blind' internal sections, that is, internal verses from odes or individual sections of a dramatic scene-complex

---

10   Attridge, *Rhythms of English Poetry*, p. 126.
11   *Ibid.*, p. 86.
12   In *Songs set by Signior Pietro Reggio* (London, 1680); Purcell's improved version appeared in John Playford's *Choice Ayres and Songs*, Book IV (London, 1683), available in a facsimile reprint introduced by Ian Spink, *Choice Ayres, Songs, and Dialogues, Books III, IV, and V* (London, 1989).
13   Henry Purcell, *Orpheus Britannicus: a collection of all the choicest songs for one two, and three voices . . . the third edition with large additions* (London, 1721; republished in 1965 by Gregg Press, Ridgewood, NJ).

Ex. 10.2 'If music be the food of love', bars 26b–35

(publ. 1655; Musica Britannica, vol. XXXIII) and in the numerous switches between triple and duple metre in Louis Grabu's 'Hark, how the songsters of the grove' (*Choice Ayres and Songs*, Book II, 1679).

On rare occasions, a number of inverted first-foot lines in a later strophe might have influenced Purcell to write the entire song in triple metre. In the first quatrain of 'Let monarchs fight for power and fame' (*Dioclesian*), the strong downbeat oriented triple metre batters the regular iambic text: the unstressed syllbles *let, for, with, their* and *and* all fall on the first count of the bar (Ex. 10.3). This extraordinary difficulty makes more sense if one imagines Purcell's having created the tune while looking at the third couplet, which begins

[|]Greatness shall [|]ne'er my [|]soul en [|]thral,
 1   4

[|]Give me con [|]tent and I have [|]all.
 1   4

Ex. 10.3 *Dioclesian*: 'Let monarchs fight', bars 1–16

or the fourth, which also has stressed syllables in first position:

> ᴵHear, ᴵmighty ᴵLove! to thee I ᴵcall;
> 1   4
>
> ᴵGive Me As ᴵtrea, and I have ᴵall.
> 1   4

Another plausible explanation for the peculiar nature of this piece, of course, is that it was a dance or a catchy tune with some words attached, whether they fit well or not – and they certainly do not, at the beginning.

Iambic lines beginning with two adjacent stressed syllables (stress in weak position 1: І І . І)

In this type of line stressed syllables appear in positions 1, 2 and 4:

> ᴵGreat ᴵminds a ᴵgainst them ᴵselves con ᴵspire
>   2   4   6   8

The most effective musical way to support the stress on the first two syllables is to position each on a primary count. A duple-metre opening with the first

Iambic lines beginning with three adjacent unstressed syllables (unstress in strong position 2: . . . |)

This final type of specialized iambic line results from initial word-strings such as conjunction/conjunction/determiner ('But while the |nymph I |thus a |dore'), primary verb[19] /pronoun/infinitive marker ('Were I to |choose the |greatest |bliss'), and conjunction/negative particle/preposition ('If not for |mine, for |empire's |sake'). In rapid conversational speech none of the three initial syllables is stressed, but in more careful declamation the speaker usually chooses one for emphasis, giving in to the strong proclivity for regular alternation of stressed and unstressed syllables felt by native English speakers.[20] A study to determine which word-classes are most likely to assume stress in these cases, along the lines of what Heinz J. Giegerich did for modern British English,[21] might be accomplished for Restoration English by examining all of Purcell's settings of long strings of nominally unstressed syllables.

In setting lines beginning with three adjacent unstressed syllables, Purcell favoured triple metre, with declamatory style a close second; lyrical duple metre is much less frequent. Triple-metre settings of iambic texts with three adjacent unstressed syllables in the opening line include 'When I am laid in earth' (*Dido and Aeneas*) and the internal section 'Were she but kind, whom I adore' in 'I see she flies me'. Examples in declamatory style are the opening of 'Whilst I with grief did on you look' and the section 'And yet this death of mine I fear' in 'No, to what purpose should I speak?'. This particular metrical preference was not universal among Purcell's contemporaries. Compare the openings of Samuel Ackeroyde's and Purcell's settings of 'Since from my dear Astrea's sight', the one in duple metre with stress assigned to the second word, the other in triple with stress assigned to the first (Ex. 10.8a–b; both songs were published in *The Gentleman's Journal*, Ackeroyde's in August of 1693 and Purcell's in December of the same year).

Trochaic lines (odd positions strong, | . | . | . |): gavotte and minuet

Purcell's settings of exclusively trochaic texts are virtually all lyrical; the few exceptions include two brief internal sections of 'From silent shades', accommodating a total of three lines of verse, and the four-line recitative 'See the

---

19 Primary verbs are forms of *be*, *have* and *do*; see Randolph Quirk *et al.*, *A Comprehensive Grammar of the English Language* (London, 1985), sect. 2.34.

20 David Abercrombie, 'A Phonetician's View of Verse Structure', in *Studies in Phonetics & Linguistics* (London, 1965), pp. 16–25.

21 Giegerich, 'On the Rhythmic Stressing of Function Words: A Modest Proposal', *Work in Progress, University of Edinburgh Department of Linguistics* (Edinburgh, 1978), vol. XI, 43–51.

Ex. 10.8a   Samuel Ackeroyde, 'Since from my dear Astrea's sight', bars 1–4

Ex. 10.8b   Henry Purcell, 'Since from my dear Astrea's sight', bars 1–8

flags and streamers curling' in *Dido and Aeneas*. Two syllable schemes are frequent in the trochaic lyrics: he set successions of seven-syllable lines ('Banish sorrow, banish care; / Grief should ne'er approach the fair') and alternating or mixed lines of eight syllables, including a feminine ending, and seven syllables ('Fairest Isle, all isles excelling, / Seat of pleasure and of love'). The latter is slightly more common than the former, preferred perhaps for the forward motion provided by the unstressed eighth syllable.

While many of the composer's trochaic settings are rhythmically complex, a significant number follow one of two basically simple schemes: the duple-metre gavotte and the triple-metre minuet. Each of these features four-bar phrases and certain characteristic rhythmic gestures.

Ex. 10.10 *King Arthur*: 'Shepherd, shepherd, leave decoying', bars 24–31

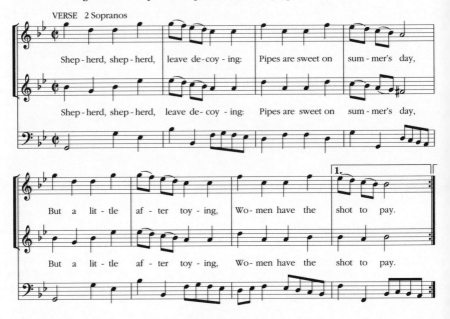

Ex. 10.11 *Dido and Aeneas*: 'Fear no danger to ensue', bars 1–8

Spink counts 'Fear no danger' as among some of the songs in *Dido* that 'show trace of a French accent'; Ellen Harris describes it as containing 'strong dance rhythms throughout' and being 'constructed in the dance pattern of a rondo'; Curtis Price characterizes it as 'balletic' and notes that it is 'frequently cited as the most Frenchified number in the opera'; Bruce Wood and Andrew Pinnock recently hailed its 'sweet parallel 3rds and distinctive rhythms'.[26] Let's call it what it is: a fashionable French *menuet en rondeau*.

[26] Spink, *English Song*, p. 223; Ellen Harris, *Henry Purcell's Dido and Aeneas* (Oxford, 1987), p. 64; Curtis Price, *Henry Purcell and the London Stage* (Cambridge, 1984), p. 249; Wood and Pinnock, 'The Dating of Purcell's *Dido and Aeneas*', p. 377.

A possible channel for this French import was Louis Grabu, who was in England in the King's service from 1665 to 1679 and again beginning in 1683.[27] Grabu's 'Hark how the songsters of the grove' (Ex. 10.12, published in *Choice Ayres and Songs*, Book II in 1679) is a two-part air, the first part of which is in triple metre and points towards the characteristic rhythms of 'Fear no danger'. In this piece the extra crotchet in the first bar accommodates an iambic inverted first-foot, eight-syllable line instead of the trochaic seven-syllable line. Purcell is quite likely to have known this piece: his important elegy on Matthew Locke appears in the same collection, along with four other songs of his. (Coincidentally, Purcell wrote his own setting of 'Hark how the songsters' for a revival of *Timon of Athens* in 1695.)

Ex. 10.12   Louis Grabu, 'Hark how the songsters of the grove', bars 1–8

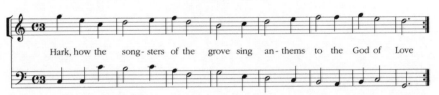

This type of minuet was popular in English song during the 1680s. In *The British Broadside Ballad and its Music*, Claude M. Simpson shows both the trochaic type – in the anonymous broadside ballad 'Joy to the bridegroom', first published in 1682 – and the iambic inverted first-foot type, in Robert King's 'He that loves best' from *Youth's Delight on the Flagelet*, 9th edn, *c.* 1690 (previously published with text in *Choice Ayres and Songs*, Book V, 1684, 7).[28] Other examples include James Hart's 'Happy is the country life' (*Choice Ayres and Songs*, Book IV, 1683, 36) and King's 'Fly from Olinda, young and fair' (*Theatre of Music*, Book I, 38, 1685). The sixth edition of *Apollo's Banquet*, published by Henry Playford in 1690, includes four labelled instrumental minuets of this type.

Not surprisingly, Purcell experimented with French dance types in the series of welcome songs designed to flatter the francophile monarch Charles II and his brother James. Purcell began cultivating both the gavotte and the minuet for trochaic texts as early as 1680, the year of *Welcome, Vicegerent*.[29]

[27] Ian Spink, 'Grabu, Louis', *The New Grove*.
[28] Claude M. Simpson, *The British Broadside Ballad and Its Music* (New Brunswick, 1966), pp. 403, 293.
[29] Rosamond McGuinness, in *English Court Odes 1660-1820* (Oxford, 1971), p. 80, refers to Locke's use of the minim–crotchet–crotchet–minim triple rhythm in an unnamed ode (presumably *All things their certain period have* of 1666), and notes its frequency in Restoration music.

'Celia has a thousand charms' (from *The Rival Sisters, or the Violence of Love* by Robert Gould, produced in 1695) include not only a contrast between trochaic and iambic but also a number of irregular iambic lines (SP = strong position, WP = weak position):

|Celia has a |thousand |charms,   [trochaic; unstress in SP 3]
 1   3   5   7

'tis |heav'n to |lie with |in her |arms;   [iambic]
   2   4   6   8

while I |stand |gazing on her |face,   [iambic; unstress in SP 2,
    2   4   6   8   stress in WP 3, unstress
                                    in SP 6]

some |new, and some re |sistless |grace   [iambic; unstress in SP 4]
    2   4   6   8

|fills with |fresh |magic |all the |place: [iambic, inverted first
 1   4   6   8   foot; stress in WP 3]

Not one of these lines is exactly like another in its stress patterns. The mixture of trochaic and iambic in the first couplet, along with the wide variety of stress/position mismatches in the remaining lines of the stanza, cries out for the musical flexibility of the declamatory style; any rhythmically patterned lyrical formula would result in a number of infelicitous correspondences between unstressed syllables and strong counts (and the opposite). The second stanza is rather more regular, with merely a few unstressed syllables filling strong positions:

But while the |nymph I |thus a |dore,   [iambic; unstress in SP 2]
    2   ·   4   6   8

I should my |wretched |fate de |plore;   [iambic; unstress in SP 2]
   2   4   6   8

for |oh! Mir |tillo, have a |care,   [iambic; unstress in SP 6]
   2   4   6   8

Her |sweetness is a |bove com |pare;   [iambic; unstress in SP 4]
   2   4   6   8

but then she's |false as |well as |fair.   [iambic; unstress in SP 2]
   2   4   6   8

That Purcell set the first, irregular stanza in declamatory style and the second, regular one in triple-metre lyrical style might inspire us to generalize this case to a principle. Anyone familiar with Purcell's work, however, would argue that he may have chosen declamatory style for the opening purely on musical grounds, since the two-part structure of declamatory followed by lyrical style is extremely common. This argument would deny a possible link between irregular verses and declamatory style.

An irregular mixture of trochaic and iambic lines is common in the recitative of *Dido and Aeneas*; the only exceptions are four successive trochaic lines at 'See the flags and streamers curling' and a few purely iambic sections, such as 'The queen of Carthage, whom we hate'. But while ten texts with mixed iambic and trochaic lines are set in declamatory style in *Dido*, another five are lyrical, in both triple metre ('Ah! Belinda, I am press'd') and duple ('Cupid only throws the dart').

In *The Fairy Queen*, by contrast, twelve of the fourteen texts with mixed trochaic and iambic lines are set in lyrical style, reflecting the general sparsity of declamatory style writing in the work. The textual type is rare in *Dioclesian* and *King Arthur*, which together include three lyrical examples and two declamatory ones. Of those instances of mixed trochaic and iambic lines outside the dramatic operas, some are in declamatory style ('Celia has a thousand charms', 'Bacchus is a pow'r divine', 'Gentle shepherds, you that know'), some in lyrical ('Ah! cruel nymph, you give despair', 'What can we poor females do', 'Sing, ye Druids, all your voices raise'). Thus no generalization is possible beyond the fact that the recitatives in *Dido* have an unusually concentrated number of lines that mix iambic and trochaic openings.[34]

Anapaestic lines with occasional iambic (and other) feet

Pure anapaestic metres occur occasionally in lyrical poetry of this time:

To the |hills and the |vales, to the |rocks and the |mountains,
     3   6   9   12

To the |musical |groves, and the |cool |shady |fountains . . .
     3   6   9   12

---

[34] Harris (*Henry Purcell's Dido and Aeneas*, pp. 37–9) comments on many features of the verse in *Dido*, including the variability of the number of stresses in each line, but does not mention the mix of iambic and trochaic lines.

Ex. 10.15   *Dioclesian*: 'Since the toils and the hazards of war's at an end'
(a) bars 18–25

Dactylic lines alternating eleven and ten syllables

This unusual type turns up in late works: the earliest example, 'What shall I do to show how much I love her', appears in *Dioclesian*. Its features are: (1) moderate triple metre; (2) four-bar phrases that alternate feminine endings (construed as a minim followed by a crotchet) and masculine ones (inevitably a dotted minim); (3) an unusually angular melody; and (4) an opening bar of equal crotchets, beginning on the first count. The next example, 'How blest are shepherds, how happy their lasses' (*King Arthur*), shares the angular melody, the four-bar phrases and many of the rhythmic characteristics of 'What shall I do'; the cadential rhythms are different, and the song begins

(b) bars 34–40

with two bars of crotchets rather than one. The third piece in the series, 'When I have often heard young maids complaining' (*The Fairy Queen*), obligingly (though presumably coincidentally) expands the equal crotchets to three bars. The rhythmic gestures common to these three pieces are shown in Ex. 10.16a–c.

Purcell may have begun the series some years earlier with an instrumental version, the Triumphing Dance of *Dido and Aeneas*. This triple-metre, ground bass dance begins on the downbeat, is organized in four-bar phrases, begins with two bars of crotchets in the melody and is remarkably angular in both ostinato bass and opening melodic phrase. It differs in that many of its

in Book I of *Choice Songs and Ayres* (1673). Three more examples of this poetic metre are represented among the texts of that collection, but none of the settings strongly resembles Purcell's; while all are in triple metre, they are saturated with dotted rhythms rather than even crotchets.

As with the trochaic minuet and gavotte, French models are to be found, though under conflicting dance names. The long choral/instrumental number in Lully's *Armide* entitled 'Suivons Armide et chantons sa victoire' is labelled a sarabande, while another prototype, 'Que devant vous' from Act 2 of Lully's *Atys*, calls itself a minuet. Louis Grabu set Dryden's text 'From the low palace of our father Ocean' in *Albion and Albanius* (1685) as the second of a pair of minuets, the first of which was instrumental.[36]

Restoration composers almost certainly thought of these kinds of pieces as minuets: the anonymous setting of a comparable dactylic text by Thomas Durfey in *Don Quixote*, Part II (1694) is labelled 'The first song to a Minuet at the Duke's Entertainment of *Don Quixote* in the first Act'.[37] Purcell himself wrote an angular, even crotchet minuet for a 1694 revival of Durfey's *The Virtuous Wife*; Durfey later used this dance as a vehicle for the partially dactylic verse 'New reformation begins thro' the Nation'.[38]

'Mad-song' stanza and the bourrée

Within English verse forms, a large group of related stanzas share the feature that, if arranged in four lines, the first, second and fourth lines have three strong positions while the third line has four. In hymnody the iambic version of pattern is called 'short meter', or 6. 6. 8. 6., as in this metrical version of Psalm 25 from Sternhold and Hopkins's *The Whole Booke of Psalms* (1601):[39]

I lift mine heart to thee,	(6.)
my God and guide most just:	(6.)
Now suffer me to take no shame	(8.)
for in thee doe I trust.	(6.)

---

[36] Louis Grabu, *Albion and Albanius: An Opera, or, Representation in Musick* (London, 1687), p. 244.

[37] In *The Songs to the New Play of Don Quixote ... Part the Second* (London, 1694), pp. 1–2. The text is

If you will love me be free in Expressing it,
and henceforth give me no cause to complain;
or if you hate me be plain in confessing it,
and in a few words put me out of my pain.

[38] Originally published in *Songs Compleat, Pleasant and Diversive . . . Written by Mr D'Urfey*, vol. II (London 1719); also available in *Wit and Mirth: or Pills to Purge Melancholy*, ed. with an introduction by Cyrus L. Day, vol. II (New York, 1959), 110–13.

[39] Thomas Sternhold, John Hopkins *et al.*, *The Whole Booke of Psalms, collected into English Meeter* (London, 1601), p. 12.

From this basic structure one need only divide the third line into two shorter ones with end rhymes and substitute some anapestic triplets to produce the limerick, an invention of the nineteenth century. An intermediate stage is represented by one of Ophelia's mad songs in the fourth act of *Hamlet*:

> And will 'a not come again?
> And will 'a not come again?
>   No, no, he is dead;
>   Go to thy deathbed;
> He never will come again.
>
> His beard was as white as snow,
> All flaxen was his poll.
>   He is gone, he is gone,
>   And we cast away moan.
> God 'a mercy on his soul![40]

Paul Fussell identifies this form, with the addition of feminine endings to all the longer lines, as 'conventional "mad-song" stanza' and attributes its origins to the early Renaissance.[41] He gives as his seventeenth-century example Durfey's 'I'll sail upon the dog-star', and indeed Durfey ran a profitable trade in this type of verse. Table 10.2 shows eleven examples, some of them internal sections, others free-standing. Those texts not part of a mad-song are clearly comic, either ridiculing the dialect of the singing character or, in the case of 'Of all our modern stories', lampooning the amorous pastoral dialogue. The great majority are matched to a bourrée tune, characterized by rapid duple metre, single upbeat (realized by one crotchet or two quavers), and a break after the second note (on the second or third count) of the second bar. Ex. 10.17 shows the beginnings of two such bourrée-songs, Purcell's 'By this disjointed matter', a section of 'Behold the man that with gigantic might' in *The Richmond Heiress*, and the anonymous setting of 'De foolish English nation' from *Don Quixote*, Part II (1694). Ironically, one of the few texts in the group that does not use a bourrée tune begins

> Of all our modern Storys
> To Minuets sung, or Borees,
>   None stir the Mood,
>   as late the Feud,
> 'Twixt *Phillida* and *Chloris*.[42]

---

40   I am indebted to Barbara Cobb for this reference.
41   Fussell, *Poetic Meter and Poetic Form*, pp. 140–41.
42   Originally published in *Wit and Mirth: or Pills to Purge Melancholy* (London, 1706; no. 210A in Cyrus L. Day and Eleanor Murrie, *English Song-Books, 1651-1702*); also available in *Wit and Mirth: or Pills to Purge Melancholy* (1959), vol. II, 44–5.

style, rapid triple (3), slower declamatory style, and slower triple (3/2) in 'Fly swift, ye hours' makes for satisfying contrasts. While one can correlate the choices for each section with semantic features in the text ('fly swift' and 'swifter than time' will hardly work in moody declamatory style or graceful gavotte), one should still be aware that features in the verse probably influenced Purcell's decision among the plausible choices. Why, for example, should the last section be in triple metre instead of duple?

In addition to focusing attention on links between poetic and musical metres, this essay has suggested that dance types were much more prominent in the composer's vocal works than has been previously noted. Performers who are immersed in these rhythms have probably known this for years, but scholars have been slow to recognize it. The music for the rustic entertainers in Act 2, scene 2 of the Dryden and Purcell's *King Arthur*, for example, is a progression of dances and dance-songs (see list below), a fact announced by the dialogue that precedes it but not mentioned in standard descriptions of the scene. According to the principles established here, the trochaic text in the middle could have been set either as minuet or as gavotte; clearly, the preceding minuet and the succeeding triple-metre hornpipe dictated the choice of the duple-metre gavotte type for effective contrast. Purcell's affection for dance types in his big stage works complicates the received idea that his later career was shaped by a turn away from French styles and towards the Italian. In addition, his employment of dance rhythms as demonstrated in the more straightforward examples discussed above prompts one to consider 'What can we poor females do', 'Oh, the sweet delights of love', and 'Leave these useless arts in loving' as expanded gavottes and 'Trip it, trip it in a ring' from *The Fairy Queen* as a bourrée run out of control.

Dance types in Act 2, scene 2 of King Arthur

1. Instrumental minuet (G major)
2. Vocal minuet, dactylic 11. 10. 11. 10.: 'How blest are shepherds, how happy their lasses', to the tune of the preceding dance

3. Instrumental gavotte: 'Symphony' (G minor)
4. Vocal gavotte, trochaic 8. 7. 8. 7.: 'Shepherd, shepherd, leave decoying', to the tune of the preceding dance

5. Vocal hornpipe: 'Come shepherds, lead up a lively measure' (G major)
6. Instrumental hornpipe, to the tune of the preceding song

Admirers of Purcell should not be put off by the idea that he wrote multiple songs on the same rhythmic framework and apparently made some of his fundamental compositional decisions virtually by rule. It may be hard to think of 'Fairest isle' as one of a long series of Purcellian trochaic minuets that began in the welcome songs of the early 1680s, or of the graceful triple metre of 'Since from my dear Astrea's sight' as a foregone conclusion having nothing to do with the emotions of the text and everything to do with the stress pattern of the first four syllables of its opening line; yet these standard responses to different verse types are as much a part of Purcell's basic technique as harmonic language or the rules of counterpoint. The establishment of these conventions detracts nothing from his accomplishment for, as in many varieties of artistic design, God is in the details; and Purcell's creative genius in fashioning those details never ceases to astound and delight.

Table 10.1   *Correlation of musical metre and style to poetic metre and stress patterns in Purcell's songs*

Poetic metre of opening line(s)	Preferred metre in lyrical style	Frequency of declamatory style
Straight iambic (. l . l)	initial sections: duple internal sections: triple or duple	frequent, especially in mixed lines of 10, 8, 6 and 4 syllables
Iambic, inverted first foot (l . . l)	before 1688: initial sections: duple internal sections: may be triple after 1688: triple	frequent
Iambic, two adjacent stresses (l l . l)	duple	frequent
Iambic, three adjacent unstresses (. . . l)	triple	very frequent
Trochaic (l . l .)	duple (often gavotte) or triple (often minuet)	very rare
Mixed iambic and trochaic lines	duple	very frequent, especially in recitatives of *Dido and Aeneas*
Dactylic, esp. 11. 10. 11. 10. (l . . l . .)	triple (even-crotchet minuet)	none
Anapaestic, often mixed with iambic feet (. . l . . l)	triple; frequently compound duple with gigue rhythms	very rare
Iambic/anapaestic 7.7.6.6.7	fast duple (bourrée)	none

forced to begin by making a number of assumptions the validity of which is now often contested – that language can refer to something outside itself, that the meaning a careful reader draws from a text may approximate that which a careful writer embodied in it, that we may escape the habits of thought and expression that prevail in our own age sufficiently to understand those that prevailed in another.[3]

Bywaters includes a level-headed half chapter on *King Arthur* drawing on Curtis Price's earlier work – though, being a professor of English, he goes further down the literary-critical path.

Such assumptions about meaning are implicit in any attempt to explain Dryden's satirical or allegorical 'intentions'. I would add a couple more. The meaning which a careful writer thinks is embodied in his text will change as he grows older and the world moves on. (This is especially true of political material.) And, where a number of careful readers agree on a meaning unimagined – dare I say 'unintended'? – by the author, it is there really and truly; no use the author denying it, or those who claim to speak on his behalf. A text may invite different interpretations at different times; or several interpretations at once. In *King Arthur* Price finds a double meaning running throughout. Dryden

> transformed what was originally a heartfelt parable of royal reconciliation into a backhanded compliment to a king for whom he did not much care. . .*King Arthur* had to be ambiguous in tone, because Dryden chose to interweave a laudatory allegory with a seditious one.[4]

The Dryden biographer James Anderson Winn goes further:

> readers of either political persuasion could interpret these lines as they pleased. . .[Dryden's] skill in recasting the opera to make it open to either a Williamite or a Jacobite reading has a beauty all of its own.[5]

I would not disagree, but there is more to say.

'King Arthur conquering the Saxons' appealed to Dryden as a subject he could write about 'for the honour of [his] native country' without having to follow historical authorities very closely. King Arthur, 'being further distant in time, gives the greater scope to my invention'.[6] He was free to make most of it up: free to draw on non-Arthurian sources for details of the plot, and for

3   *Dryden in Revolutionary England* (Berkeley and Los Angeles, 1991), p. x.
4   *Henry Purcell and the London Stage* (Cambridge, 1984), p. 318; 'Political Allegory in Late-Seventeenth-Century English Opera', in *Music and Theatre: Essays in honour of Winton Dean*, ed. Nigel Fortune (Cambridge, 1987), pp. 1–29.
5   *John Dryden and His World* (New Haven and London, 1987), p. 449.
6   From the preface to the playbook (1691).

'more poetical' flesh to cover the plot's bare bones. Source hunting is an interest few will admit to these days. Still, I do think it helps to know the background reading that Dryden may have done to prepare himself and the sort of reading that will have coloured other people's reactions to his work when it first appeared publicly, either in print or on stage. Searching for *King Arthur* cribs, I have made some interesting finds.

Margaret Laurie's preface to the revised edition of *The Works of Henry Purcell*, vol. XXVI, pointed the way: 'Dryden wrote . . . *King Arthur* in 1684, to celebrate the twenty-fifth anniversary of the Restoration, which would take place the following year.' Now the Restoration was a process spread out over months: more convenient to celebrate would be the event in which it culminated – Charles II's coronation on 23 April 1661 – St George's Day. On Charles II's coronation medal the king is pictured shepherding his flock (a suggestive image, if one considers the fifth-act masque in *King Arthur*). The date 23 April 1661 was fixed indelibly in the popular consciousness. The saintly connection supplied a patriotic theme for dozens of third-rate poets and ballad-mongers. Coronation Day was marked each year in towns up and down the country with bell-ringing and bonfires. James II was crowned on 23 April 1685, following his brother's shrewd example – unlike William and Mary, who chose 11 April.

Let us consider the very beginning of the opera:

ACT I. SCENE I.

Enter CONON, AURELIUS, ALBANACT.

CON. Then this is the deciding Day, to fix
   Great Britain's Scepter in great *Arthur*'s Hand.

AUR. Or put it in the bold Invaders gripe. . .

AUR. Well have we chose a Happy day, for Fight; . . .

CON. Because this day
   Is Sacred to the Patron of our Isle;
   A Christian, and a Souldiers Annual Feast.

ALB. Oh, now I understand you, This is
   St. *George* of *Cappadocia*'s Day. . .

St George's Day – 'Sacred to the Patron of our Isle' and, as it happened, 'Sacred to the Coronation of his Majesty Charles the II'. At the very beginning Dryden nails his colours firmly to the mast. Act 3, scene 2, where Emmeline, blind from birth, is miraculously cured and looks for the first time on Arthur her true love, refers unambiguously to the Restoration.[7]

---

[7] The keywords are in **boldface** type.

MER[LIN].　My *Philidel*; go Meritorious on . . .
　　　　　and with these **Soveraign** Drops
　　　　　Restore her Sight.
　　　　　　　　　　　Exit MERLIN *giving a Vial to* PHILIDEL. . . .
　　　　PHILIDEL *approaches* EMMELINE, *sprinkling some of the*
　　　　　　Water over her Eyes, out of the Vial.
PHIL.　　　*Thus, thus I infuse*
　　　　　These **Soveraign** *Dews*. . .

Compare Edmund Waller's poem 'To the King upon his Majesty's Happy Return':

> Great Britain, like blind Polypheme, of late,
> In a wild rage, became the scorn and hate
> Of her proud neighbours . . .
> But you are come, and all their hopes are vain;
> This giant isle has got her eye again.

On to Act 5, scene 1, where Arthur and the Saxon king Oswald face each other in single combat. Perhaps that refers to the complex negotiations between King and Parliament to effect the Restoration Settlement. One should note that Abraham Cowley, in his unfinished epic treatment of *The Civil War*, 'associated the struggle of the British and Saxons with the conflict between the King and Parliament . . . a very natural parallel since the Stuarts had emphasized their British descent, and Parliament was basing its claim to power upon the ancient rights of the Saxons'.[8] Dryden broadly hinted that he made the same association when he chose the name Oswald for his Saxon hero. Oswald had appeared before, in Sir William Davenant's unfinished heroic poem *Gondibert* (publ. 1651, repr. 1673), as a prince of the Lombard royal line, second only to Duke Gondibert in point of valour, dangerously ambitious and without his rival's statesmanlike qualities. Davenant compares the two much as Dryden does his Saxon Oswald and King Arthur. King Aribert – lacking a male heir – chooses Gondibert to wed his daughter Rhodalind and so, in due course, to inherit the crown; whereupon Oswald, urged on by his advisers, takes up arms to press his rival suit. The same happens in *King Arthur*. After some discussion, Oswald and Gondibert agree to settle the matter in a hand-to-hand fight – so do Arthur and Oswald in *King Arthur*. Both Oswalds are defeated. Oswald in the Davenant poem is killed outright (the hero goes on to further adventures); Dryden's King

---

[8]　Roberta Florence Brinkley, *Arthurian Legend in the Seventeenth Century* (Baltimore, 1932), pp. 102–3.

Arthur disarms Saxon Oswald and magnanimously releases him. Still, Dryden's indebtedness to Davenant is clear. Davenant's modern editor David Gladish links Oswald with Oliver Cromwell in his tentative '"key" to the characters in *Gondibert*;[9] and it seems to me that Dryden's Saxons – another Oswald at their head – may very well represent whiggish parliamentarians: still alive, because of course they were; beaten, but invited by an 'all-forgiving King'[10] to share in the fruits of his victory.

> [MERLIN]   To Osw. Nor thou, brave Saxon Prince, disdain our Triumphs;
> Britains and Saxons shall be once one People;
> One Common Tongue, one Common Faith shall bind
> Our Jarring Bands, in a perpetual peace.

Here in outline is a Restorer's reading of *King Arthur* to set beside the already familiar Jacobite and Williamite interpretations. In 1952 Samuel Kliger praised the skill with which Dryden 'merges the ideas of Saxon democracy and of the Royalist conceptions . . . attached to the Arthurian tradition . . . Merlin sums up the political significance of the play when he prophesies a combined British and Saxon future.'[11]

The sacrifice scene, Act 1, scene 2, is difficult to fathom without knowing Dryden's main source. He claimed in the preface to the libretto to have 'employ'd some reading . . . to inform myself out of *Beda, Bochartus*, and other Authors, concerning the Rights and Customs of the Heathen Saxons'. In fact practically all the ritual detail came from a far handier source (which unaccountably Dryden forgot to mention): Aylett Sammes's *Britannia Antiqua Illustrata* (1676). 'The Sculpture representing the Temple of Thor, with whom is placed Woden and Frigga [= Freya].' The gods are seated on a couch – rather a decadent pose, as Sammes concedes, showing their suscept-ibility to Roman influence in mid-career. Formerly the Saxons 'represented their Idols standing, and set them upon Pillars and Obelisks'; and Woden, father to Thor, occupied the place of honour. Compare Dryden's stage direction: '*The Scene represents a place of Heathen worship; The three Saxon Gods,* Woden, Thor, *and* Freya *placed on Pedestals. An Altar.*' More from Sammes:

> When they were to consult of matters of weight and importance, besides the inspection of Beasts Intrails they especially observed the neighing of Horses; For this purpose the whitest that could be pickt out were kept at the publick charge in Groves and Parks set apart from them.

---

9   *Sir William Davenant's Gondibert,* ed. D. F. Gladish (Oxford, 1971), p. xv.
10   *Threnodia Augustalis,* line 257; *The Poems of John Dryden,* ed. John Sargeaunt (Oxford, 1910), p. 111.
11   *The Goths in England* (Cambridge, Mass., 1952), p. 193.

> *Tanfan* was their God of Lots, to whom they addressed themselves to interpret future Events . . . [If a sacrifice] was performed to the honour of *Woden*, according to his own institution, yet the particular determining of the party most acceptable might be the particular office and imployment of *Tanfan*.
>
> In the Laws of *Friesland* . . . there is one yet extant concerning the manner of Casting Lots . . .

Most telling of all is Sammes on Valhalden – Valhalla:

> they believed that after death they were to go into *Wodens* Hall, and there drink Ale with him, and his Companions, in the Skulls of their Enemies. To this end they imagined a certain Goddess called *DYSER*, employed by *Woden*, to convey the Souls of the Valiant into his drunken Paradice.

Sammes prints the 'Death Song of Ragnar Lothbrok' in runic characters, with a rhyming translation.

> *We have stood true to* Snick *and* Snee,
> *And now I laugh to think,*
> *In* Wodens *Hall there Benches be,*
> *Where we may sit and drink.*
> *There we shall Tope our bellies-full*
> *Of Nappy-Ale in full-brim'd Skull.*
>
> *Methinks I long to end,*
>   *I hear the* Dyser *call;*
> *Which* Woden *here doth send*
>   *To bring me to his Hall.*
> *With Asians there in highest Seat,*
>   *I merrily will quaff,*
> *Past-hours I care not to repeat,*
>   *But when I die I'll laugh.*

Now compare the corresponding scene in Dryden:

> GRIMBALD *goes to the Door, and Re-enters with 6 Saxons in White, with Swords in their hands. They range themselves 3 and 3 in opposition to each other. The rest of the Stage is fill'd with Priests and Singers.*
>
> Woden, *first to thee,*
> *A* **Milk-white Steed** *in Battle won,*
> *We have Sacrific'd.*
>   CHOR.   *We have Sacrific'd.*
>   VERS.   *Let our next oblation be,*
>   *To* Thor, *thy thundring Son,*
>   *Of such another.*

CHOR. *We have Sacrific'd.*
VERS. *A Third; (of* **Friezland** *breed was he,)*
To Woden'*s Wife, and to* Thor'*s Mother* :
And now we have atton'd all three
We have Sacrific'd.
CHOR. *We have Sacrific'd.*
2 VOC. **The White Horse Neigh'd aloud.**
To Woden *thanks we render.*
To Woden, *we have vow'd.*
CHOR. *To* Woden, *our Defender.*
[The four last Lines in *CHORUS.*
VERS. **The Lot is Cast, and Tanfan** *pleas'd*:
CHOR. *Of Mortal Cares you shall be eas'd,*
Brave Souls to be renown'd in Story.
Honour prizing,
Death despising,
Fame acquiring
By Expiring,
Dye, and reap the fruit of Glory.
Brave Souls to be renown'd in Story.
VERS. 2. *I call ye all,*
To Woden's *Hall;*
Your temples round
With Ivy bound,
In Goblets Crown'd,
And plenteous Bowls of burnish'd Gold;
Where you shall Laugh,
And dance and quaff,
The Juice, that makes the Britons bold.

The six Saxons are led off by the Priests, in Order to be Sacrific'd.

Sammes pokes fun at the 'Death Song' – 'as good Verses as Ale could inspire' – and pictures King Lothbrok as a drunken oaf, but it is no mere 'bacchanal', nor is Dryden's re-write (and Purcell's setting of it). Woden demands a very high price for admission to his beer-hall: a valiant death in battle. The Saxon warrior-heroes look foward manfully to their reunion in Valhalla, without a drink in sight. Price remarks that 'a dichotomy of tone pervades the sacrifice scene, and the music leaves a modern audience puzzled by the difference between what they see and what they hear'.[12] Acqaintance with Dryden's source helps solve the problem.

---

[12] *Henry Purcell and the London Stage*, p. 300.

The final masque is conjured up by Merlin to celebrate 'The Wealth, the Loves, the Glories of our Isle', the charmed future to which Britons can look forward; and it ends, predictably, with a hymn to the Order of the Garter, that 'most noble *Order . . . [exceeding] in Majesty, Honor, and Fame, all Chivalrous Orders in the world*'.[13] There was ample precedent for a Garter-finale. To end Thomas Carew's Whitehall masque *Coelum Britannicum* (1633) the clouds part revealing 'a troope of fifteene starres, expressing the stellifying of our British Heroes' – the brightest of all hanging over the King and Queen, seated in state – and below it, 'a farre off, the prospect of Windsor Castell, the famous seat of the most honourable Order of the Garter'. The final scene in Dryden's *Albion and Albanius* is strikingly similar:

> *In the Air is a Vision of the Honors of the Garter* [including the Garter Star, of course – pictured in many a pub sign]; *the Knights in Procession, and the King under a Canopy: Beyond this, the upper end of St.* George's *Hall.*

No doubt Dryden had *Coelum Britannicum* in mind: the old masque was better known than it deserved to be, since it had been mis-attributed to Davenant and reprinted in the 1673 folio edition of his works.

Given the intimate connection between *Albion and Albanius* and *King Arthur*, perhaps one should not be surprised to find the same emblems used at the climactic moment in both for essentially the same purpose. In *Albion and Albanius*, Fame standing on a globe (emblazoned with the Arms of England) sings to the glory of Charles II who, in the person of Albion, has just been 'adopted' as a god, and lifted up to heaven in a 'very glorious Machine' sent to collect him:

> FAME.   Renown, assume thy Trumpet!
> From Pole to Pole resounding . . .
> Great *Albion*'s Name shall be
> The Theme of Fame . . .
> Record the Garters Glory:
> A Badge for Hero's, and for Kings to bear . . .
> And swell th'Immortal Story . . .

A full chorus repeats everything Fame sings, with dancers joining in to end the opera. Compare the words of the final chorus in *King Arthur*, with the Garter-revealing stage direction and a little introductory dialogue:

> The Scene opens above, and discovers the Order of the Garter.

---

[13] Selden, quoted in Elias Ashmole, *The Institutions, Laws, and Ceremonies of the Most Noble Order of the Garter* (London, 1672), p. 190.

Enter Honour, *Attended by* Hero's.

MERL. . . . Now look above, and in Heav'ns High Abyss,
Behold what Fame attends those future Hero's.
Honour, who leads 'em to that Steepy Height,
In her Immortal Song, shall tell the rest.
(Honour sings.)

1.

HON. *St. George, the Patron of our Isle,*
A Soldier, and a Saint,
On that Auspicious Order smile,
Which Love and Arms will plant.

2.

Our Natives not alone appear
To Court this Martiall Prize;
But Foreign Kings, Adopted here,
Their Crowns at Home despise.

3.

Our Soveraign High, in Aweful State,
His Honours shall bestow;
And see his Scepter'd Subjects wait
On his Commands below.

A full Chorus of the whole Song: After which the Grand Dance.

Here are verses 'clearly referring to William';[14] 'Foreign Kings [pay]
obeisance to King William III'[15] – an allusion to William which, 'though
superficially laudatory, may easily be construed as scathingly ironic'.[16] The
source-hunter can supply an amusing gloss from Elias Ashmole's monumental folio volume *The Institutions, Laws, and Ceremonies of the Most Noble
Order of the Garter* (1672):

> *The Institution of the Order of the* Garter . . . *The* Honor *and* Reputation
> *thereof*. . . It hath been honored with the Companionship of divers *Emperors,*
> *Kings,* and *Sovereign Princes* of *Christendom,* who reputed it among their
> greatest honors, to be chosen and admitted thereinto; insomuch as some of
> them have with impatience courted the honour of *Election.* For we find
> remaining upon this *Registry* of *Honor,* eight *Emperors* of *Germany,* three
> *Kings* of *Spain,* five *French Kings,* two Kings of *Scotland,* five Kings of
> *Denmark,* five Kings of *Portugal,* two *Kings* of *Sweden,* one *King* of *Poland,*
> one *King* of *Aragon,* two *Kings* of *Naples,* besides sundry Dukes and other
> *Free Princes,* as one *Duke* of *Gelderland,* one *Duke* of *Holland,* two *Dukes* of
> *Burgundy,* two *Dukes* of *Brunswick,* one *Duke* of *Milan,* two *Dukes* of *Urbin,*

14 Winn, *John Dryden,* p. 448.   15   Price, *Henry Purcell,* p. 316.
16 Bywaters, *Dryden in Revolutionary England,* p. 91.

one *Duke* of *Ferrara*, one *Duke* of *Savoy*, two *Dukes* of *Holstein*, one *Duke* of *Saxony*, and one *Duke* of *Wertemberg*, seven *Counts Palatines* of the *Rhyne*, four *Princes* of *Orange*, and one *Marquess* of *Brandenburgh* . . . It entitles those *Knights* and *Noblemen*, whose virtue hath raised them to this degree of honor, to be *Companions* and *Fellows* with *Emperors* and *Kings;* a Prerogative of an high nature, and a reward for greatest merits.

The 'four Princes of Orange' mentioned here pre-date William III as crowned King of England and head of the Order *ex officio*. Dryden's reference to 'Foreign Kings', in a Garter context, would have been perfectly intelligible even in 1684.

There is no doubt that Dryden's audience in 1691 would have seized on 'Foreign Kings' as a reference to William, as modern critics have also done. But whether Dryden wrote it with William in mind is far from clear. Seemingly the most obvious 1691 addition to *King Arthur* may be no such thing. This final chorus may have been taken over from Dryden's original draft – the draft of an opera written to eulogize Charles II. It may have come to mean something new and subversive in completely different political circumstances, but with the words unchanged. In fact, as Price has suggested, not much re-writing need have happened at all.

Dryden's preface to *King Arthur*, published with the text of the opera in 1691, is worth a close reading:

> I wrote it, seven Years ago . . . But not to offend the present Times, nor a Government which has hitherto protected me, I have been oblig'd so much to alter the first Design, and take away so many Beauties from the Writing, that it is now no more what it was formerly, than the present Ship of the *Royal Sovereign*, after so often taking down, and altering . . . [is] the Vessel it was at the first Building.

Cutting would explain the sad demise of 'so many Beauties'. Dryden does not say that his dramatic verse was marred by party-political re-writing, only that beautiful parts of the original draft were taken away: 'not to offend the present Times', he was obliged to alter the design, to make (or to agree to) structural changes. Students of dramatic opera are used to structural changes made at a late stage in the production process, changes in the running order to solve logistical problems which only became apparent during rehearsal. Sometimes it is possible to work out what these changes were and consider undoing them, where the printed word-books and independently authoritative musical manuscripts disagree, or where the music sources show signs of disturbance. *King Arthur* is in 'disarray', it has been claimed: very revealing disarray, when one has learned how to read the evidence.

Dryden pointed to a number of cuts (one can only guess where the knife went in); but he also complained that in places he had been 'oblig'd to cramp [his] Verses' in obedience to the composer's wishes, bending the 'Rules of Poetry' to produce a serviceable libretto.

> I flatter my self with an Imagination, that a Judicious Audience will easily distinguish betwixt the Songs, wherein I have comply'd with [Purcell], and those in which I have followed the Rules of Poetry, in the Sound and Cadence of the Words.

In the *King Arthur* word-book, then, one can expect to see four different classes of song text:

1. lyrics written back in 1684; Purcell set some of them, 'humour[ing] the poet's invention' – but he ignored others as unsuitable for music on Dryden's own admission;
2. lyrics originally written in 1684, revised in 1691 following Purcell's advice;
3. lyrics completely new in 1691;
4. lyrics not by Dryden at all; the fifth-act dialogue 'You say 'tis love' is labelled 'SONG by Mr. *HOWE*'.

Dryden, in the preface to *Albion and Albanius*, hinted at a set of 'rules which I have given to myself in the writing of an opera in general, and of this opera in particular'; rules he is likely to have followed in the writing of *King Arthur* too – at least in those parts of it which he wanted set to music:

> 'Tis no easy matter in our language to make words so smooth, and numbers so harmonious, that they shall almost set themselves, and yet there are rules for this in nature, and as great a certainty of quantity in our [English] syllables, as either in the Greek or Latin. . . I may, without vanity, own some advantages which are not common to every writer, such as . . . the knowledge of the Italian and French language, and the being conversant with some of their best performances in this kind; which have furnished me with such variety of measures, as have given the composer, Monsieur Grabut, what occasion he could wish to show his extraordinary talent in diversifying the recitative, the lyrical part, and the chorus.

Dryden's experience with *Albion and Albanius* persuaded him that a librettist's job was to write verses with varying line lengths, stress patterns and rhyme schemes, which a composer 'exactly express[ing his] sense' would set mostly as recitative or arioso: Dryden would never have imagined that full-blown arias rose spontaneously from the pages of his libretto and 'almost set themselves'.

But the poetical variety which Dryden accounted such a virtue in 1684 – providing Grabu with a steady stream of musical inspiration – was not at all what Purcell wanted seven years later. There is very little recitative or arioso in the *King Arthur* score: instead, a succession of songs and choruses, making much slower progress through the word-book than Dryden had anticipated. Purcell's compositional techniques were not those for which the libretto had been designed. Extensive cuts were inevitable. Dryden saw that the words were printed, even if Purcell had not set them, so readers could compare those songs in which he had 'followed the Rules of Poetry' with those wherein he had complied with Mr Purcell's stern demands. It is a pity that he did not distinguish them in the way Davenant did in *Salmacida Spolia* (1640): '[A Song] Inviting the Kings appearance in the Throne of Honor. To be printed, not sung.' There is probably a lot less missing music for *King Arthur* than many authorities have supposed: in fact there is the opposite problem of redundant printed lyrics. Compare (A) 'O sight, the mother of desires' from the restoration scene in Act 3, for which no Purcell setting survives, and (B) 'How happy the lover', the Passacaglia in Act 4. Keywords are in bold:

(A)   MAN SINGS.   *O Sight, the Mother of Desires,*
                              What Charming Objects dost thou yield!
                              'Tis sweet, when tedious Night expires,
                              To see the Rosie Morning guild
                              The Mountain-Tops, and paint the Field!
                              But, when Clorinda *comes in sight,*
                              She makes the Summers Day more bright;
                              And when she goes away, 'tis Night.
        CHOR.   *When Fair* Clorinda *comes in sight,* &c.
        WOM. SINGS.   *'Tis sweet the Blushing Morn to view;*
                              And Plains adorn'd with Pearly Dew:
                              But such cheap Delights to see,
                              Heaven and **Nature,**
                              Give each **Creature;**
                              They have **Eyes,** *as well as we.*
                              This is the Joy, all Joys above
                              To see, to see,
                              That only she,
                              That only she we love!
        CHOR.   **This is the Joy, all Joys above,** &c.
        MAN. SINGS.   *And, if we may* **discover,**
                              What Charms both Nymph and **Lover,**
                              'Tis, when the Fair at Mercy lies,

> *With Kind and Amorous Anguish,*
> *To Sigh, to Look, to Languish,*
> *On each others Eyes!*
> CHOR. OF ALL *And if we may discover, &c.*
> MEN & WOM.

I.

(B) SONG.

> *How happy the **Lover**,*
> *How easie his Chain*
> *How pleasing his Pain?*
> *How sweet **to discover!***
> *He sighs not in vain.*
> *For Love every **Creature***
> *Is form'd by his **Nature**;*
> *No Joys are above*
> *The Pleasures of Love.*

II.

> *In vain are our Graces,*
> ***In vain are your Eyes,***
> *If Love you despise;*
> *When Age furrows Faces,*
> *'Tis time to be wise.*
> *Then use the short Blessing:*
> *That Flies in Possessing:*
> *No Joys are above*
> *The Pleasures of Love.*

This rhyme-recycling suggests that 'How happy the lover' began life as a metrically more regular re-write of 'O sight', suitable (as 'O sight' plainly is not) for a strophic setting and probably meant to replace 'O sight' in Act 3. I think it was relocated in Act 4 rather later.

Evidence in the musical sources supports this theory. Music for the first five lines of stanza II, 'In vain are our Graces', is missing or garbled in three otherwise reliable manuscripts; and these same manuscripts – musical continuity notwithstanding – transfer the whole of the second stanza to Act 5. Why? Well, in Act 4 'How happy the lover' follows hard on the heels of 'Two daughters of this aged stream'. The two daughters are soprano duettists, sirens who 'arise from [a pool of] Water . . . [and] show themselves [naked] to the Waste'. They would hardly have had time to dry off, dress decently as woodland nymphs and re-enter at once for 'How happy the lover' – which had therefore to be performed two principal sopranos short. Purcell's setting of stanza II, needing another three solo sopranos, was probably more than the chorus could manage unaided. So stanza II was cut. Where Purcell's music for the first stanza finished, someone wrote 'end of Act IV', sensibly recording their decision not to run on to the end of the movement. It is hardly surprising that later copyists, transcribing the whole lot, should mistake this stage direction and begin Act 5 where Act 4 appeared to end – cutting the Passacaglia in two. 'Blunders' like this gladden the heart of an imaginative editor.

One approaches *King Arthur* expecting great things: it has been billed as a 'momentous collaboration' between the foremost composer and the foremost dramatic poet of the age; 'a work unique in English music history, indeed without parallel anywhere. Though it is primarily an entertainment, it remains a unified work, unlike *The Fairy Queen*, and a truly poetic stage piece, unlike *Dioclesian*.[17] I think Zimmerman overstates the case. In this essay I have tried to show how the 1691 *King Arthur* – like *The Fairy Queen*, like *Dioclesian* – was adapted from a script written sometime before. True, *King Arthur* 'is unique among Purcell's semi-operas in that it was designed from the first as such';[18] true, too, Dryden was alive and well when *King Arthur* went into production and available for consultation (unlike Shakespeare, Fletcher or Massinger). But the textual evidence does not suggest that Dryden substantially re-worded his original draft. Smoother versions of some of the lyrics were made grudgingly – modern music 'cramped' his poetical style; and Purcell probably did not set all the songs. Another author altogether supplied words for the prominently placed fifth-act duet. An imposing chorus planned for Act 3 was perhaps relocated in Act 4, more for practical than for artistic reasons. In short, pressures of production were as much responsible for the way *King Arthur* looked in 1691 as was Dryden himself.

---

[17] Franklin B. Zimmerman, *Henry Purcell, 1659–1695: His Life and Times*, rev. edn (Philadelphia, 1983), p. 191.
[18] J. A. Westrup, *Purcell*, rev. edn by Nigel Fortune (London, 1980), p. 131.

12

King Arthur's journey into the eighteenth century

ELLEN T. HARRIS

Dryden and Purcell's *King Arthur* ranks as one of the greatest and best-known 'Dramatick Operas'. First performed in 1691, it continued to be produced throughout the decade. At its first major revival in 1736, the work remained largely unchanged. In contrast, a Dublin performance in 1763 included a significant number of alterations. David Garrick and Thomas Arne made a much more extensive revision in 1770; performed over three seasons, this version was revived in 1781. Then, in 1784 it was greatly shortened and compressed by John Kemble and Thomas Linley into a two-act afterpiece entitled *Arthur and Emmeline*, which was performed until 1791. Many of the practices of revision revealed in this history of *King Arthur* are presaged in Restoration revisions of Shakespeare, especially of *The Tempest*, on which Dryden's *King Arthur* appears to have been modelled, and paralleled in the eighteenth-century revisions of Purcell's *Dido and Aeneas*. In this essay, therefore, the eighteenth-century adaptations of *King Arthur* will be examined, not only to analyse the transformation of a single work, but also to study the process of revision as it relates to other operatic adaptations.

KING ARTHUR AND SHAKESPEARE

Although the only one of Purcell's large dramatic works for the professional stage that is not an adaptation from an earlier play, *King Arthur* nevertheless bears a close relationship to Shakespeare's *Tempest*, especially Restoration versions. For example, the characters closely parallel one another.[1] In both a good magician (Prospero/Merlin) works with a good 'airy spirit' (Ariel/Philidel) to overcome the usurper or invader (Alonzo/Oswald) and unite the leading young man (Ferdinand/Arthur) with the innocent young woman

[1] See Curtis Price, *Henry Purcell and the London Stage* (Cambridge, 1984), pp. 295–6.

(Miranda/Emmeline) who has 'never seen a man', with the difference that Emmeline is actually blind. In both cases, the good characters must contend with an earth-bound evil spirit (Caliban/Grimbald) who in *King Arthur* takes orders from an evil magician (Osmond).

There are also parallels in action, such as when the airy spirits use song to lead the confused leading men: Ariel sings 'Come unto these yellow sands' and 'Full-fathom five' to Ferdinand, and Philidel sings 'Hither this way' and 'Come follow me' to Arthur. Smaller points of comparison include the acting out of events only referred to in Shakespeare. For example, in *The Tempest*, Prospero accuses Caliban of having sought 'to violate the honour of my child', but in *King Arthur* Osmond is openly depicted attempting to ravish Emmeline. Further, in *The Tempest* Prospero describes finding Ariel imprisoned in a tree where Sycorax, Caliban's mother, had placed him twelve years before; hearing his moans, Prospero had released him. In *King Arthur*, when Arthur acts to destroy the enchanted forest by cutting down the 'queen of all the grove', he is deluded into believing that Emmeline is imprisoned in the tree, and her illusion moans and shrieks when the tree is hit.

King Arthur reveals especially close connections with *The Tempest* of 1670,[2] which is not surprising given that Dryden had a major hand in that production.[3] He gave Miranda a sister (Dorinda) who also has never seen a man. The two discuss what a man must be like (end of Act 1). Similarly, in *King Arthur*, Emmeline talks to her attendant Matilda about what she thinks men must be like (Act 2, scene 5). Even more closely parallel, Emmeline and Dorinda both compare holding their lovers' hands to holding their fathers':

> EMMELINE   ... When my father clasps my hand in his,
> That's cold, and I can feel it hard and wrinkled,
> But when you grasp it, then I sigh and pant,
> And something presses to my heart.   (1, 2)
> DORINDA   I've touched my Father's and my Sister's hands
> And felt no pain; but now, alas! there's something,
> When I touch yours, which makes me sigh ...   (2)

Finally, *King Arthur* also exhibits affinity with the 1674 operatic adaptation of *The Tempest*, with which Shadwell has been credited (or, rather accused) but which Dryden must have known well, perhaps as a participant. Especially

---

2   *The Tempest, or the Enchanted Island. A Comedy.* This adaptation, published in 1670, was first acted in 1667.

3   The 1670 version was based in part on the work of Charles Davenant. The musical revision of this text in 1674 has sometimes been attributed to Thomas Shadwell. The settings long thought to be by Purcell were probably composed after 1710 by John Weldon. See Margaret Laurie, 'Did Purcell Set *The Tempest?*', *Proceedings of the Royal Musical Association* 90 (1963–4), 43–57.

striking is the similarity between the closing masques. In the 1674 *Tempest* when all is resolved, Prospero entertains the assembled group with a masque that includes Neptune, Amphitrite, Oceanus and Tethys with attendant sea-gods and sea-goddesses. Neptune calls upon Aeolus to calm the winds, and Aeolus responds:

> You I'll obey, who at one stroke can make,
> With your dread Trident, the whole Earth to quake.
> Come down, my Blusterers, swell no more,
> Your stormy rage give o'r.
> Let all black Tempests cease –
> And let the troubled Ocean rest:
> Let all the Sea enjoy as calm a peace,
> As where the Halcyon builds her quiet Nest.

The chorus then sings, "Sound a calm". In *King Arthur* the final masque begins with Aeolus, who sings:

> Ye Blust'ring Brethren of the Skies,
> Whose Breath has ruffl'd all the Watry Plain,
> Retire, and let Britannia Rise,
> In Triumph o'er the Main.

Followed by:

> Serene and Calm, and void of fear,
> The Queen of Islands must appear.

Beyond this direct parallel, however, the additions, revisions and cuts throughout the 1674 musical version of *The Tempest* anticipate the kinds of alterations made in the first one hundred years of *King Arthur*.

THE 1770 REVIVAL OF *KING ARTHUR*

The 1770 revision of *King Arthur* by Garrick and Arne[4] and the anonymous 1774 adaptation of Purcell's *Dido and Aeneas*[5] both reflect a growing interest in England of the music of the past. The Academy of Ancient Music, which sponsored revivals of *Dido* in 1774 and 1787, was flourishing; in the 1768 book of repertory entitled *The Words of Such pieces as are most usually performed by the Academy of Ancient Music*, 2nd edn, Purcell's works are given special emphasis. Also during this period, the Handel Commemoration Festival of 1784

---

4   *King Arthur: or, the British Worthy . . . the Music by Purcell and Dr. Arne* (London, 1770).
5   See Ellen T. Harris, *Henry Purcell's Dido and Aeneas* (Oxford, 1987), pp. 124–47, for a detailed study of late eighteenth-century adaptations of the opera.

included the greatest number of musicians known at that time to have been assembled, and Dr Samuel Arnold began but did not complete the first collected edition of the music of Handel between 1787 and 1797. In 1789 Charles Burney published *A General History of Music from the Earliest Ages to the Present Period*.[6]

Garrick, who is particularly remembered for his Shakespearean revivals and the realism of his acting, was himself an important part of the revivalist tradition. Arne was among the leading composers in England. They collaborated on a number of ventures, and part of their correspondence concerning *King Arthur* survives.

In the first extant letter, Arne expresses his judgement of Purcell's score and outlines his plans for the adaptation:

> David Garrick, Esq. Sir, – A due attention to your Commission having gone hand in hand with what fancy and judgment I may be thought to possess in my profession, I thought it necessary to lay before you a true state of the merits and demerits of the Musical Performance, you are about to exhibit in King Arthur. To attain a certain rectitude, in judging of this matter, I have not only, with the utmost care and candor inspected the Score of Purcell's composition; but attended two rehearsals of it . . .[7]

As it happens, Arne's judgement was contemptuous and his plans for revision extensive. He writes of the first act that the 'long' sacrifice scene ('Woden first to thee') is 'necessary to be deliver'd in' music; if performed as written, it 'may have a solemn and noble effect', provided the following air ('I call you all to Woden's Hall') 'be perform'd as I have new compos'd it'. He argues that Purcell's version (for countertenor) 'is intirely out of Mrs. [Sophia] Baddeley's compass, very indifferent, and no way proper for a woman, where a troop of warriors are assembled, to bribe their idols for success in battle'. Arne writes that his version of 'I call you all' for the bass Samuel Champness (who according to the 1770 playbook played Aeolus), 'being highly spirited, will carry off with an éclat, an (otherwise) dull, tedious, antiquated suite of Chorus'. This substitution was not included in the final version. Arne

6   See William Weber, *The Rise of Musical Classics in Eighteenth-Century England: A Study in Canon, Ritual, and Ideology* (Oxford 1993) for a thorough discussion of the discovery and development of England's musical past. See also Ellen T. Harris, 'Handel's Ghost: The Composer's Posthumous Reputation in the Eighteenth Century' in *Companion to Contemporary Musical Thought*, ed. John Paynter et al. (London, 1992), pp. 208–25, for a discussion of the growth of historical interest in music, especially Handel's.

7   Printed in Hubert Langley, *Doctor Arne* (Cambridge, 1938), p. 68, and P. T. Dircks, 'Thomas Arne to David Garrick: An Unrecorded Letter', *Theatre Notebook* 30 (1976), 87–90. See also James Boaden, *The Private Correspondence of David Garrick*, 2 vols. (London, 1831–32), and *The Letters of David Garrick*, ed. David M. Little and George M. Kahrl, 3 vols. (Cambridge, Mass., 1963).

concludes his discussion of Act 1 with a request that the final song and chorus, 'Come if you dare, our trumpets sound', also be replaced; Purcell's version is 'tolerable, but so very short of that Intrepity and Spirited defiance pointed at by Dryden's words and sentiments, that, I think, you have only to hear what I have compos'd on the occasion, to make you immediately reject the other'. Again, Arne's version was not chosen; like Purcell's, it would have been sung by tenor Joseph Vernon, who was assigned the role of Honour.[8]

Arne writes of the second number in Act 2, 'Let not a moonborn elf mislead you', as sung by Grimbald, that 'after the two first bars of Purcell [it is] very bad, and out of Mr. Champnes' [sic] compass of voice. – Hear mine'.[9] Like the previous suggestions, however, this was not enacted.

At this point, Arne simply summarizes his critique of Purcell and his plans for adaptation as follows:

> All the other Solo Songs of Purcell are infamously bad; so very bad, that they are privately the objects of sneer and ridicule to the musicians, but, I have not meddled with any, that are not to come from the mouths of your principal Performers. I wish you wou'd only give me leave to *Doctor* this performance, I would certainly make it pleasing to the Public, which otherwise, may have an obstruction to the success of the Revival. It is not *now* my intention to new set many things, mention'd in our original plan; but to put it in the power of your principal performers to make a proper figure, by opening and adorning the most entertaining points of view, wherein *they* are to appear . . .[10]

King Arthur does not crop up again in his correspondence until 1775 when Arne complains to Garrick that he has been of late 'neglected'.[11] Garrick responds that Arne seems 'more inclined to the theatre of Covent-Garden than that of [Garrick's] Drury-Lane', and gives as evidence Arne's music for *Elfrida* (written in 1772 for Covent Garden).[12] Arne's rebuttal, which concerns *King Arthur*, deserves quotation in full:

> I must beg your permission to assure you that you are greatly mistaken in two points. First, when you imagine that I have the least partiality either in favour of the other theatre or its patentees: next in saying that the music in 'Elfrida' is much superior to the music I composed for you in 'King Arthur'. The principal songs, which for air and mastership I have never excelled,

---

8   Arne identifies the intended singer in a letter to Garrick of 24 August 1775. See Langley, *Arne*, p. 80.
9   According to the 1770 playbook and the printed score, Grimbald was sung and acted by Charles Bannister. It is not clear if the singer was changed during rehearsal or whether Arne was simply mistaken, since both Bannister and Champness were basses.
10   As quoted in Langley, *Arne*, p. 69.
11   21 August 1775: Langley, *Arne*, p. 77; Boaden, *Correspondence*, vol. II, 78.
12   24 August 1775: Langley, *Arne*, p. 79; Boaden, *Correspondence*, vol. II, 79; *The Letters of David Garrick*, letter 934, vol. III, 1029.

have *not* been performed. They were written for the late Mrs. Arne [Mrs Michael Arne, née Elizabeth Wright], and fashioned to her sweet voice, and glaring abilities. Mr. Arne expected, from the music and her performances of it, that they would be productive of the highest pleasure, that a judicious audience ever received from either of our endeavours, and several eminent masters thought as he did: but when those *coups de maitre* came out of the mouths of persons who could neither sing in time nor tune, nor turn out one *jeu de la voix* in them, the result was much the same as if an approved author had written a fine part for _____ . . . Champness's songs, the chorus in the first scene of Mr. Vernon's 'Come, if you dare', and several other things that employed my utmost efforts, were laid aside, in favour of Purcell's music, which (though excellent in its kind) was Cathedral, and not to the taste of a modern theatrical audience. But never was my surprise greater than when I perceived that a drama so fertile of invention and elegant in poetry . . . should . . . fail in making that impression on the public, which the managers had an undoubted right to expect.[13]

The Arne and Garrick correspondence reveals tensions over the extent to which *King Arthur* was to be revised. Apparently Arne's 'original plan' was 'to new set many things' (letter of 1770), but this was rejected. If Arne actually wrote many pieces specifically for Mrs Arne, who died on 1 May 1769, then the planning for the production must have started no later than early in 1769, and perhaps as early as 1768. Possibly her death delayed the first performance on 13 December 1770. Even after the production was in rehearsal, however, Arne continued to urge changes that Garrick declined to accept. In his 1770 letter, Arne, after hearing two rehearsals, describes the effect of various pieces, difficulties singers were having with range and style, and the privately shared negative attitude of the musicians. On the evidence of the printed score, Garrick remained unyielding to Arne's entreaties.

However, the printed score and libretto illustrate that this *King Arthur* was far from pristine Purcell. Not only are there musical changes, but Dryden's text is altered as well. Thus, it is hard to tell what caused the supposed failure of the 1770 production.[14] Perhaps Garrick made too many changes, or Arne

13 3 September 1775: Langley, *Arne*, pp. 79–80; Boaden, *Correspondence*, vol. II, 85. See also Richard Luckett, '"Or rather our musical Shakspeare": Charles Burney's Purcell', in *Music in Eighteenth-Century England*, ed. Christopher Hogwood and Richard Luckett (Cambridge, 1983), pp. 59–77, for a detailed discussion of eighteenth-century views of Purcell. Note especially, as regards Arne's comment that Purcell's music is 'Cathedral', that Thomas Gray wrote of the 1736 revival of *King Arthur* that 'the songs are all Church-musick' (pp. 68–9).

14 According to *The London Stage 1660–1800*, Part 4: *1747–1776*, ed. George Winchester Stone, Jr. (Carbondale, 1962), vol. III, 1518ff., *King Arthur* received nineteen performances in 1770–71 season, none in the 1771–72 season (it was scheduled twice and deferred due to illness) and four in the 1772–73 season. The first season was hardly shameful, but neither was it record-breaking. Richard Cumberland's *The West Indian*, another Garrick première of 1770–71, saw twenty-eight performances (*The London Stage*, Part 4, vol. III, 1496).

was right in arguing that contemporary taste demanded even more changes or, as Arne also argued, the substitution of Mrs Baddeley as the principal female singer after the premature death of the inestimable Mrs Arne significantly weakened the performance of his own music. It may be indicative, given Arne's concerns about Mrs Baddeley's singing of 'I call you all to Woden's Hall', that according to the 1770 playbook this was performed by Mr Vernon and in the published score it is given to a Mr Kear;[15] the apparent reassigning of this piece to three different singers indicates some difficulty in finding a performer who could do justice to Purcell's setting.[16] After the deaths of Arne in 1778 and Garrick in 1779, *King Arthur* was revived in 1781, and Vernon may have been the only principal singer retained.[17] Shortly thereafter, *King Arthur* was further adapted by Kemble and Linley as a two-act entertainment entitled *Arthur and Emmeline* that played from 1784 to 1791 as an afterpiece in thirty-one performances with twenty-four different plays.[18] A study of these various adaptations reveals a continuing tradition of methods of revision and much about late eighteenth-century taste.

GARRICK'S ADAPTATION OF DRYDEN

Arne's deprecation of Purcell closely parallels the low opinion in which Dryden was held at the same time. For example, in a 1761 pamphlet addressed to Garrick and intended to encourage the revival and performance of the plays of Philip Massinger, Dryden is heavily criticized:

15 James Thomas Kear was a regular singer with Drury Lane company at this time. See Philip Highfill, Jr., Kalman A. Burnim and Edward A. Langhans, *A Biographical Dictionary of Actors, Actresses . . . in London, 1660–1899*, vol. VIII (Carbondale, 1982), 277–8.

16 Roger Fiske, *English Theatre Music in the Eighteenth Century*, 2nd edn (London, 1986), p. 616, describes Mrs Baddeley's voice as particularly appropriate to the 'slow pathetic song'. If this is the case, then the coloratura written for Mrs Arne would certainly have been inappropriate for her voice. Furthermore, Fiske (p. 638) describes Vernon's voice as 'unappealing in quality'. As if this did not bode badly enough, there were apparently problems with the acting as well; the Hopkins Diary records of the first performance (13 December 1770) that 'Miss Hayward play'd Emmeline very bad', as quoted in *The London Stage*, Part 4, vol. III, 1518.

17 *King Arthur: or, the British Worthy . . . by David Garrick, Esq . . . the Music by Purcell and Dr. Arne* (London, 1781). The playbook gives Vernon in the case list, but *The London Stage*, Part 5: *1776–1800*, ed. Charles Beecher Hogan (Carbondale, 1968), vol. II, 468, states that by this time Vernon had left the stage and suggests that this role was probably taken by Charles Dubellamy, a singer of 'much merit' (*A Biographical Dictionary*, vol. IV, 478–80). Bannister retained the speaking role of Grimbald but probably did not sing. Also, Mrs Wrighten, who played one of the attendant spirits and one of the sirens in 1770, substituted in 1781 at the last minute, apparently in a subsidiary vocal role.

18 Two distinct playbooks survive: *Arthur and Emmeline. A Dramatic Entertainment in Two Acts, Taken From The Masque of King Arthur . . . the Music by Purcel and Dr. Arne* (London, 1784); and *Arthur and Emmeline. An Entertainment of Two Acts, Abridged From The Masque of King Arthur . . . by David Garrick, Esq.* (London, 1786).

Indeed the Heroick Nonsense, which overruns the Theatrical Productions of Dryden . . . must nauseate the most indulgent Spectator. [Footnote:] Nobody can have a truer Veneration for the Poetical Genius of Dryden, than the Writer of these Reflections; but surely that Genius is no where so much obscured, notwithstanding some transient Gleams, as in his Plays; of which He had Himself no great Opinion.[19]

Not surprisingly, Garrick's changes to Dryden's text of *King Arthur* are extensive. These include transposition of scenes, elimination of text, addition of text and substitutions.

These methods were, of course, long common to adapters of musical-theatrical works, including Dryden himself, and often made for the same reasons. Perhaps, given that *King Arthur* resembles Shakespeare's *The Tempest*, especially in Dryden's version (and the operatic revision of 1674), there is some poetic justice in Garrick's revamping of Dryden. For example, transposition of material to create spectacular endings is common. In the 1674 *Tempest*, the scenes of Act 2 are transposed so that the first, which concludes with a masque of devils, could end the act, and this revision was enabled by moving one of the second act scenes to the beginning of Act 3. Thus what in 1670 was a sequence of four scenes became in 1674 the following sequence: Act 2 (1670) scenes 3–4–1; Act 3, scene 2 (and continuing). The earliest revision of *Dido and Aeneas*, when the opera was incorporated into Shakespeare's *Measure for Measure* in 1700, also illustrates the same tendency towards transposition with the same result. The two scenes of the second act of the first known production of 1689 were reversed, thus placing the spectacular scene with the witches at the end rather than the beginning of the act. And in the late eighteenth-century scores this effect is maintained despite a return to the original order, simply by appending the witches' scene to the end of Act 1. Similarly, the mythological prologue of 1689 was in 1700 removed to the end, thus providing a celebratory concluding musical masque to *Measure for Measure*, much as 'The Masque of Neptune and Amphitrite' is added to the end of the 1674 *Tempest*.[20]

Garrick similarly begins his revision of *King Arthur* by eliminating the 1691 spoken prologue and transposing the action in Act 1 so that the work begins in an operatic fashion with the musical scene of sacrifice for the Saxons, only then followed by Dryden's original first scene in which the

---

[19] [George Colman], *Critical Reflections on the Old English Dramatick Writers* (London, 1761), pp. 16–17.

[20] See Harris, *Henry Purcell's Dido and Aeneas*, for a more detailed discussion of the revisions to this opera. See also Price, *Henry Purcell and the London Stage* and Eric Walter White, 'New Light on *Dido and Aeneas*', in *Henry Purcell (1659–1695): Essays on his Music*, ed. Imogen Holst (London, 1959).

history and background to the story of Arthur and Emmeline is recounted in spoken dialogue.[21] This history is capped with an abbreviated version of Dryden's original ending to Act 1, the song 'Come if you dare'. Thus in Garrick's operatic version, *King Arthur* begins in music, and both scenes of the first act end with a song and chorus, the first with 'I call you all to Woden's Hall' and the second with 'Come if you dare'.

In Dryden's Act 1 the pantomime battle between Oswald's Saxons and Arthur's Britons separates the sacrifice scene and the victory song, 'Come if you dare'. In Garrick's version, these musical numbers are already separated by a spoken scene, and Garrick reinterprets 'Come if you dare' as the Britons' battle preparation, parallel in function to the Saxons' sacrifice. Thus the fighting is transposed to the opening of Act 2, providing, as in Act 1, for a spectacular stage scene rather than spoken text at the opening of the act. Arne's march 'for the Entry of the Warriors' printed at the end of the 1770 score was probably used at this point.[22]

Dryden's opening speech of Act 2, 'Alas, for pity, of this bloody field', is then slightly altered and set by Arne as recitative, followed by the air 'O peace descend' to a text newly written by Garrick.[23] Thus, even after the battle was transposed to begin the second act, Garrick still made revisions so as to begin the 'spoken' part of the act with song. Then follows Dryden's unaltered text, including the spoken dialogue between Merlin and Philidel, the scene in which Arthur is led through the woods (with the Purcell settings of 'Hither this way' and 'Let not a moon-born elf', and Arne's revision of 'Come follow me'), and the concluding pastoral masque with Arne's wholly new setting of 'How blest are shepherds' and Purcell's original 'Shepherds leave decoying'. The final text of this masque, 'Come, shepherds, lead up a lively measure', is given by Garrick but not included in the 1770 score. It is not clear whether Purcell's setting was performed, but one may assume that a

---

21 John Buttrey has recently argued (Purcell Conference at Oxford, September 1993) that the first two scenes of *King Arthur* are incorrectly reversed in the 1691 playbook. If so, then the 1770 version is a 'correction' rather than a 'revision'. However, all intervening playbooks maintain the 1691 ordering until 1770.

22 *The Songs Airs Duets & Choruses in the Masque of King Arthur . . . Compos'd by Purcel and Dr. Arne* (London, n.d.).

23 O Peace, sweet Peace, descend,
Of human woes the friend,
O charm to rest this troubled isle,
And o'er the land propitious smile;
Thy smile can chase these clouds away,
From darkest night bring forth the day.
O peace, sweet peace, appear,
And plant thy olive here.

new setting was not contributed, as that certainly would have been published. The text appears in the 1781 playbook but is eliminated from the later condensed version *Arthur and Emmeline* (1784 and 1786).[24]

Act 3 begins as in Dryden with a scene in which the Britons are rebuffed by the magic charms of the Saxons. There is no known music for this scene either by Purcell or Arne, but it is possible that some music accompanied it in both versions.

In the second scene of Act 3, Arthur goes with Merlin and Philidel to restore the sight of Emmeline. She and her handmaiden Matilda are now prisoners of the Saxon chief Oswald. In Dryden's text this scene contains three significant musical numbers: two airs for Philidel ('We must work, we must haste' and 'Thus I infuse') and an extended scene for airy spirits beginning 'O sight, the mother of desires'. No setting by Purcell survives for any of these texts, and the 1770 score contains newly written compositions for each by Arne. In addition, Garrick follows the 'recitative' for Philidel, 'We must work', with a new song, 'To virtue with rapture', also set by Arne.[25]

Act 3 concludes with Osmond's magical presentation for the newly sighted Emmeline of the Frost scene as in Dryden, although Garrick omits the final air by Cupid, 'Sound a parley'. Dryden gives an indication for a dance at the end of this act, and in Purcell's version the third act tune is a hornpipe. In the Arne publication, a 'Country Dance' by Charles Dibdin given at the end of the score is cued for the 'end of the 3d. Act'.

Act 4 begins with a short scene between Osmond, who is hoping to satisfy his lust for Emmeline, and Grimbald, who warns him that Merlin's magic is overpowering them. The body of the act, however, depicts Arthur's foray into the enchanted forest with the intent of destroying the magic spell. His

---

[24] The inclusion of this piece in a manuscript now in the Folger Shakespeare Library (Washington, D.C.), entitled 'Musick in King Arthur, omitted in Dr. Arne's publication', lends credence to the possibility that this music was not performed even though the text is included in the 1770 playbook. This manuscript bears the book-stamp 'W Watts 1789', which provides a *terminus post quem* and places the copy within the general time period of the performances. Of course, as the inscription of the manuscript indicates, it includes music not in Arne's *publication*, and thus may not reflect the performances at all; see also note 53.

[25] To virtue with rapture I bear
  The balsam to heal, the cordial to cheer,
  When vice is oppressing,
  Pursuing, distressing,
  Just Heav'n with virtue takes part;
  For sorrow and sadness,
  Bring comfort and gladness,
  To close ev'ry wound of the heart.

determination is tested first by two syrens and then by woodland nymphs and sylvans, all of whom sing their temptations. Garrick omits the text for the first air sung by one of the syrens, 'O pass not on'. Since there is no surviving music by Purcell, it may never have been set. There seems to have been some confusion over what would be included of the following scene for the nymphs and sylvans. Garrick includes 'How happy the lover', 'For love every creature', 'No joys are above', and omits 'In vain are our graces', but the Arne score includes only 'How happy the lover' and 'In vain are our graces'; this discrepancy is discussed below. After this scene, Dryden calls for a pantomime showing Arthur breaking the magic spell. Garrick follows this with a victory song for Philidel and chorus, again providing a way to end the act with sung music; although this text is not set in Arne's score, it remains in the published texts of every subsequent revival (1781, 1784 and 1786).[26]

Dryden's fifth and last act concludes with a masque in praise of Britain. Garrick shortens or eliminates most of this. The opening air sung by Aeolus, 'Ye blust'ring brethren of the skies', is retained, but the following text beginning 'Serene and calm' is cut from nine to two lines, thus matching that portion set by Purcell (according to the surviving sources). The following texts are then cut completely: 'Round thy coast', 'For folded flocks' and 'Your hay it is mow'd'. 'Fairest isle' is retained (in Purcell's setting); then 'You say, 'tis love creates the pain' is cut. The final text, 'St George, the patron of our isle', is newly set by Arne to conclude the masque.

ARNE'S REVISION OF PURCELL

Arne's contribution, thus, was not minimal. Unlike Garrick's adaptation, which involved both cuts and additions (but little alteration of remaining Dryden text), Arne took the opportunity to revise Purcell's score and clearly proposed more changes than Garrick could accept. He added a solo to 'Come follow me' (Act 2), newly set 'How blest are shepherds' (Act 2) and 'St George, the patron of our isle' (Act 5), and composed a new overture and two hornpipes (one of which probably served as an act tune for Act 4) to replace Purcell's instrumental music. He also added settings for texts by Dryden for which no Purcell setting survives: 'Alas the horror' (originally 'Alas, the pity') (Act 2), 'We must work' (Act 3), 'Thus I infuse' (Act 3), 'O sight, the mother of desires' (Act 3) and contributed settings for newly added texts by Garrick: 'O

26   PHILIDEL: Victory! victory! Vice is in chains,
                      Victory! victory! Virtue reigns!
         CHORUS: Victory! victory!

peace descend' (Act 2) and 'To virtue with rapture' (Act 3). He may also have set Garrick's 'Victory' at the end of Act 4, as the text is retained in later versions even though it does not appear in the 1770 score. Beyond all of these revised and added settings, however, Arne is undoubtedly also responsible for the extensive cuts to 'Come if you dare' (Act 1), 'Come follow me' (Act 2) and 'How happy the lover' (Act 4), as well as for the small editorial changes in many of the other pieces.[27]

The small changes parallel those made in *Dido and Aeneas* four years later and can be discussed in specific categories.[28] In both works, rhythms are simplified:

Ex. 12.1 'Let not a moonborn elf'

Short–long rhythms on the beat are frequently eliminated (even though Arne himself uses them in his own compositions):

Ex. 12.2 'Let not a moonborn elf'

Ex. 12.3 'No part of my dominion'

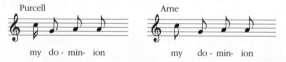

And regular groups of notes in short–short–long patterns are reversed to long–short–short:

Ex. 12.4 'The lot is cast'

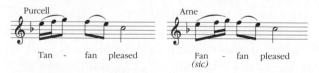

---

27 As with Mozart and Mendelssohn, Arne's musical contributions to posterity are better judged in his original work than in his revisions. See Jane H. Adas, 'Arne's Progress: An English Composer in Eighteenth-Century London', Ph.D. thesis, Rutgers University (1993), for a reappraisal of Arne's original compositions.

28 See Harris, *Henry Purcell's Dido and Aeneas*, pp. 124–47. The revisions in *King Arthur* are far less extensive.

Ex. 12.5 'The lot is cast'

Underlay is altered so that words are set on, rather than ahead of, the beat:

Ex. 12.6 'Let not a moonborn elf'

And melismas are shortened:

Ex. 12.7 'What ho'

Ex. 12.8 'No part of my dominion'

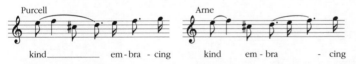

Among the more extensive revisions, Arne added a solo to 'Come follow me' based on Purcell's chorus. Arne models his setting on Purcell's melody for the most part, but his harmonies are more closely restricted to the tonic and dominant. Also, the harmonic rhythm is much slower. Arne thus reinterprets many of Purcell's melody notes as non-harmonic tones, and the ornamental nature of the melody is strengthened by added graces and lengthy coloratura runs.

In the first line of Arne's 'Come follow me', where the melody is borrowed intact, Arne not only adds appoggiaturas in two places but re-conceives a number of the scale tones as passing notes in a phrase that extends the dominant over two bars before cadencing to the tonic (D major). In Purcell's setting, there is harmonic change on every melody note, also leading to the tonic.

Ex. 12.9   'Come follow me'

In the second line, Arne also alters the melody, to which he again adds appoggiaturas, and sets the line to a series of alternating tonic and dominant chords, again cadencing to the tonic. Purcell once more changes the harmony on every melody note, this time directing the line towards arrival in E major, a secondary dominant.

Ex. 12.10   'Come follow me'

Arne then adds a vocal melisma on 'follow' that effects a modulation to the dominant (A major) and cadences to the dominant of that key (E major).

Ex. 12.11 'Come follow me'

The dominant is confirmed in the next phrase, a repetition of the second line of text, which ends the first part of the song. In Purcell's chorus, this section ends on the tonic.

Purcell begins the second section in the tonic. The words 'No goblin or elf shall dare to offend ye' are at first presented by the bass alone. When the full chorus enters, there is a modulation to the dominant, after which an instrumental interlude returns to the tonic. The setting of the last section, beginning 'We brethren of air', offers a dramatic contrast to the previous text in its presentation by treble voices only. It moves successively through the supertonic, submediant, dominant, supertonic, subdominant, dominant and tonic (D major).

In his version for soprano solo, Arne combines these texts (without an instrumental interlude), gives them a consistent dotted rhythm borrowed from Purcell's 'No goblin' setting and maintains the dominant key (A major) with references also to its minor tonic and major dominant.

Ex. 12.12 'Come follow me'

Once again, Arne prepares the final cadence of this section with a long melisma.

Ex. 12.13 'Come follow me'

that at - tend___

to the kind

The entire text is then repeated, the second phrase returning to the tonic, which is then maintained throughout. Arne provided further coloratura runs for Mrs Baddeley on the words 'bear' (twice) and 'kind'. The last two of these conclude on high A, as did the melisma on 'attend' given above.

Ex. 12.14 'Come follow me'

kind___

he - roes will bear___

Arne's solo adaptation of Purcell's chorus is in 'slow-movement sonata form'.[29] 'Come follow me and greensward all your way shall be' is set in the tonic. A vocal run on 'follow' moves to the dominant, and a final phrase confirms the modulation with a cadence in the dominant. The second section or theme sets the words 'No goblin or elf shall dare to offend; we brethren of air you heroes will bear to the kind and the fair that attend'. Again the cadence to this section is confirmed with a long vocal run that leads to the close in the dominant. Without an intervening development section, there is a quick return to the tonic and the two thematic areas are immediately recapitulated in that key. The extensive coloratura additionally relates this section formally (but not harmonically) to an ornamented *da capo* repetition.

29   Charles Rosen, *The Classical Style* (New York, 1972), p. 306, n. 2, where the term is used to describe 'Là, ci darem la mano' from *Don Giovanni*.

In Purcell's setting, the opening melody of a downward octave scale and the points of arrival in various keys depict the sense of 'Come follow me'. Furthermore, the distinct and varied vocal ranges of 'No goblin' and 'We brethren of air' not only represent the relative regions in which these beings reside but also represent the spirit rising from the abyss into the light. Arne's setting eliminates both the tonal variety and distinctive ranges of the Purcell, but also represents the sense of 'Come follow me' primarily through vocal pyrotechnics and large-scale form. Arne follows this solo with a significantly shortened version of Purcell's chorus, concluding with the first four bars of the instrumental interlude cadencing in the tonic – a contraction that is musically sensible given the changes in the air.

'Come if you dare', to take a different example, seems to have been cut for dramatic reasons. In 1691, Dryden prefaced this song with the following stage direction: 'A Battle supposed to be given behind the Scenes, with Drums, Trumpets, and Military Shouts and Excursions: After which, the *Britons*, expressing their Joy for the Victory, sing this Song of Triumph.' In 1770, Garrick uses a shortened version of 'Come if you dare' as a rallying song to conclude the first act. The second act begins with the battle, followed not by a song of victory as in Dryden, rather by a prayer for peace; Garrick only gives the Britons a victory chorus at the end of Act 4 when they have truly won. Thus Purcell's battle music is eliminated (bars 81–115), as is all that follows: the third strophe tells how 'The fainting Saxons quit their ground' and the fourth celebrates 'Now the victory's won'. The truncated chorus thus ends with the setting of 'And pity mankind that will perish for gold', providing less than half of Purcell's original. The textual adjustment is also made in the 1770 playbook.

In the fourth act, Purcell's lengthy passacaglia 'How happy the lover', depicting Arthur's temptation by the woodland nymphs (after he successfully resists the sea nymphs), is extensively cut. Dryden's stage direction reads: 'As he is going forward, Nymphs and Sylvans come out from behind the Tree, Base [sic] and two Trebles sing the following song to a Minuet.' There follow two nine-line strophes, with the refrain, 'No joys are above / The pleasures of love'. Dryden adds before the first strophe: 'Dance with the Song, all with Branches in their Hands', and following it: 'The Dance continues with the same Measure play'd alone.' Purcell's setting opens with a fifty-six-bar instrumental prelude with fourteen repetitions of the four-bar passacaglia, which is heard in different registers, varied, and in inversion. Arne reduces this to the first four repetitions during which the bass remains unchanged. Arne then provides Purcell's solo and chorus setting of the first five lines of the first strophe. At this point Purcell includes another long ritornello (bars 90–134). Arne gives only the last nine bars of this (two repetitions of the bass and a cadence to the tonic). He skips the setting of the final four lines of the strophe (bars 135–97), but includes the setting of the entire second strophe, 'In vain are our graces' (bars 198–242 in Purcell). Arne thus preserves less than half of Purcell's lengthy original and apparently cuts both dances.

In the 1770 playbook there are no directions for dance during the passacaglia, and the song text is cut, but not in the same manner as in the score. The first strophe is given completely, and the second strophe not at all. Seemingly, then, the revision was not made for dramatic reasons, as in 'Come if you dare', but rather simply to shorten this long entertainment unified by the ostinato bass. 'Oft she visits' in the 1774 *Dido and Aeneas*, an entertainment for the hunting party sung by the Second Woman over a recurring bass, was similarly truncated.[30] That these changes seem to represent a late eighteenth-century English impatience with dance-oriented operatic tableaux built on repeating basses in the style of the great chaconnes of Lully's operas is confirmed by Charles Burney:

> The composing songs on a *ground-base*, was an exercise of ingenuity, in which Purcell seems to have much delighted; but though it was as much a fashion in his time . . . yet the practice was Gothic, and an unworthy employment for men possessed of such genius and original resources.[31]

In Act 2 Arne completely resets 'How blest are shepherds'. The six-line text has the rhyme scheme *ababcc*. Like Purcell, Arne breaks the text after the first (unrhymed) couplet, dividing the song into two parts, but Arne only sets the first four lines.[32] The second section of Purcell's setting is therefore twice as long as the first, with an intermediary cadence in E minor, whereas in Arne's setting the two sections balance exactly. Both composers set the song in G major.[33] Although in similar metres (Purcell 3/4; Arne 6/4), the two settings display different accent patterns in relation to the text. Whereas Purcell follows the dactylic metre of the poem, Arne chooses instead to accent the strong word in each of the first two lines. Purcell stresses these words with pitch.

> How blest are Shepherds how happy their Lasses,
> While Drums & Trumpets are sounding Alarms!

---

30   See Harris, *Henry Purcell's Dido and Aeneas*, pp. 140–4, for an analysis of this revision.
31   Charles Burney, *A General History of Music*, ed. Frank Mercer (New York, 1935), vol. II, 394.
32   Not only is the full text of the first strophe printed in the 1770 playbook, but the complete second strophe is printed in both the playbook and the published score. In both strophes, however, the musical setting can only be of the opening quatrain.
33   In the Arne score, 'How blest are shepherds' is published with the incorrect key signature of two sharps.

Ex. 12.15   'How blest are shepherds'

Purcell's setting, which conforms to the metric accent and still emphasizes the appropriate words, is more lilting and less plodding than Arne's which is hardly a 'correction'.[34] Rather it is a simplification of rhythm, metre, form and harmony. Compare in Ex. 12.15 the different rhythmic settings of 'their', and the text painting that Purcell indulges in for the phrase 'while drums and trumpets' and the word 'sounding'. In addition to truncating the text, Arne also eliminates Purcell's choral repetition.

The final set of strophes sung by Honour are also newly composed by Arne. In Dryden's text, this song is preceded by a stage direction for 'a Warlike Consort', which Purcell supplies, followed by 'A full Chorus of the whole Song: After which the Grand Dance'. The two surviving settings of the first strophe attributed to Purcell are doubtful, but both are solos in the treble clef.[35] The second and third strophes, a complete chorus with full orchestra and two obbligato trumpets in binary form with cadences throughout to C major, are probably authentic. In contrast, Arne provides a straightforward, strophic setting with each solo line followed immediately by a choral response; it too is accompanied by full orchestra and two obbligato trumpets. Perhaps the lack of an original Purcell setting of the first strophe encouraged Arne to replace this number. At any rate, once the first strophe was newly composed, this setting and not Purcell's was used for the remaining two strophes as well.

---

[34]   Fiske, *English Theatre Music*, p. 360, gives text-setting as the reason for Arne's resetting, implying that Arne sought to correct Purcell.

[35]   *The Works of Henry Purcell*, vol. XXVI, rev. A. Margaret Laurie, 168–71 and 205.

In a number of cases Arne supplies music where there is no Purcell setting, or at least no surviving setting. At the beginning of Act 2, for example, the text 'Alas, for pity' is re-conceived as a recitative (with its text altered to 'Alas the horrors') and followed by Garrick's new air 'O peace descend'. In the 1691 playbook there is nothing to suggest that 'Alas, for pity' was sung. In decasyllabic blank verse, these verses are not set off nor in italic as are the sung texts. This is also true in the 1770 playbook where, however, 'O peace descend' in rhymed couplets of mixed length is called 'A Song', indented and set in italic. Because in the published score the text of 'Alas, for pity' differs slightly from the 1770 playbook (which follows Dryden's 1691 text in content, typography and layout), the textual alteration and musical adaptation was probably Arne's idea.[36] Perhaps Garrick's new song text led him to consider setting the previous text as recitative; indeed, something similar occurs in Act 3. There is no reason to believe that Purcell ever set 'Alas, for pity', nor was the recitative–song pair performed after the 1770 performance and 1781 revival. In the *Arthur and Emmeline* revisions of 1784 and 1786, the new air is omitted and the preceding text is cut in half and undoubtedly spoken, not sung.

The accompanied recitative, for Mrs Baddeley in the role of Philidel, is unremarkable. With a four-bar instrumental introduction largely in unison and beginning in C minor, it comes to rest briefly on B♭ major in the second bar and cadences in G minor. For the first two bars the dynamics alternate *forte* and *piano* every half bar, after which the introduction dies away to *pianissimo*. The accompaniment is of little interest once the singer enters, and the voice depicts neither the sense nor the rhythm of the text:

[36] Dryden/Garrick version:

> Alas, for pity, of this bloody field!
> Piteous it needs must be when I, a spirit,
> Can have so soft a sense of human woes!
> Ah! for so many souls, as but this morn
> Were cloath'd with flesh, and warm'd with vital blood,
> But naked now, or shirted but with air.

Arne version (original spelling and punctuation):

> Alass. the Horrors of this bloody Field
> Horrid it needs must be. When I, a Spirit,
> can have so soft a sense of Human woes.
> Ah. For so many Souls as but this Day,
> were cloath'd with Flesh, and warm'd with Vital Blood.
> But naked now. Or Shirted but with Air.

Ex. 12.16 'Alas the horrors'

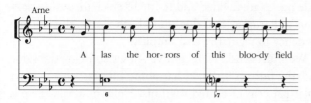

The setting largely depends on a dotted quaver – semiquaver pattern with static accompaniment:

Ex. 12.17 'Alas, the horrors'

The following song, 'O peace descend', for Philidel was undoubtedly also sung by Mrs Baddeley. It is set in binary form in E♭ major, with the first statement of text moving from the tonic to the dominant. The second setting of the text is truncated and moves from the dominant back to the tonic. Appropriately for this sombre text, there is little in the way of coloratura.

In Act 3, Arne sets a second recitative–aria pair; again the recitative text, 'We must work', is derived from Dryden and the air, 'To virtue with rapture', newly written by Garrick. In this case the recitative is indicated in the 1691 playbook as sung text; in rhyming seven-syllable lines, it is indented and set in italic type. However, there survives no Purcell setting of this or either of the other original song texts from the scene in which Emmeline's sight is magically restored. 'Thus I infuse' is set as a self-standing recitative for Mrs Baddeley, and 'O sight, the mother of desires' (shortened text) is set as a recitative–aria pair for the 'Attendant Spirit', Mrs Wrighten. This repeated effort to create recitative–aria pairs also occurs in the 1774 *Dido and Aeneas*, where previously single pieces are divided and retitled as recitative and aria.[37] Like the other revisions to harmony and rhythm in both works, this restructuring illustrates a tendency to regularize and simplify.

Arne's setting of 'We must work' as recitative shows some of the same characteristics of 'Alas, the horrors': it lacks harmonic interest, and the text setting falls into regular patterns of dotted rhythms. Here, however, there is some text painting in the orchestral accompaniment. Note in Ex. 12.18 the orchestral response to 'sprite', 'glimmer' and 'run'.

Ex. 12.18 'We must work'

'To virtue with rapture' is set, like 'Come follow me', as a highly ornamented air in slow-movement sonata form. The text is divided into two unequal sections, the first consisting of the first two lines. This is set simply in B♭ major. The text is then broken up into smaller bits modulating to the dominant and leading into a long vocal run on 'bear' that is played out over a dominant in the new key (F major). The second section (or theme) is based on the remaining six lines of text. This remains largely in F major and culminates with a long vocal run on the word 'heart'. There immediately follows a recapitulation of the first and second sections in the tonic. After the 1781 revival of the 1770 production, this recitative–aria pair, including Dryden's original spoken text, was cut.

After Emmeline's sight is restored and she sees her attendant Matilda and her lover Arthur for the first time, Philidel calls forth 'Airy forms' to

---

37 See Harris, *Henry Purcell's Dido and Aeneas*, pp. 144–6.

'congratulate' Emmeline on her 'new-born eyes' and to show her what she has gained 'by sight restor'd' ('O sight, the mother of desires'). In 1691, Dryden included the stage direction, 'Airy Spirits appear in the Shapes of Men and Women'. The first eight lines of text are cued 'Man sings', with a choral repetition of the last four lines. Then a 'Woman sings' the next ten lines with a choral repetition of the last four lines. Finally, a 'Man sings' the last six lines, which are repeated by a 'Chor. of all Men & Women'.

In Garrick's version, this text is shortened and redistributed: the last six lines are eliminated, and the first two sections of text are simply 'Sung by Mrs. Wrighten'. A choral entry is signalled on the last (newly written) line, but since the stage direction is altered to 'Airy Spirits appear in the shape of Women', a women's chorus must have been intended rather than the mixed chorus called for in Dryden's text. In Arne's setting, however, there is no chorus and the first two sections of text are set respectively in recitative and song.

The song is set as a binary form without large-scale textual repetition. The first section comprises the first six lines, modulating from the tonic (G major) to the dominant; the second section sets the last four lines modulating back to the tonic. There are long vocal runs on 'light', 'love' and especially on 'eyes'.

Ex. 12.19 'O sight, the mother'

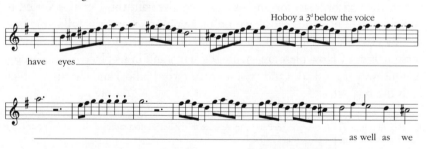

The reasons for Arne's revisions, deletions and additions to Purcell's score are apparent. In some cases they directly follow Garrick's revisions, such as the restructuring of scenes in Acts 1 and 2. More often, however, there is an attempt to bring Purcell's score up to date. This is done through small stylistic revisions to melody and rhythm, slowing down the harmonic rhythm, truncation of a long and varied scene unified by a passacaglia bass, and the attempt to create recitative–aria pairs whenever possible, either with new text or by re-conceiving Dryden's, or both. In short, Arne attempts and often succeeds in transforming Purcell's seventeenth-century baroque score into an example of the classical style.

THE LATER VERSIONS

In 1784 *King Arthur* was revised yet again, being greatly shortened and compressed into a two-act afterpiece entitled *Arthur and Emmeline*. John Philip Kemble, who played Arthur in all of the performances over the next seven years, is credited with the adaptation, and Thomas Linley made the necessary musical adjustments.

> At Drury Lane a great deal of pains had been taken with a masque called Arthur and Emmeline, an alteration of Dryden's King Arthur, or the British Worthy. Miss Farren was the heroine, and her innocent blindness interested in a very high degree. Kemble sustained Arthur in a most chivalrous style, and the Grimbald and Philidel of Bannister and Miss Field (not to speak it profanely) formed no despicable stage companion to the magic of the Tempest. Linley made some tasteful additions to the divine music of Purcell.[38]

The 1784 and 1786 playbooks indicate that this version remained relatively stable.[39]

The opening sacrifice scene is shortened by the omission of 'The white horse neigh'd' and 'The lot is cast'. (In 1786, however, 'The white horse neigh'd' re-appears in the playbook.) 'I call you all to Woden's Hall' is also eliminated, so that the sacrifice scene ends with 'Brave souls'. The Britons' 'Come if you dare' is given in the shortened form created by Arne. After the battle, the text of 'Alas, for pity' is shortened by half; this clearly reverted to speech, as half of Arne's music would make no sense, and the following new text by Garrick for the aria 'O peace descend' is omitted. The entire pastoral masque is cut ('How blest are shepherds', etc.) and in its place is a new song, 'Come away from shades and cool fountains' for Philidel and chorus,[40] which ends the first act.

---

[38] James Boaden, *Memoirs of the Life of John Philip Kemble*, 2 vols. (London, 1825), vol. I, 225.

[39] According to *The London Stage*, Part 5, there were thirty-one performances of *Arthur and Emmeline* over six seasons, the last being 1790–91.

[40] PHILIDEL. Come away,
    From shades and cool fountains,
    Bright Spirits of Day,
    Who gild the high mountains.
CHO. We come, we obey,
    With delight we attend thee.
PHILIDEL. To fair Emmeline bear
    Your heav'n born treasure,
CHO. Come away, we obey!
PHILIDEL. With fair Emmeline share
    Your pure light, love, and pleasure.
CHO. Lead on, point the way,
    With delight we attend thee,
    Lead on, point the way,
    Love to light shall befriend thee.

The second act begins with the infusion scene. 'We must work' is omitted, and the scene begins with a spirit singing 'O sight, the mother of desires'. As the text is the shortened version of Arne's setting, this is undoubtedly what was sung. The infusion itself is still marked with the text 'Thus I infuse', but the following Frost scene is omitted completely. Similarly, the temptation scene for Arthur is emasculated. There are no songs for the sirens and only 'How happy the lover' remains for the nymphs and sylvans. However, Garrick's victory chorus, for which no music survives, is retained, and a new song for Philidel precedes it, 'Iopeans fill the sky'.[41] This and 'Come away from shades and cool fountains' were probably written by Kemble and set by Linley.[42] The final masque of Britain follows exactly from the Arne and Garrick version.

The version of *Arthur and Emmeline* that appears in the 1798 edition of the dramatic works of David Garrick honours these changes by and large, but it also eliminates the only remaining section of the passacaglia, completing a process begun in 1770.[43] 'Serene and calm' is also omitted following 'Ye blust'ring brethren'. It is hard to know, however, whether or not these additional cuts reflect the stage version after 1786. If so, then from 1770 to 1798 the process of cutting continued with few reprieves, and new additions were as likely to receive the axe as Dryden and Purcell's originals. By 1798, Arne's settings of 'Alas the horrors', 'O peace descend', 'How blest are shepherds', 'We must work' and 'To virtue with rapture' had all been cut. 'Come follow me', 'O sight, the mother of desires' and 'St George' probably remained as Arne had set them. 'Thus I infuse' may not have been sung: in the 1798 edition it is clearly not indicated as a song.

Of course, in the absence of a score, much rests on educated guesswork. To take a single example, one copy of 'Fairest isle' that survives in an eighteenth-century songbook preserves the tune not in Purcell's original triple metre, but in duple cut time.[44] Whether this represents a version ever performed on the stage or simply an odd private variant, perhaps for instruction, is impossible to tell.

---

[41] Iopeans fill the skies,
The monster is in chains;
Beneath my feet he lies,
Virtue triumphant reigns!

[42] See Boaden, *Kemble*, vol. I, 225. Kemble also revived *The Tempest* in 1789 retaining Dryden's addition of Dorinda from 1670 and the masque of Neptune and Amphitrite from the 1674 operatic version, as well as adding new songs of his own.

[43] *The Dramatic Works of David Garrick, Esq.* (London, 1798), vol. III, 109–34.

[44] Yale University, Beinecke Rare Book and Manuscript Library, Osborn Shelves Music Ms. 25: 'anonymous collection of English songs, melodies, and solfège exercises.'

Ex. 12.20 'Fairest isle'

Fair-est isle all isles ex-cell-ing Seat__ of plea-sures and__ of loves

Ve-nus here will choose her dwell-ing and__ for-sake__ her Cyp - rian groves

Cu-pid from his fa-vorite na-tion care__ and en-vy will__ re-move

jea-lous-y that poi - son pas-sion and__ des-pair__ that dies__ for__love

THE INTERIM YEARS

Arne's extensive contributions to the important scene in which Emmeline's sight is restored and the lack of any Purcell settings for it raises many questions that go beyond the history of the 1770 revision. Did Purcell ever set the songs in this scene? Could he not have wanted to use music for this magical restoration? If Purcell did set these songs, when and how were they lost? Could Arne's settings be based on Purcell's originals, as is 'Come follow me'? Although none of these questions can be answered definitively, an examination of the interim revivals and a glance at the sources of Purcell's music provide some clues.

King Arthur was a popular work that saw a number of important revivals between the première in 1691 and the Arne/Garrick revision of 1770. The major revivals of 1695 and 1736, as determined by surviving playbooks, closely follow the original in all details. The 1736 production differs primarily in its title: *Merlin: or, The British Inchanter and King Arthur, The British Worthy*, which emphasizes the magical rather than the historical and heroic elements of the story.[45] Not surprisingly, given the title, this production emphasized new and spectacular scenic effects that were widely praised. Like

---

[45] The Giffard who produced this revival is variously identified as Henry or William. For the record, Arne in his letter of 3 September 1775 attributes the production to Henry (Harry). (*A Biographical Dictionary*, vol. VI, 201–3, attributes the revival to William.)

the 1695 revival, however, it seems to have stuck closely to the original text and score.

The first important revision of *King Arthur* was for Dublin in 1763.[46] Arne apparently refers to this production and the earlier performances of 1736 in a letter of 3 September 1775 in which he defends his hand in the 1770 adaptation:

> But never was my surprise greater than when I perceived that a drama so fertile of invention and elegant in poetry, which brought so much to Harry Gifford [in 1736], and lately in Dublin should (though strongly performed at a vast expense at Drury-lane) fail in making that impression on the public, which the managers had an undoubted right to expect.[47]

Text changes in the 1763 version seem to presage the Arne/Garrick adaptation. The 1763 text adds new songs to Acts 1, 2 and 5, thus setting a precedent for Garrick's additions in 1770. In Act 1, a song for a priestess, sung by Signora Christina Passerini,[48] follows 'I call you all' before the battle.[49] In Act 2, after 'Let not a moon-born elf' and before the reprise of 'Hither this way', the song 'This way turn' is added, also for Passerini.[50] And in Act 5, a new recitative and duet are added for 'Signora and Master Passerini' after 'Fairest isle'.[51] None of these songs is maintained in later revivals.

---

[46] *King Arthur: or, The British Worthy. A Dramatick Opera . . . By Mr. Dryden* (Dublin: James Hoey, 1763): exemplar in British Library. A second, slightly different, version of this performance is preserved in an alternative printing from the same year: *King Arthur: or, The British Worthy. A Masque . . . Altered from Dryden. The Music by Purcell* (Dublin; J. Potts, 1763). The Potts version appears to predate the Hoey, in which all the changes are integrated into the text; Potts indicates deletions with virgole ('Such passages as were tiresome to the *Auditor* are therefore marked thus ' ' and omitted in the Representation') and the additions are given on an extra page at the end: exemplar in Regenstein Library, The University of Chicago; the exemplar in the British Library is lacking the added page.

[47] Langley, *Arne*, p. 80; Boaden, *Correspondence*, vol. II, 85.

[48] Passerini was a leading soprano who came to England in 1751 and sang frequently in Handel's oratorios; see Winton Dean, 'Passerini' in *The New Grove*, vol. XIV, 275.

[49] This song appears only in the Hoey playbook (see n. 46):

> Pow'rs, who take a dreadful Pleasure,
> In the Steel-form'd Array of Fight;
> Trumps that sound their warlike Measure,
> Rout and Ruin, Fear and Flight!
>
> To our wonted Fame restore us!
> Give the *British* Host to yield;
> Cause their Squares to sink before us!
> Theirs the Flight, and ours the Field!

[50] This way turn, the Fiends avoiding,
Or in Bogs and Pits you'll fall,
Once decoy'd in,
There destroy'd in,
Merlin can't your Doom recall.

[51] There is also an added recitative that precedes this duet:
DUET: By Signora and Master Passerini.

The 1763 version shows significant cuts as well. In Act 3, for example, 'We must work', 'O sight, the mother' and 'Sound a parley' are left out. Each of these movements is also altered or deleted in the Garrick/Arne version: 'We must work' is newly set by Arne as recitative, 'O sight, the mother' is shortened and completely set anew and 'Sound a parley' is omitted. Similarly, in 1763 as in the Garrick/Arne version, 'O pass not on' is omitted from Act 4, and in Act 5 'Serene and calm' is shortened[52] and 'Round they coast', 'For folded flocks', 'Your hay it is mow'd and 'You say 'tis love' omitted. Thus the 1763 version may have played a major part in both Garrick's and Arne's choices for 1770.

The three songs in the infusion scene missing from Purcell's setting are particularly vexing. Arne's recitative settings of 'We must work' and 'Thus infuse' and his alteration of 'O sight, the mother of desires' into a recitative–aria pair in contrast to the longer text and alternating choral format described by Dryden are unlikely to have been based on Purcell settings, as is, for example, Arne's revision of 'Come follow me'. However, the Folger manuscript in which are compiled Purcell's settings which Arne shortened, eliminated or replaced includes no settings of these pieces.[53] The elimination of two of these three songs in the Dublin performance also tends to confirm a lack of surviving musical settings by Purcell at least by this time. The text of the third song, 'Thus I infuse', is included in the 1763 playbook no doubt because it describes the moment of the magical restoration, but it probably was declaimed in speech rather than sung.

HE	Love and Beauty when united,
	Rule supreme in ev'ry Heart;
SHE	You're forgot, and I am slighted,
	Pow'rless both, when once we part,
HE	For you, with me,
SHE	For I, with you;
BOTH	With you, with you
	The Subjected World Subdue,
	Gods and Mortals we keep under
	Never, therefore, let us sunder.

[52] Not in Hoey; in Potts the deletion is indicated by virgole.

[53] This manuscript contains 'Come follow me – We brethren of air', 'Symphony – How blest are shepherds', 'Shepherds leave decoying' and 'Come shepherds lead up' from Act 2, 'Sound a parley' from Act 3, 'Two daughters of this aged stream', and 'How happy the lover – For love every creature – No joys are above – In vain are our graces – Then use the sweet blessing' from Act 4, and 'Round thy coast', 'For folded flocks', 'You say 'tis love' and 'St George' (based on the following) and 'Our nations not alone appear' from Act 5. That the complete 'Come if you dare' does not appear from Act 1 may mean that part of the beginning of this manuscript is lost, but there is no reason to suppose that the songs from the infusion scene in Act 3 would not have been included had they existed.

Anonymous eighteenth-century settings of all three songs are preserved in a Gresham College Library manuscript of *King Arthur*, which preserves most of Purcell's original; but these stylistically modern compositions, with written-out keyboard accompaniments, seem to offer yet another indication that Purcell settings for these songs were lacking. Unfortunately, this manuscript cannot be associated with a specific performance and is only generally datable to the late eighteenth century.[54] The Gresham settings were certainly not used in the Garrick/Arne version, and since 'We must work' was cut in the performances of *Arthur and Emmeline* and two of the three songs were cut in the 1763 Dublin version, the Gresham settings cannot relate to these performances either.[55]

That these three song texts were not exclusively associated with Purcell's *King Arthur* can be adduced from their use in other works. The first such borrowing occurs in the operatic version of Shakespeare's *A Midsummer Night's Dream*. Entitled *The Fairies*, it was composed by John Christopher Smith and produced by Garrick at Drury Lane, first on 3 February 1755. In the last act of the opera, as Oberon drops a magic potion in the eyes of Titania in order to free her from her 'blind' love of a 'patch'd fool', the libretto gives him these words:[56]

> This, this I'll infuse
> Whose sovereign dews
> Shall clear each film that cloud her sight;
> And you her crystal humours bright,
> From noxious vapours purg'd and free,
> Shall be as you were wont to be.

The different dramatic context explains the few changes from Dryden's original text:

---

[54] *The Works of Henry Purcell*, vol. XXVI, rev. A. M. Laurie, xi. This manuscript is now housed in the Guildhall Library, London.

[55] The Gresham College manuscript, quite apart from the three songs in the infusion scene, does not relate to any of the playbooks from 1763 and later. The music is revised throughout, but the alterations include no wholesale omissions, substitutions or additions. Thus, the manuscript may be considered an attempt at authenticity, at least compared to Garrick and Arne's version. Because both 'Come if you dare' and 'O sight, the mother of desires' adhere to the shortened versions of Garrick's text, and 'O sight, the mother of desires' is written as a solo song, as cued in Garrick, this manuscript can safely be dated after 1770. Further, the stylistic changes so closely parallel those made in the 1774 *Dido and Aeneas* that its origin within the Academy of Ancient Music at about the same time seems probable.

[56] *The Fairies. An Opera. Taken from A Midsummer Night's Dream, written by Shakespear . . . The Music composed by Mr. Smith* (1760; facsimile reprint, London 1969), p. 43.

Thus, thus I infuse
These Soveraign Dews.
Fly back, ye Films, that cloud her sight,
And you, ye Crystal Humours bright,
Your Noxious Vapours purg'd away,
Recover, and admit the Day.
Now cast your Eyes abroad, and see
All but me.

In the libretto of *The Fairies* this text is not given as a song, and in the 1755 published score there is no setting.[57] Once again, as in the 1763 Dublin performance of *King Arthur*, the evidence seems to point to this text being spoken rather than sung as an air or even accompanied recitative.

Apparently the success of *The Fairies* led quickly to another Shakespearean opera, for a year later Garrick produced Smith's *Tempest* at Drury Lane; it opened on 11 February. In the first act, as Prospero discusses his plans with Ariel, he sings 'We must work, we must haste'. Here Dryden's text is largely preserved intact, the only significant change coming in the last line: '*Osmond* will be here anon' (Dryden); 'Naples will be here anon' (Smith).[58] In this case, Smith provides an elaborate setting for soloist and full orchestra, including strings, with violins doubled by oboes, two horns and two bassoons. The aria is a so-called 'modified da capo': the first A section cadences in the dominant, the B section is modulatory and cadences on the dominant and the second A section (not a repetition of A1) is the tonic throughout.[59] The text setting, vacillation between major and minor, harmonic rhythm, orchestration and form confirm Smith's rather than Purcell's authorship (see Ex. 12.21).

Of the various surviving eighteenth-century settings of the three songs in the infusion scene, none seem to derive from an original Purcell setting. 'We must haste' was set most often. 'Thus I infuse' survives in two settings (Gresham and Arne), but perhaps even more interesting are three other cases in which these verses were not given heightened musical settings: in the 1756 operatic version of *A Midsummer Night's Dream (The Fairies)* by Smith, in the Dublin 1763 performance and in the 1798 edition of Garrick's works.

---

57   *The Fairies* [.] *An Opera. The Words taken from Shakespear &c. Set to Music by Mr. Smith* (London, n.d.).
58   *The Tempest. An Opera. Taken from Shakespear . . . The Songs from Shakespear, Dryden, &c. The Music composed by Mr. Smith* (London, 1756), p. 6.
59   This form is sometimes described as deriving from the curtailment of the traditional five-part *da capo* that occurs by placing the B section in between the two written-out statements of A and foregoing the signed *da capo*, a process that occurs in some of Handel's scores. For a discussion, see Eric Weimer, '*Opera seria' and the Evolution of Classical Style: 1755–1772* (Ann Arbor, 1984), pp. 16–17 and 27. For discussion of modified *da capo* arias in Handel's *Belshazzar*, see David Hurley, 'Handel's Compositional Process: A Study of Selected Oratorios', Ph.D. thesis, University of Chicago (1991), pp. 322–6.

Ex. 12.21 'We must work'

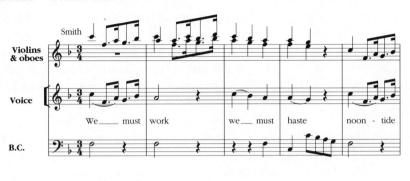

Obviously, 'O sight, the mother of desires' was intended for song, as is evident from Dryden's explicit directions for men's and women's choirs and soloists. Arne's version sets a shorter text in a completely different way and, because this text is given in all following playbooks up to 1798, it is likely that Arne's version was used. The Gresham College setting is also a solo song based on this shorter text and does not likely derive from a putative Purcell setting. Although it is possible to imagine that Purcell might never have set 'We must haste' or 'Thus I infuse' it is less easy to imagine that he would ignore the large-scale potential of 'O sight, the mother'. Still no Purcellian setting of these three songs survives in any of the manuscript sources for *King Arthur*, the earliest of which has been dated 1699. Therefore, one has to assume that if original Purcell settings were lost, they were lost early on when *King Arthur* was being frequently performed and well before the extensive revisions discussed above. There is a parallel with *Dido and Aeneas*, for which there is no Purcell setting of the witches' chorus that ends the second act. In this case, however, the earliest surviving source dates from after 1777,[60] and there are no substitute settings for the eighteenth-century productions nor is the text found in other works.

King Arthur saw many transformations during the eighteenth century. In 1736 it was revived seemingly intact. The 1763 Dublin performance, by contrast, contained significant alterations, including both extensive cuts and additions of new songs for the lead soprano. These alterations in turn served as a model for Garrick and Arne's thorough-going revision of *King Arthur* in 1770, although more generally their textual alterations follow methods of revision familiar since Dryden's day and their musical revisions follow a pattern of late eighteenth-century improvements that can also be seen in *Dido and Aeneas* from 1774. Furthermore, Garrick's productions of John Christopher Smith's *Fairies* and *Tempest* not only relate historically to such operatic adaptations of Shakespeare as the Restoration operatic version of *The Tempest*, which directly influenced the original *King Arthur*, but both of Smith's operas also contain added text from *King Arthur*. Moreover, Garrick and Arne's *King Arthur* of 1770 did not end this series of adaptations. First it was revived in 1781, after its adapters' deaths, but then it too was subject to extensive revision by yet another pair of adapters: in 1784 John Philip Kemble and Thomas Linley continued the process begun at least by 1763. Their version, *Arthur and Emmeline*, sustains more cuts, not only of Dryden and Purcell, but also of Garrick and Arne, and contains additions by Kemble and Linley.

It may seem ironic that a classicizing tradition at the end of the eighteenth century would lead to revivals and revisions rather than to reconstruction, but indeed, this is only one side of the story. The Folger Library manuscript, containing all of Purcell's music omitted by Arne, and the Gresham College manuscript with its complete, albeit stylistically revised, version of *King Arthur*, illustrate a competing trend in the other direction. Such 'revisionist' and 'authentic' trends have continued to exist side by side, and their separate proponents typically argue their methods on the same grounds: the preservation

---

[60] Harris, *Henry Purcell's Dido and Aeneas*, p. 45, n. 2.

of the original work. As we have seen in the 1770 revival of *King Arthur*, Garrick and Arne themselves disagreed as to the extent of necessary revisions, with Arne stating that it needed significant alteration to make it 'pleasing to the Public'. In an era more attuned to 'authentic' readings, it may seem tempting to pillory Arne for his treatment of Purcell's score, but he was no more or less abusive to Purcell than Mozart was to Handel or, some years later, Mendelssohn to Bach. Indeed, throughout the nineteenth century, the dual trends of modernization and authenticity continued with near equal strength, the first largely in performance and the second especially in the great monumental editions, including the Purcell Society Edition begun in 1878.

In this century it has sometimes seemed that the authenticity movement has finally prevailed, but in opera the compromise between modernization and authenticity has achieved widespread popularity and notoriety. Peter Sellars's stagings of operas by Handel, Mozart, Wagner and Sullivan offer only one obvious example of a trend that may have a distant forebear in the spectacular 1736 production of *King Arthur* that used original text and music. The 'improved' Purcell of the late eighteenth century is clearly of historical interest and, like Mozart's revisions of Handel, not without musical interest as well. Just as the authenticity movement of this century depends on historical reconstruction but also reveals much about the taste and culture of our times,[61] so *King Arthur*'s eighteenth-century journey reveals a methodology of revision that links this work theatrically through Dryden and Garrick to late seventeenth-century revisions of Elizabethan drama and musically through Arne and others to late eighteenth-century taste.

---

61 See *Authenticity and Early Music*, ed. Nicholas Kenyon (Oxford, 1988), especially the essays by Richard Taruskin and Robert P. Morgan.

A portrait of Henry Purcell

JANET SNOWMAN

The small watercolour portrait of Henry Purcell reproduced as the frontispiece to this volume is in the collection of the Royal Academy of Music, London. Although it dates from the late eighteenth century and is much less grand than the oils now in the National Portrait Gallery, its provenance, which can be well documented, sheds light on other, earlier images of the composer.

The Royal Academy of Music painting has, at some stage, suffered from damp; there is evidence of staining in the background and the rear of the frame seems to have been affected as well. Excluding the gilded frame, which itself has slight damage and an old repair, the painting measures 13.24 × 11 cm. Examination of the rear wooden panel reveals various inscriptions. The first, 'Henry Purcell', appears in ink in the top third of the panel: it is apparently a transfer or copy of Purcell's own signature (see ill. A.1). At the bottom of the frame the following is written: 'This belonged to Dr Philip Hayes, Professor of Music at Oxford, afterwards to Isaac Pring, Organist of New College, who gave it to me. G. Heathcote, New Coll. 1799.' Between these inscriptions is pencilled 'Harry Plunket Greene 1930–36' (the Irish baritone and specialist in English song, married to Maud, second daughter of Sir Hubert Parry), followed, in the same hand, by 'Ray Riddell, 1936–'.

Of the persons named on the back cover of the painting, Philip Hayes (1738–97) owned one of Purcell's great autographs (now British Library R.M. MS 20.h.8), which had passed to Purcell's son and grandson before it came into his own possession before he presented it to King George III. Isaac Pring (1777–99) was assistant organist to Hayes at Oxford in 1794 and succeeded him on his death in 1797 as organist of New College. He graduated at Oxford in March 1799 and died of consumption in the same year. Neither the will of Gilbert Heathcote (d. 1829) nor that of Harry Plunket Greene (d. 1936) mentions the small watercolour, and a trawl

A.1 Transfer or copy of Henry Purcell's signature. From watercolour portrait of composer, Royal Academy of Music, London

through the Wills and Admonishments Registers in Somerset House from 1936 has shed no light on Ray Riddell.

Franklin B. Zimmerman, in *Henry Purcell, 1659–1695: His Life and Times* (2nd rev. edn, 1983), reproduces as Plate IIIK a copy of an engraving described as 'Henry Purcell, Musician & Actor, from the original picture in Dulwich College', engraved by W. N. Gardiner, 1794. Malcolm Rogers of the National Portrait Gallery has confirmed that the Royal Academy of Music's watercolour is the work of Sylvester Harding, which was copied as an engraving by William Gardiner in 1794. The painting shows a young man with red lips and blondish, curly hair, head and bust in an oval, against a blue-grey stipple background, looking head left and wearing a black tunic with a cowl neck over a white collared garment. On removal of the back board, the inscription 'Henry Purcell from S. Harding' appears in ink in the bottom right-hand corner.

A.2 Engraving of Henry Purcell (1794), British Museum

From about 1775 Sylvester Harding (1745–1809) – artist, publisher, musician and actor – made watercolour copies of old portraits which from 1786 he published with his brother Edward in various historical and other illustrated works from their shop in Fleet Street. Many of these were engraved by Bartolozzi, Delatre, Gardiner and others. In 1792 they moved their premises to 102 Pall Mall, where they carried on a successful business, which included publication of *The Economy of Human Life* with plates by Gardiner from designs by Harding (1799), *Shakespeare Illustrated by an Assemblage of Portraits* (1793) (which includes composers) and the *Biographical Mirror* (1795), with essays by F. G. Waldron, author of *The Shakespearian Miscellany* (1802).

The Department of Prints and Drawings of the British Museum and the National Portrait Gallery possess various small watercolour portraits by Harding. In most cases these are far more highly-coloured and refined than the Purcell, though some use the same stippling effect in the background. It is interesting to note that whilst the faces and clothing are drawn and painted with some delicacy, Harding's management of the sitters' hands in the portraits he copied often looks peculiar.

Frequently cited as the place of publication of the engraving 'Henry Purcell, Musician & Actor' is the *Biographical Mirror*, 'comprising a series of Ancient and Modern English Portraits of Eminent and Distinguished Persons from Original Pictures and Drawings', 1795. But a copy of the engraving in the British Museum Department of Prints and Drawings gives 1 November 1794 as the date of publication (see ill. A.2). Examination of all three copies of the *Biographical Mirror* in the British Library (each in three parts bound in one volume) reveals no sign of the Purcell engraving. The third volume, published in 1810, a year after Sylvester Harding's death, includes forty extra plates intended for an additional volume which never appeared. Included in the first volume are engraved portraits of Edward Alleyn and Michael Drayton, each 'from an original picture in Dulwich College'. Comparing the two Purcell images, one will notice that the one in the watercolour has longer nose, a more pronounced curl on the forehead, with more prominence of the lines of the curling hair and a less-rounded left cheek.

A hundred years ago William H. Cummings wrote: 'Dulwich College, down to the year 1794, possessed a portrait of Purcell; in that year it was copied by Harding and engraved. Unhappily the interesting and valuable original has disappeared, no one knows when or how.'[1] In a later article

1   'Portraits of Purcell', *The Musical Times*, 36 (1895), 735–6.

William A. Shaw noted, 'The only other authentic type of Purcell portraiture is that furnished by the engraving by W. A. Gardiner in 1794, after a drawing by S. Harding, taken from the original, then at Dulwich.'[2]

Another reference to this missing portrait is found in the *Catalogue of Engraved British Portraits Preserved in the Department of Prints and Drawings in the British Museum*, vol. III (1912); the engraved copy is listed as 'H[ead] L[eft], directed and looking to L[eft]; oval. From picture formerly at Dulwich College, Plate to Harding's *Biographical Mirrour*, 1794, engraved by W. N. Gardiner.' The lost work is also mentioned in the *Dictionary of National Biography*, under Purcell: 'The other portraits said to have been formerly at Dulwich College, have vanished . . .'

The archives of neither the Dulwich Picture Gallery nor Dulwich College have any record of such a picture of Purcell ever having been in their possession. It is obvious, however, that both the engraving and the Royal Academy of Music's watercolour are related in type to the anonymous portrait in the National Portrait Gallery, formerly attributed to Sir Godfrey Kneller (NPG Catalogue no. 2150). A major difference is that the undergarment worn in the Harding image is not present in the National Portrait Gallery's painting. David Piper, in *A Catalogue of Seventeenth-Century Portraits in the National Portrait Gallery, 1625–1714*, has the following to say about this portrait:

> A signed statement by Joah Bates (1741–99) was formerly on the back; according to this, the portrait was given by Purcell to his friend John Church and was given by the latter's granddaughter, Mrs Strutt, to Joah Bates. Engraved, when in the possession of Edward Bates, by W. Humphreys. From Bates's descendants it was brought by Mr Henry Littleton; sold with the effects of A. H. Littleton (Elliott, Son and Boyton), 16–17 March 1915, bought by William Barclay Squire, by whom it was bequeathed to the Gallery; accepted by the Trustees, 1927. Another version, of very similar quality, was sold at Sotheby's 18 June 1947, lot 25e, from the collection of G. W. Hastings of Great Malvern; a chalk drawing, in the British Museum, is of much livelier quality than either of the paintings and may be the original study from life. This portrait type is traditionally ascribed to Kneller, but has probably nothing to do with him. The sitter's youthful appearance suggests a date early in the 1680s, but this may be a posthumous image. The identification is traditional, and the features, while obviously idealised, agree well enough with those in established portraits. W. N. Gardiner's engraving, 1794, suggests that a variant of this type may then have been at Dulwich College; it is now not traceable.

2   'Three Unpublished Portraits of Henry Purcell', *The Musical Times*, 61 (1920), 588–90.

The Royal Academy of Music's watercolour is obviously also derived in type from the chalk drawing, head half-turned left, and slightly thrust forward, wearing long curling hair or wig, only partly indicated (black chalk, retouched on the jaw, on a lilac/peach colour paper with some rusting; 40.1 × 27.2 cm). The artist named on the mount is 'Sir Godfrey Kneller', and the drawing was also at one time attributed to Jonathan Richardson the Elder. It is now considered to be a copy by a follower of John Closterman. This portrait was purchased by the British Museum from Edward Cheney through Sotheby's (Sale 4 May 1885, lot 995, not mentioned, with drawings attributed to Jonathan Richardson).

The National Portrait Gallery file also contains an extract from a letter by William Cummings of the Chapel Royal to George Grove, dated 31 December 1880, which says, 'I have today been to the College [Dulwich] and with Dr Carver have looked at all the portraits now left there. "Henry Purcell Musician and Actor" was undoubtedly there in 1794 but when or where it went no-one knows – I have a copy of the engraving published in the year named.'

The National Portrait Gallery also has a 'Grangerized' version of *The Early Diary of Frances Burney, 1768–1778*, ed. Annie Raine Ellis (1889), with additional illustrations, comprising engravings, watercolours and drawings of the period, collected by F. Leverton Harris. The Gardiner engraving is pasted into the preface (unfortunately, once again the source of the original painting is not given); the book also contains early engravings of William Hayes, William Hey(a)ther, Charles Burney, Ben Jonson, Haydn, Handel, Blow, Arne, Jane Austin, Guy's Hospital for Incurables, and a humorous portrait of Handel's singer Giulia Frasi.

Finally, there is mention of a watercolour portrait of Purcell (holding a scroll) by Thomas Lowe after Closterman that was auctioned at Philips in 1987 (lot 51): 'Signed and inscribed on an old label on backboard "Copied expressly for Mr Enoch Hawkings, Gentleman of Her Majesty's Chapel Royal, and Lay Clerk of Westminster Abbey."' A file note by a member of the National Portrait Gallery staff says that this was not thought to be related in type to any known image of Purcell, although this would seem by description to have been a copy of the Closterman portrait now in the possession of the Royal Society of Musicians.

Index

Index